State and Regional Nationalism

State and Regional Nationalism
Territorial Politics and the European State

Michael Keating
Professor of Political Science
University of Western Ontario

HARVESTER · WHEATSHEAF

NEW YORK   LONDON   TORONTO   SYDNEY   TOKYO

First published 1988 by
Harvester · Wheatsheaf
66 Wood Lane End, Hemel Hempstead
Hertfordshire HP2 4RG
A division of
Simon & Schuster International Group

© 1988 Michael Keating

All rights reserved. No part of this publication may be reproduced, stored in a retrieval system, or transmitted, in any form, or by any means, electronic, mechanical, photocopying, recording or otherwise, without the prior permission in writing, from the publisher.

Printed and bound in Great Britain by
Billing & Sons Ltd, Worcester

British Library Cataloguing in Publication Data

Keating, Michael, 1950–
State and regional nationalism:
territorial politics and the European state.
1. Western Europe. Regionalism
I. Title
352'.0073'094
ISBN 0-7450-0272-2

1 2 3 4 5   92 91 90 89 88

Contents

Preface	vii
1. Introduction	1
Theories of Territorial Politics	1
The Resurgence of Peripheral Politics	8
Territorial Management	18
2. The Creation of of the State	25
The Making of the United Kingdom	25
France—The Myth of the Nation-State	33
Spain and the Empire	36
The Unification of Italy	40
3. The National Revolution	46
Nationalism and the State	46
France—The Consolidation of the Jacobin State	49
Spain—The Failure of the National Project	51
The Making of Italy	53
The United Kingdom—A Multinational State	56
The Economic Revolution	58
The Cultural Revolution and the Assertion of Identity	66
The Survival of the Periphery	77
4. The Revolt of the Periphery	79
The Mobilisation of the Periphery	79
The Crisis of the United Kingdom	80
The Disintegration of Spain	97

France	108
Italy and the *questione meridionale*	113

5. Territorial Management in the Postwar Era — 121
Territorial Integration in Postwar Europe — 121
Territorial Management in Postwar Britain — 125
France—The Survival of the Notables — 131
Italy—The New Clientilism — 135
Spain—The Extermination of Regions — 141
The Resilience of Territory — 144

6. The Politics of Regional Development — 147
The Growth of Regional Policies — 147
The Rise and Fall of Regional Planning — 157

7. The New Territorial Politics — 167
The Crisis of Territorial Representation — 167
The Return of Territorial Politics — 171
The United Kingdom — 174
France—The New Regionalism — 200
Spain—The Re-emergence of the Regions — 211
Italy—The Exception to Prove the Rule — 230

8. The State and the Regions — 235
Configurations of Territorial Politics — 235
Regional Government — 240

Bibliography — 245
Index — 263

Preface

In some respects, the origins of this book go back to the 1950s when, as a child growing up in the North of England with an Irish father and Scots mother, I first became aware of territorial politics, if only in the domestic context. Later, as an undergraduate at the University of Oxford, I learnt the Westminster view of the constitution, for only with the explosion of Scottish, Welsh and Irish nationalism in the early 1970s was the politics of non-metropolitan Britain taken seriously by academia. Even then, there was a tendency to regard the periphery as quaint, backward or boring and its politics as deviant from the normal, civilised mode. Similar attitudes are found in other European countries. The central argument of this book is that the regionalism and nationalism of the periphery are not atavistic throwbacks but rational responses to the growth of the modern state and can only be understood as such. Territorial relationships are a constant factor in politics, though changing in form and their means of expression over time.

I have chosen to examine this theme in four countries, the United Kingdom, France, Spain and Italy since these are the four large unitary states of Europe, all have experienced territorial challenges and all have sought to establish devolved regional governments in the post-war years. Other cases could doubtless be added but at the cost of a loss of the detail which is essential for the analysis and a risk of overgeneralisation. I have also chosen to include some historical analysis since, while history does not 'explain' the present, it is essential to its understanding. This is not a complete theory and history of regionalism and peripheral nationalism. That would be a massive undertaking and would include dimensions neglected here. My intention has been more modest, to examine some themes neglected in previous debate on the topic and, particularly, the interaction between regional mobilisation and the power structures and policies of the central state.

The work for this book was done between 1985 and 1987 with travel funds provided by a Leverhulme Trust fellowship. Earlier work on France was supported by the Nuffield Foundation and the Economic and Social Research Council. Many colleagues have helped with advice, contacts and hospitality. Barry Jones and other members of the Political Studies Association work group on UK politics have contributed greatly to my thinking. I am grateful, also, to Francesco Merloni and Vincenzo Santanonio in Rome; Elizabeth Keating and Luis Moreno in Madrid; Antonio Perreira-Menaut in Pamplona; Francesc Pallares in Lérida; Jacques Leruez in Paris; Paul Allies and colleagues in Montpellier; Vaughan Rogers in Edinburgh. Library staff have been most helpful at the University of Strathclyde; Virginia Polytechnic Institute and State University; National Library of Scotland; Fondation Nationale des Sciences Politiques, Paris; University of Barcelona; Centro de Investigaciones Sociológicas, Madrid; European University Institute, Florence; Istituto di Studi sulle Regioni, Rome; Centre International de Documentation Occitane, Béziers; and the University of Montpellier. I am indebted, too, to the Department of Political Science, Virginia Polytechnic Institute and State University which provided the time to write the book while I was visiting professor in 1987–8.

Michael Keating
Blacksburg, Virginia
December 1987.

1
Introduction

Theories of Territorial Politics

Territory is part of the very essence of the state, one of the dimensions of its authority. The creation of states involves first the acquisition of territory, then the imposition of authority within it. Recently, scholars have recognised that the management of territory to retain that authority is an important task of the contemporary state. Yet the processes by which states acquire, consolidate and retain their territorial authority remains a subject of controversy, especially since the wave of 'peripheral nationalist' movements which, confounding most orthodox wisdom, swept through advanced western countries in the 1960s and 1970s. The re-emergence of peripheral nationalism not only upset many of the textbook theories of politics in western nations. It also proved an uncomfortable experience for scholars and teachers brought up within 'national' traditions which took for granted the existing state order, allowing only the existence of boundary problems in places like Northern Ireland, Alsace–Lorraine or the Alto Adige. So a tendency developed to regard peripheral nationalism either as a pathological condition, a malfunction of the modern state, or as an archaic throwback, a temporary regression in political development. Once the impact of the new peripheral nationalisms was fully felt, some observers veered to the other extreme, seeing the breakup of the existing states of Europe as a natural and proper result of contemporary political trends. They, too, were confounded by the resilience of the state in the face of these challenges. What is needed in the late 1980s is a set of theories which, avoiding the perils of overdetermination, explain both the eruption of territorial protest at some times and its subsidence at others.

For a long time the dominant theory of the formation and consolidation of states was that of 'diffusionism' within a 'centre–periphery' model. In essence, this holds that societies and states are formed around central points which assimilate the peripheries around them to their own values to form a common social, economic and political system. Sociological versions of diffusionism, while evocative, are sometimes highly abstract and difficult to test in practice. Shils (1975, p. 3), for example, holds that

> Society has a center . . . . The central zone is not, as such, a spatially located phenomenon. It almost always has a more or less definite location within the bounded territory in which the society lives. Its centrality has, however, nothing to do with geometry and little with geography. The center, or the central zone, is a phenomenon of the realm of values and beliefs. It is the center of the order of symbols, of values and beliefs, which govern the society.

The values are those of elites in politics, economics, education and other public spheres, which legitimate the distribution of roles and rewards in society. Rulers will seek to extend the value system throughout society, while the development of unified economic systems, political democracy, urbanisation and education will, by bringing more of the population into contact with one another, create a greater acceptance for it. The process may not always be smooth. Indeed, in the initial stages of contact, the contrast between peripheral and central values may be a source of conflict and even, in the case of territorial peripheries, secession; but secession is rare and, at least in territorially compact societies, integration is the norm.

Shils is careful not to confine the notion of peripherality to the territorial dimension and allows for groups which are socially and economically peripheral but located within the territorial centre. As our present interest is in territorial integration, however, we shall limit the discussion to those elaborations of the theory which define centre and periphery in geographical terms. Several scholars have traced the processes by which territorial integration has come about, separating the spheres of economics, culture and politics. Integration is seen as a process whereby 'backward' territories, peripheral both geographically and socially, acquire the values of the centre and enter into the national economic and political system. Traditional structures in the periphery are marked by primitive technologies, a largely self-sufficient agriculture, local and small-scale cottage industry, rural settlement patterns, religious belief, minority languages and a social hierarchy with status based on ascriptive values rather than achievement. Economic development challenges this by substituting scientific knowledge for traditional technology and commercial production for subsistence farming, while introducing mechanisation and specialisation in industry (Smelser, 1966). Industrial capitalism and urbanisation are key agents of change, starting in the central territories, breaking social structures based on kinship, traditional obligation and ascriptive values and replacing them with the exchange relationships characteristic of modern capitalist society. As people are drawn into towns, old community patterns are broken up. Modern communications and education break down peripheral languages and cultural patterns. Finally, the mass politics of modern society, especially as the franchise is expanded, comes to revolve around economic questions dividing the interests of economic sectors (for example agriculture and industry) or of classes (workers and employers), while issues of ethnic or religious identity become less salient. These new issues, being economic in nature, are amenable to negotiation and compromise within a political system based on exchange and value consensus. The development of organised labour movements reinforces integration, given labour's interest in national wage bargaining to prevent undercutting and in national regulation of working conditions.

This process can, it is conceded, produce acute conflicts. Upwardly mobile elements from the periphery may feel aggrieved at the disdain still shown them by central elites. Peasant farmers and feudal landowners, small-scale manufacturers and traders in the periphery may all feel threatened by modernisation, large-scale capitalist production and competition in national markets. Religious elements in the periphery may fear the arrival of secular values from the centre. All these may fuel peripheral protest and revolt during the modernisation phase but this will eventually be stilled by the advance of integration or the secession of the deviant territory to produce, in the words of a leading diffusion theorist, 'sovereign governments which have no critical regional or community cleavages' (Deutsch, 1966, p. 80).

There is a strong element of economic and social determinism in many versions of the diffusionist model, with political forms being seen as moulded by the underlying economic and social forces. So, while Deutsch recognises the role of politics and military force in making communities, he insists that

> Governments can modify communities, and they can make communities in rare and favourable situations; but on the whole it is communities which make governments, or rather, it is the distribution of communities at any one time which both offers and limits the opportunities for governments to consolidate and extend their power. (Deutsch, 1966, p. 79)

The relationship between economic and social and political/military factors in the making of states remains a contentious issue but diffusionism places the major emphasis on the former. Though the mechanism of defeat for the periphery may be military suppression, this merely accelerates the inevitable since economic and social modernisation holds no place for backward elements.

This diffusionist view of the world suffers from a number of problems, at both the theoretical and the empirical levels. At the theoretical level, most versions of the theory are highly value-laden and often appear to be attempts to show how the 'backward' nations of the Third World can aspire to the more advanced social systems of the West. It is also uni-directional. Political development is seen as an irreversible process leading to ever-higher planes of social organisation, the highest being the liberal democracies of the 'Anglo-Saxon' countries. This owes a great deal to the western concept of 'progress' to the 'wishful thinking' of liberals (Lijphart, 1977) in its implication that the 'irrational' elements of pre-modern political and social arrangements will necessarily give way to the individualistic and exchange-based arrangements of the contemporary western society.

Some liberals also find the intellectual legacy of the 'nation-state' idea, itself often a combination of scholarship and propaganda, difficult to shake loose. They believe that only where the 'nation', defined in terms of culture and self-identification, corresponds to the state can a truly liberal politics, free from oppression and the problems of permanent minorities, thrive. By a reversal of the argument, it is often then assumed that, where stable liberal democracies exist, this must be because a 'nation state', with a culturally homogeneous population, has been established. Demands from groups within the state to be regarded similarly as constituting the primary group and perhaps even a nation of their own, thus cause liberals acute discomfort and are often dismissed as irrational, reactionary or 'artificial'. Other liberals insist on dismissing the political demands of the peripheries as 'inward-looking' and an affront to the universalist ideas of liberalism, ignoring the fact that their own 'universalism' is tightly bounded by the existing state and may amount to nothing more than metropolitan chauvinism—some of the most parochial thinking in the world is to be found in the common-rooms of Oxford and the salons of Paris—while the latter may be more genuinely international in outlook. This leads us to another weakness in much of diffusionist theory, the assumption that the process of integration and normative equalisation will take place within and across the politically defined state. It is equally possible in theoretical terms to see it operating at a higher or a lower territorial level, but the fact that scholarship has so often been bounded by 'national' ways of thinking and that data tends to be available in sets based upon state units does not encourage scholars to look for it elsewhere. As MacLaughlin (1986) notes, many nineteenth-century geographers were so tied to the state-centred approach that they became instruments in the formation and maintenance of the 'nation-state' itself. In many instances, the idea of national integration has been self-proving.

Diffusionism is also an important strand in orthodox Marxism, with its emphasis on the progressive role of capitalism and the bourgeoisie in producing economic plenty while creating the conditions in which the sole basis of social and political conflict is that between capital and labour. The role of capitalism in eroding traditional and localist values was noted by Marx and Engels in the *Communist Manifesto*. Marxist tendencies to reduce all social relations to class ones often obscure the independent effect of territorial solidarities which, at various moments, have been the more powerful force. Nairn (1981) is an exception, breaking with traditional Marxism by seeing nationalism itself as the driving force in the 'normal' mode of development, not just in former colonies of the Third World but in western Europe as well.

Finally the diffusionist model fails to give sufficient attention to political calculation. The ideology of nationalism, such a powerful force in building nations, is not merely the product of a cultural diffusion from the core, assimilating peripheral territories to a common value system. It may be consciously used by political elites to create a common value system, using the mechanisms of communication, education and administration. So the political act of state creation may come first and the sense of national identity be created later by public policies and partisan activity (MacLaughlin, 1986). As Breuilly (1985) notes, nationalism is essentially a form of politics. Nation-building is an activity suiting the interests of key groups at various historical moments and it cannot be seen apart from this essentially political function.

Not all writers on the theme of integration have been deterministic. Lipset and Rokkan (1967, p. 12), while using a centre–periphery model, note that circumstances differ among states and that much depends on the timing of the process of 'territorial unification, the establishment of legitimate government and the monopolisation of the agencies of violence, the take-off toward industrial growth, the development of popular education and the entry of the lower classes into politics.' The process of modernisation may leave its traces in territorial and cultural conflicts which persist into industrial society but territorial resistance to incorporation is still seen as the result of an incomplete modernisation and the isolation of the periphery from the centre. Specifically, they concede that territorial politics may develop where there is a heavy concentration of a distinct culture in the periphery; where there are few ties of communication, alliance and bargaining experience toward the national centre and more toward external centres of cultural or economic influence; and where there is minimal economic dependence on the metropolis. In other words, where the process of modernisation has been incomplete and the periphery has remained isolated, a distinctive territorial politics may persist.

Rokkan and Urwin (1983) retain the centre–periphery model but, instead of postulating just one type of centre–periphery relationship, point out that centre–periphery linkages can take a whole variety of forms. They plot three dimensions to nation-building, military-administrative system-building, economic system-building and cultural system-building. These dimensions are, of course, common to all our models but here each is seen as independent of, though influenced by, the others. So a conquered periphery may be able to escape economic dependence on the centre or cultural assimilation. In contrast to the orthodox Marxist view of the primacy of the economic, no one dimension is seen as determining (Rokkan, 1981); rather, territorial politics will be the outcome of an interplay of all three. This will be an important element in our analysis for we shall encounter times and places where the locus of political and economic power in societies have not coincided. We do not always see a 'modernising' core confronting a 'backward' periphery. In the case of Spain, we will see a politically dominant core confronting an economically more advanced periphery. Even within a single dimension, it is not always the core which is 'advanced' and the periphery 'backward'. In nineteenth-century Britain, democratic forces on the periphery came into collision with an archaic and, in many respects, pre-democratic state form. Lipset and Rokkan (1967) similarly point to the complexity of forces involved in the process of nation-building, identifying seven types of political, religious and economic elites. The differing strengths of the various formations in different territories in turn introduce a territorial dimension into politics. In Lipset and Rokkan's (1967, p. 12) view, this is a subordinate theme in party alignments and 'purely territorial oppositions rarely survive the extension of the suffrage.' A central argument of the chapters which follow here, on the other hand, will be that territorial conflicts have persisted into modern industrial society and taken on new forms.

Other writers have cast doubt on the simplification of territorial cleavages in terms of centre and periphery. Certainly, there is a danger of methodological determinism in the choice of the framework and the associated choice of the units of analysis. As Folz (1981) points out, it is often only with the benefit of hindsight that we know which 'centre' actually triumphed. A similar problem arises with peripheries. Rose and Urwin (1975) also question the centre–periphery dichotomy, noting that states may have multiple centres (as in the USA or Canada) or have neither centre nor periphery (as Germany or Switzerland). In any case, 'centre' itself is a relative and value-laden term in places like Northern Ireland where the main question at issue is whether the centre should be seen as London or Dublin.

Despite these problems the centre–periphery model is a useful analytical tool, and modified to take account of particular national circumstances and the differing meanings of centrality in the cultural, economic and political spheres, it is used quite extensively in the chapters which follow. The model itself, though, tells us nothing about the content of centre–periphery interactions and these will require detailed examination in order to provide substance to the model.

The Resurgence of Peripheral Politics

The main shortcoming with the diffusionist model of nation-building remains empirical, its inability to predict or explain the resurgence of territorially-based oppositions in western countries. These new movements have taken a variety of forms and to attempt a comprehensive definition or typology at this stage would be self-defeating since we intend to arrive at this inductively, examining the development of territorial movements in context and analysing their aims and strategies. These aims may be cultural, economic, political or all three and range from lobbying within the existing constitutional system for cultural recognition or economic resources, through campaigning for varying degrees of autonomy to demands for separatism and the creation of a new nation-state.

Postponing the categorisation of territorial movements also helps avoid a methodological trap which has defeated several previous attempts at theorisation. Some authors have insisted on a rigorous distinction between nationalism, seen as separatism, and mere regionalism, which might be content with limited autonomy. Connor (1977) distinguishes in this way between 'ethnonationalism', which denies the legitimacy of the existing state and is separatist, and regionalism, which recognises the state and merely seeks autonomy within it. Others have pointed out the obvious difference between lobbying a central government for favours, which not only recognises the legitimacy of the centre but suggests that its distributive capacity should be strengthened, and demands for regional autonomy which could weaken that capacity. These are valid points to make at the political level but for the purposes of analysis they too often prejudge the case. Regional political movements have to play on several strands of regionalism at once and the strains which this causes are very often the source of their weakness. Few movements have an absolutist attitude to the existing state and the wish to substitute a new state for the old is merely one possible form of rejection of the existing order. Some movements want to replace it with a more loosely structured Europe of the regions, rejecting in the name of self-determination, the state nationalist ideology used to legitimate the existing order.

Great confusion has been sown by a failure to distinguish movements for the creation of unitary nations and movements of the periphery formed precisely to resist this. Both types of movement may call themselves nationalist, but paradoxically many of the regional 'nationalists' are antinationalist in the classic sense of the term. This is because they do not believe that every group calling itself a nation should have a separate state but are prepared to coexist within a looser governmental arrangement with other 'nationality' groups. Some have eventually moved to separatism under the circumstances of events but others have not. Some quite happily demand greater autonomy and redistribution of resources at the same time, using one strand or other depending on the needs of the moment. Others show great ingenuity in intellectual square-circling.

Apart from its use and abuse by political movements, the word 'nationalism' has differing connotations in various European languages. In Italy it is almost invariably confined to the nationalism of the Italian state, rather than the autonomist, irredentist and separatist movements of the periphery. In Spain on the other hand, the term is used very loosely, sometimes limited, apart from the Spanish nation itself, to movements of the 'historic nationalities' of Catalonia, the Basque Country and Galicia, sometimes extending to regions such as Valencia (Alcarez, 1985) and Andalusia (Aumente, 1980). In the United Kingdom the term is more often used for separatist movements of the periphery than for attitudes to the state. Indeed, the United Kingdom lacks even a term for the common 'nationality' of its citizens. As Rose (1982a, p. 11) puts it, 'no-one ever speaks of the "Ukes" as a nation'. In France official attitudes have until recently made the use of the term 'nationalism' to refer to anything but greater France almost impermissible. This imprecision of language and the varying uses of terms prevent us from postulating a rigorous definition of nationalism at the outset of the investigation. In the chapters which follow, the term nationalism will be used with the appropriate prefix where this usage is common, for example to refer to the movements of Scotland and Catalonia after the turn of the century but not to Sicily, but this is not to assume that movements sharing the term have more in common with each other than any of them do with movements merely calling themselves regionalist. Only in the last chapter is a typology of movements presented, following the historical and political analysis of their development and aims.

Sometimes movements are distinguished by whether or not they have an 'ethnic' base. Unfortunately, the concept of ethnicity is even more slippery than that of nationalism. The most clearly differentiated ethnic groups in western Europe (Afro-Caribbean, Asian, Arab, Jews) are not territorial at all and have formulated no demands for institutional reform let alone political separation.

So we will limit our examination to territorial movements

aimed at securing recognition in the form of cultural or economic concessions and/or regional autonomy. Explanations of this phenomenon have all been based on a rejection of the diffusionist model. Of course, we have noted that the diffusionist model does have a place for territorial conflict in the process of nation-building, as the modernising forces of the centre come into contact with the traditional elements on the periphery and some attempts have been made to rescue the diffusionist model by moving back the date of national integration. Lijphart (1977) points out that Deutsch allows in his model for cases in which centre–periphery exchanges and transactions develop faster than normative integration, and himself adapts this idea to explain the resurgence of 'ethnic' conflict in recent years. According to Lijphart, the real penetration of the periphery by central values occurred not during the industrial revolution but since the Second World War, with the development of modern communications, arousing a sense of ethnic identity which had always existed but had been dormant in the absence of external challenge. In fact, the development of national economies and administrative systems in the late nineteenth centuries did produce territorial conflicts comparable in many ways to those occurring with the economic modernisation and state expansion of the post Second World War period. The main problem with the diffusionist model, however, is not its locating the process of national integration in the wrong century but its assumption that contact will necessarily produce integration albeit sometimes after a period of conflictual adjustment. An alternative set of theories predicts just the opposite.

Most of these are based on the idea that groups in the periphery perceive themselves to be deprived, usually economically but, in some versions, culturally or politically, relative to those in the centre. Economic development and industrialisation occur unevenly across territories and increased contact between the periphery and the centre merely exacerbates conflict by facilitating comparisons. There are a number of problems with this as a general explanation of the resurgence of territorial politics. There is a poor relationship empirically between relative economic deprivation and peripheral mobilisation. Regional nationalism is stronger in Catalonia, a relatively well-off part of Spain than in the relatively impoverished Italian Mezzogiorno. Nor does a resurgence of territorial identity always coincide with a relative downturn in the regional economy. On the contrary, it has often been associated with a relative improvement. Within regions, it is not usually the most deprived individuals who are most supportive of territorial political movements. Even if one concedes a link between economic deprivation and territorial assertion, it remains a poor predictor of political behaviour, for there are several ways in which individuals and groups could react to a perception of deprivation. They could see the problem as lying in the weakness of the local private sector and seek to develop a native capitalism. They could seek stronger representation in central government; or they could seek political autonomy or independence to gain control of local natural resources or pursue different economic policies. All these have happened in various circumstances.

One set of theories which seeks to link the issue of relative deprivation to a pattern of political activity and a political programme is that of 'internal colonialism', an idea going back to the work of the Italian Marxist Gramsci (1978a,b) and later developed by Latin American sociologists, and in the European context by Lafont (1967) and Hechter (1975). Internal colonialism retains the concepts of centre and periphery but denies the diffusionist process. Instead, it holds that capitalism and state power at the centre, developing first, subordinate the periphery to their needs just as European colonialism subordinated its territories in Asia and Africa. Inhabitants of the periphery are given subordinate economic, social and political roles, producing a 'cultural division of labour', in which 'ethnic' identity and social class coincide. Industry in the periphery develops in a dependent mode, largely confined to primary production of materials processed in the centre or other activities serving the central economy. Economic power is retained in the centre where decisions about investment, credit and wages are made. The spatial pattern of development in the periphery is skewed to the needs of the centre, with activity concentrating along the borders. Contact between centre and periphery in this model leads not to national integration but to increased differentiation as the periphery is forced into its subordinate role. Its inhabitants are kept in their place through systems of discrimination, which in turn reinforce their sense of ethnic identity. Solidarity among the working classes of centre and periphery is inhibited by the relatively favourable conditions of the former, allowing capitalist interests to divide and rule. At some point, this leads to a reaction in the periphery and to a territorial/ethnic mobilisation.

Attempts to apply the internal colonial model in Western Europe have encountered major empirical problems. Lafont's ideas enjoyed a vogue in France during the 1960s following the Algerian conflict which had obscured the distinction between state-building and colonialism—Algeria, seen by the world at large as a colony, was claimed by the *Algérie Française* party as an integral part of the state. In the United Kingdom, Ireland has historically hung between the status of colony and part of the state. Elsewhere, though, the distinction is clear and western European governments have not practised against their own indigenous citizens the sort of racial exclusiveness found in colonial situations in South Africa or in the old south of the United States. Racial tensions have arisen where different groups have mixed within the same areas but not to any great degree between territorially-based groups. In France, it is now generally accepted that internal colonialism was as much a political rallying cry as a rigorous academic analysis. It helped reconcile Marxism and socialism generally with opposition to the nation-state when this was proving politically desirable but intellectually problematic by portraying the periphery not as a den of backwardness and reaction but as an exploited class with revolutionary potential.

Hechter's analysis has been widely criticised both on basic conceptual grounds and for its faulty methodology (Page, 1978). Hechter himself (1985) has modified it in relation to Scotland, recognising that it was not a colony. He still insists on a cultural division of labour, but concedes that this may be a 'segmental' one, in which groups are occupationally specialised rather than a hierarchical one in which some groups occupy subordinate positions. Scottish nationalism is then explained by the need to preserve a Scottish monopoly of occupations such as law, from which English competitors are excluded. This is to rescue the theory by emptying it of its original content. For now it is being claimed that far from being colonised, the Scots, or at least sections of them, actually enjoy a high degree of self-government. Even in this form the theory is weak, since in Scotland as in other societies, those who enjoy a high degree of autonomy and self-regulation under the existing constitutional arrangements tend to be most opposed to political autonomy, which would expose them to a higher degree of control from other social interests within the local society.

Nairn (1981) also challenges the diffusionist model and emphasises the uneven development of capitalism and the clash of interests which this generates. While the dominant forces of the centre might claim to be bringing enlightenment and progress to the periphery, in practice this 'progress puts powerful, even deadly weapons in the hands of this or that particular 'advanced' area. Since this is a particular place and people, not a disinterested centre of pure and numinous culture, the result is a gulf (far larger than hitherto and likely to increase) between the leaders and the hinterland' (Nairn, 1981, p. 97). Peripheral nationalism emerges from the struggle of groups on the periphery to control 'progress' and impose their own terms on it. In Nairn, it is the peripheral bourgeoisie which leads the reaction to centralised development, coopting the popular masses in its support.

Lijphart (1977) provides a different version of uneven development, distinguishing between 'horizontal' social groups (socio-economic classes) and 'vertical ethnic' groups which may include all socio-economic strata. In some circumstances, the vertical ethnic groups are 'horizontalised', becoming effectively a social class. This is akin to the cultural division of labour argument in the internal colonial model and is equally difficult to demonstrate in practice.

Whatever their weaknesses as general explanations of territorial politics, these theories do point to the fact that industrialisation and capitalism do develop unevenly. This can, in turn, throw up a whole array or relationships between centre and periphery in the course of development, modernisation and change. There is not just a contrast between rich and poor, dominant and dominated. Territories differ in the balance between agriculture and industry, in their dependence on foreign trade or internal markets and these differences themselves may change in incidence, intensity and salience over time, with important implications for public policies and the social interests which can gain from them. As Agnew (1987) notes, even the uniform signals of modern mass culture can spark off differing reactions in different territories. Only thus can one explain the increased localisation of politics in the United States within the last generation. This in itself is perhaps too wide an argument for our present purpose, since the differential effects of national policies does not always spark off territorial political movements. Demands for new policies or a restructuring of power relationships can as easily assume a class or sectoral base. For it to assume a territorial form, a sense of regional identity is needed. Smith (1981) challenges Nairn's materialist explanation of territorial mobilisation by asking why the unevenness of capitalist development should correspond to cultural divisions unless the cultural divisions were already present to guide the process of capitalism. If so, then a cultural rather than a purely material explanation of the process is needed.

This sense of identity can take a whole variety of forms. Some writers fasten on the ethnicity as the essential element. Esman (1977b, p. 377) claims:

> Indeed, so compelling are the normative claims of ethnic self-determination that nowhere in contemporary Europe have regional grievances been successfully exploited except where they enjoy an ethnic base. Thus, while economic conditions in northern England have been as bleak as in neighbouring Scotland, they have not resulted in the organisation or expression of politically significant grievances. There is even evidence of attempts to invent or rediscover an ethnic base for regional claims (Occitania for example) in order to legitimate them externally and enhance their capacity to promote internal mobilisation.

The problem here is that ethnicity is not defined independently of the phenomenon which it is supposed to explain. The dictionary definition of 'ethnic'—'concerning nations or races'—is not much more helpful. If we identify race with ethnicity, we must include non-territorial groups but rule out most of Europe's peripheral nationalisms which, with some exceptions like the nineteenth-century Basque movement, have been at pains to deny any racial basis. In the case of Scotland, cited by Esman as an example of ethnic nationalism, there are at least two separate 'ethnic' groups (Anglo-Saxon and Celtic) each of which arguably has more in common racially and linguistically with its neighbours in other countries (England and Ireland) than with the other Scottish group. Hechter (1975) assumes from the outset that the component parts of the United Kingdom correspond to ethnic entities, but when the need to measure ethnicity arises is forced to use culture as a proxy for ethnicity and then religion, along with language, as a proxy for culture. This prevents one from using religion or language as independent variables of analysis or as the basis for competing explanations of the findings. Wherever it occurs in the literature on territorial movements in Europe, indeed, ethnicity seems to refer to a syndrome of cultural, linguistic, historical and religious traits and a consequent sense of collective identity. So Neilsson (1985, p. 26) writes that

> The characteristics connoted by an *ethnic group* include such social category attributes as common racial identity, culture (including language and religion), kinship, social customs, history, and stable geographic contiguity.

In other words, ethnicity is not the independent variable explaining group identity but is itself the *explicandum*, the very problem which needs to be explained.

It makes more sense, therefore, to talk simply of identity, the ways in which it is forged and maintained and the ways in which it can become politically salient. Where groups of people sharing cultural, linguistic or religious traits or common economic interests are concentrated in particular territories, a sense of collective identity may develop. In the diffusionist vision, these are usually seen as relics of the past, the product of isolation from the mainstream of development. If we abandon the diffusionist assumption, however, we can see that identity is constantly being made and remade and there is no remorseless trend towards universal value systems. A sense of history does appear as an important element in many cases of regional mobilisation, with the sense of identity rooted in an independent past—but it does not have to be accurate history or even based on a real hankering for the past. Historiographers of the periphery may recreate the past to suit the needs of the present, competing versions of history becoming weapons in the political battle over the form of the state.

Other markers of identity may be institutional, whether in politics narrowly defined or in the wider field of 'civil society'. In some instances, state-building has left intact separate collective institutions, such as the Scots legal and educational systems or the Basque *fueros*. In others, political developments since incorporation have brought into being distinctive institutions such as the Welsh Office or the *Cassa per il Mezzogiorno*. So territorial distinctiveness is not always and necessarily a throwback to the past. New identities can be formed in the present as well as old ones rediscovered. The central state itself may also serve to stimulate regional identity by organising administration on a regional basis and effectively inviting people to articulate their demands in a regional framework. One element of political modernisation theories is relevant here, too, though not in the sense in which it has usually been presented. The development of participative political cultures and exchange relationships may be a prerequisite for the emergence of liberal democratic politics—but it does not necessarily entail state integration. Rather, in a number of cases, it has favoured the politicisation of regional identity and the emergence of the region as a framework for political action.

The politicisation of regional identities which may hitherto have existed only at the cultural level or within the institutions of the civil society is a complex process understandable only within the context of individual states, though as we shall see there are strong common features in all our cases. In particular, political regionalism has followed the breakdown of the prevailing arrangements for 'territorial management' and the politicisation of territory, a major theme of the remainder of this book.

Territorial Management

Some of the sociological approaches to the question of national integration have been criticised not only for their determinism but also for the assumption that changes in the economic and social structures are the independent variable in the process, with political activity following from this. Another perspective sees political activity and public policy as critical to the process of mobilisation (Cameron, 1974). We shall give a prominent place to the role of public policy in structuring territorial politics in the four countries to be studied. Some policy problems are found to be very similar across the four states, though the central responses might differ. Others are distinctive, the product of individual national economic, social, cultural or physical conditions. The efforts of central elites to cope with the territorial dimension of policy problems and to contain territorially-based challenges to the central power structure is what we shall call 'territorial management'. A focus on territorial management has another advantage in that we are not obliged to assume that, because territories attached to the central state are politically quiescent for long periods, this is a sign of political integration of the periphery to the centre. It may be due to the displacement of regional identity into non-political channels or the success of central elites in the management of non-integrated territories. Such a perspective also allows us to break with the assumption that political development is a once-for-all process. In fact, successive changes in the role and functions of the state have necessitated successive restructurings of central–periphery relations—and the needs of the 1990s may lead to further changes. So peripheral regionalism is not necessarily a relic of the past, evidence of incomplete modernisation. Indeed, in some cases it may be possible to reverse the old orthodoxy which saw peripheral assertion as a 'revolt against modernity' (Lipset, 1985) and see it as a mechanism used by dynamic, modernising forces against an archaic centre. We shall see that both in the nineteenth century and in the latter half of the twentieth century, territorial/regional identity and its political expression have often been stronger in economically more advanced and urbanised areas and among younger and better-educated elements of the population. There is, indeed, no reason why the pattern of power relationships and policy choices of the modern state should not bring into being new territorial challenges or revive sentiments of territorial identity which have been long dormant.

Territorial management and the structuring of centre–periphery relationships are central concerns of the French school of organisational analysis. Their work is very detailed and complex but essentially rests on the assertion that, contrary to the 'Jacobin' myth of unity, the French system of government is a mechanism for managing territorial and social diversity (Crozier and Friedburg, 1977). Grémion (1976) examines the political and bureaucratic linkages between local and central elites and the intricate patterns of conflict, collusion and collaboration which develop through them, concluding that the universal rules of the centre dissolve into particularism at the periphery as uniform central regulations encounter local conditions. Dupuy and Thoenig (1985) present a highly pluralistic view of the French system of government and see this as a necessary adaptation of the administration (the eschew the term 'state') to the reality of social diversity.

Other studies have examined the role in territorial management and representation of Scottish politicians and administrators (Keating, 1978; 1985b), of Italian parties and politicians (Tarrow, 1977; Graziano, 1984) and of the *caciques* of monarchical Spain (Carr, 1975). In all these cases, it is precisely the lack of political integration which permits the territorial representative or administrator to mediate, adapting the universal rules of the modern state to the conditions of the periphery. To the diffusionist school, this is merely an aspect of the modernising process. The *cacique*, *notable* or *notabile*, whose distinctive style is based upon individual relationships, clientilism and patronage, operates at the boundaries of traditionalism and modernisation for a transitional phase while the cultural, economic and political assimilation of the periphery takes place. In due course, he will give way to the mass politics of parties and classes. Increasingly, however, attention has been drawn to the persistence of distinctive patterns of territorial representation, often overlooked in the 1960s and 1970s because they operated not through separate regional parties but within the mainstream parties of the state.

Central–local bureaucratic and political linkages and their role in managing or, as the case may be, exacerbating centre–periphery conflict will be a major theme of this work, though the sociology of organisations approach on its own is inadequate. Tarrow (1977) has criticised the French school for its neglect of the content of policy as an element influencing the pattern of relationships and of the position of social and economic groups which are relegated to the 'environment' in which bureaucratic decision-making takes place. Médard (1981) similarly draws attention to the need to examine the *notable*'s sociological background and his relationship to the power structure.

An adequate understanding of territorial politics must take account of both macro and micro-politics. Within each periphery is a complex social and economic structure with linkages to external centres of economic power, to the state and to political parties, trade unions and other interest groups operating at the state level. It is invariably a gross oversimplification to talk of a balance of power or of wealth between the centre and the periphery. Rather, different groups within the periphery will have an interest in different patterns of centre–periphery relations in the economic, cultural and political spheres. Some groups might favour separatism and free trade while others seek protectionism within the larger state and yet others want vigorous centralised regional policies. Occasionally, an overwhelming common interest might submerge these differences. Minority language or cultural groups may develop a sense of territorial identity and press for self-government to give this expression. Alternatively, they may settle for a policy of cultural pluralism within the unitary state, which would protect their primary interest while avoiding the dangers of political or economic isolation. Politically, dominant groups and parties within the periphery might see an interest in a degree of self-government which could allow them to pursue their preferred policies though in opposition at the national level. Groups which are in the minority within the periphery may by the same token prefer centralisation. Elected representatives and territorial administrators may favour a system of administrative decentralisation in which they are the privileged channels of centre–periphery exchange and can insulate themselves to a degree from both central and local control. Privileged groups within the periphery may wish to maintain the distinctiveness of their territory, and so their monopoly position, but also resist political decentralisation which would subject them to local popular control. Political machines and bosses may see opportunities for patronage and clientilism in the complexity of centre–periphery relations.

All this can change over time because of changes in the conditions of the periphery, in policies at the centre or in the international environment. These can upset existing patterns of territorial representation and administration, as can regime changes and national party realignments, allowing territorially-based political movements to emerge. These are not mere irrational throwbacks, the rejection of 'modernity'. On the contrary, they may have a rational basis (Rogowski, 1985; Polese, 1985), seeking a redistribution of power and wealth in favour of specific groups or the achievement of substantive policy goals. The creation of the state has itself historically involved a complex pattern of winners and losers and changes in circumstances can alter the balance of benefits derived from particular constitutional arrangements. Pressures for territorial autonomy stem from a perception of the policy benefits to be obtained and not simply from abstract issues of identity. So the analysis must encompass these policy issues.

The resulting territorially-based political movements face a series of dilemmas as to their aims and strategies. They must present a convincing programme for institutional change and establish their appeal to a sufficiently large constituency. In the short run, this presents little difficulty. Demands for regional autonomy can be bracketed with demands for more resources behind a coalition of territorial defence, despite the inherent contradictions. If the movement is to progress beyond the stage of mere protest, however, there is a need to spell out the programme in more detail and this can fragment the coalition. The same applies to substantive social and economic policies. In the protest phase, the movement can function as a 'catch-all' but eventually choices must be made, at the risk of alienating part of the constituency. This must be done in the face of competition from ideological, sectional and class-based parties who may be able to absorb some of their demands. We need to examine how far state-wide parties and bureaucratic elites can make the necessary policy concessions and how far these serve merely to reinforce territorial movements. Policy concessions may be at the cost of considerable internal tension, as they attempt to reconcile these with their overall policy programmes. In the process of mobilisation and bargaining over public policies, though, territorial solidarities may be created within, or in opposition to, the 'nation-state', not as a mere hangover from the past but in the contemporary circumstances of advanced industrial societies.

Another theme to be explored is the way in which the central state itself has restructured territorial governance in pursuit of its own objectives. Regionalism in various forms has been an important instrument of governments seeking to engage in economic intervention, to improve administrative efficiency and reduce overload at the centre, to coordinate their own activities and those of other agencies as well as to satisfy autonomist demands from the periphery. The region has, too, been a level at which new economic forces as well as various types of bureaucratic interest have sought freedom of operation. This has left the term 'region' itself as a rather ambiguous one (Hebbert, 1987), impossible to define in a purely geographical sense but to be seen rather as a meeting-place for a variety of political forces, an arena for various types of intervention. Attempts to institutionalise the region in Europe, while often presented in technical terms, have therefore involved struggles over power and control of resources which in turn have heightened the sense of territory and its political salience.

Exploring these issues requires an adequate sample of cases. Many studies of national integration and territorial mobilisation are highly abstract, drawing on extremely large numbers of cases in the hope of generating general theories. This is a minefield of problems. The level of abstraction required often means that it is virtually impossible to apply the resultant models to particular cases. Without such a theoretical framework on the other hand, one is left with nothing but a pile of raw data. Other work has confined itself to individual case-studies, denying the validity of comparison and insisting on the uniqueness of the case in question. This fails to develop theory or to illuminate processes which may well be common to several cases. This study opts for a middle course, selecting four countries, the United Kingdom, Italy, France and Spain, which have sufficient in common in their historical experience, constitutional structure, economic systems and political practices to allow of comparison and which have experienced similar policy problems in recent years. At the same time, they contain peripheries with contrasting histories, traditions, cultures and political and economic forces, prompting differing responses from time to time from the central state. The peripheries examined are Ireland, Scotland and Wales (for the UK); Brittany and Languedoc (for France); Catalonia, the Basque Country, Galicia and Andalusia (for Spain); and the Mezzogiorno (for Italy). The aim is to examine the cases in their own contexts as well as to draw some general lessons about territorial politics in western European states and the responses of state elites to it.

In the next chapter we examine the construction of the four states in the study, seeing them essentially as dynastic creations. Nation-building is seen as a separate matter and this is examined in Chapter 3 in the three areas of politics, economics and culture, adapting the terms 'national revolution' and 'industrial revolution' (Lipset and Rokkan, 1967) and adding a cultural revolution as an analytically separate element. The national revolution refers to the efforts of central elites, in the eighteenth and nineteenth centuries, to establish common institutions based on consistent val˙˙es within the four states. The industrial revolution refers to the spread of industrialisation, capitalism and market relationships in the eighteenth and nineteenth centuries, the new classes which they spawned and the effects of this on the territorial balance. Of course, the national and industrial revolutions are intimately linked, but the link is not a deterministic one and it is useful to keep the processes analytically separate. The cultural revolution refers to the efforts to unify state territories linguistically and culturally, seen much more as a strategy of political elites at the centre than as a process of natural osmosis resulting from contacts between centre and periphery. The process succeeded in some measure but encountered a powerful reaction in the form of peripheral cultural and linguistic revivals.

Together, these processes, which are intricately connected, are seen to have consolidated rather than eroded territorial identities at the sub-state level, giving them a contemporary meaning and relevance. Chapter 3 also examines the ways in which the late nineteenth-century state, even while promoting national integration, was able to accommodate these identities through mechanisms of territorial management. The explosion of peripheral nationalism in the late nineteenth and early twentieth centuries is examined in Chapter 4 and the re-establishment of territorial management systems after this in Chapter 5. Chapter 6 looks at a central element of territorial management in the post-Second-World-War era, the growth of regional policies and regional planning. Chapter 7 examines the breakdown of territorial management systems in the 1960s and 1970s, the emergence of territorial political movements and the response of the central state. Chapter 8 looks at the configurations of regionalist and peripheral nationalist movements in the 1980s and at the success of regional government in re-establishing stable patterns of territorial politics.

A recurrent problem in the study of comparative politics is whether to proceed thematically or by country. A thematic treatment risks neglecting the interrelationship of elements within national contexts. A country approach, on the other hand, makes difficult a comparison of policies and institutions. I have attempted to get the benefits of both by mixing comparative analysis with accounts of developments within each of the four countries. So each chapter will have sections on the four countries but, to preserve some thematic coherence and continuity, they are not always in the same order. Inevitably, there is an unevenness in the treatment of the four countries since issues have differed in their importance at different times and different places and the coverage must reflect this.

2
The Creation of the State

All the four states being considered were dynastic creations. This is not to deny the importance of economic, cultural or physical factors in facilitating dynastic consolidation, but it does put political factors in first place. In three cases, we can trace the emergence of the state back to the sixteenth century. The process often consisted of the expansion of power from a core area, the seat of monarchical government but the process was far from smooth or inevitable. In some instances, we see the expansion of royal power through a territory, imposing uniform norms and creating a unified political system. In others, we see the often haphazard acquisition of territories with their own civil and legal institutions, which are attached to the core territory without being fully assimilated. In the case of Britain, we see representative institutions emerging at the level of the state, implicating economic and social elites in the process of state formation. In the case of France, the agency of state-building is absolute monarchy, while in Spain attempts to create absolute monarchy are frustrated by essentially territorial resistance. In Italy, there was no process of state formation at all in the period in question.

The making of the United Kingdom

In England, the re-establishment of monarchical authority after 1485, the breakdown of feudalism and economic expansion provided the basis for the consolidation of the

English state. The destruction of the power of territorial magnates was followed under Henry VIII's minister Thomas Cromwell by an attack on the supranational authority of the Papacy and the economic power of the religious orders. This did not lead to absolute monarchy under the Tudors, for the Henrician settlement was carried out in alliance with the 'gentry', the landed classes coming to dominate the countryside and state sovereignty was vested not in the monarch but in the Monarch-in-Parliament. Attempts in the civil wars of the seventeenth century to alter this pattern were ultimately unsuccessful and the settlement of 1688 confirmed the oligarchical regime under a constitutional monarch. It is unclear just how far Thomas Cromwell had a strategic vision and certainly he was more of a monarchist than an oligarch but the implications of his work, the creation of a unitary state were truly revolutionary (Elton, 1977). It laid the basis of the oligarchical power system which was to dominate British politics for three centuries and of the constitutional doctrine of parliamentary sovereignty which has prevailed to this day.

English constitutional practice succeeded in the creation of a unitary state, with no competing centres of power internally or externally but without an absolute monarchy, a centralised bureaucracy or, for many years, a standing army. While London was the centre of political activity and the Crown-in-Parliament the sole source of legitimate authority, most of the humdrum business of administration was devolved to local collaborators, Justices of the Peace, local squires, themselves part of the ruling oligarchy represented in Parliament. As a consequence, there did not develop a sharp distinction between 'state' and 'society' since the state was based on monarchical power together with the collaborative territorial/parliamentary elite and 'society' was identified with the latter. For the same reasons, there was no distinction between the 'nation' and the state as thus defined (Breuilly, 1985), hence the ability of constitutional theory to invest sovereignty, externally and internally defined, in the institution of Parliament and the failure to develop a theory of nationalism apart from this. What was to be even more remarkable was the translation of this constitutional order into a modern urbanised, industrial society in which working-class interests were staking a claim to influence.

Another reason for the failure to develop an English nationalist identity was that England was not to remain a state into the age of nationalism but was transformed into the United Kingdom by union with its neighbours and simultaneously became the centre of an overseas empire. Wales was attached to England after the defeat of the incipient nationalist movement in the fourteenth century. The 1536 Act of Union largely assimilated it into England in economic, legal and political terms and started a period of dominance by the anglicised gentry. Welsh identity was preserved largely by the Welsh language, itself safeguarded by geographical remoteness and by the class differences between the anglicised gentry and the natives but the lack of distinctive institutions inhibited the expression of political issues in Welsh terms.

In Scotland an independent state had emerged from the wars of independence of the fourteenth century and a precocious statement of nationalist ideology had even been produced in the Declaration of Arbroath. With a weak monarchy and recurrent internal divisions, it lurched between dependence on England and on France until the triumph of the Protestant Reformation and the defeat of Mary Stuart determined alignment with the former. The Union of the Crowns of 1603 tied Scotland's fortunes to those of England during the civil tumults of the seventeenth century while Scottish parliamentary institutions atrophied, enjoying only a brief revival before 1707. The causes and effects of the Union of Parliaments in that year have never ceased to arouse controversy. Nationalists focus on the extent of bribery of members of the Scots Parliament as the key factor in securing the passage of the Union. Certainly, bribery was extensive, in accordance with the best eighteenth-century practice, but in its absence it is unlikely that the result would have been radically different. There appears to have been little popular enthusiasm for the Union—even discounting the unrepresentative nature of the anti-union Edinburgh mob. On the other hand, Union resulted from political developments within Scotland. It was not imposed by force of arms and is certainly not to be seen as a colonial annexation. Economic factors played an important part in its making. After the failure to establish a Scottish colony at Darien, the Scots merchant classes wanted access to English colonial markets which only union could bring. Influential groups in Edinburgh also feared the return of the Stuart dynasty which they associated with absolute monarchy, Catholicism and the French alliance.

Where the framers of the Union might be criticised is in their lack of constitutional imagination. The Act of Union is an extremely untidy compromise. For the dominant Scots classes, what mattered was to secure economic union with access to colonial markets while at the same time preserving vital elements of Scots civil society such as the separate church establishment, the local administration of the royal burghs and the legal system. A Parliament was seen as less crucial in those days, though it may seem obvious to a modern observer that, without political institutions, these guaranteed rights might prove impossible to maintain. For English politicians, a Scottish Parliament represented a possible centre for Jacobite intrigues (Harvie, 1977), and after a half-hearted plea for federalism, the Scots negotiators accepted the full union under a single parliament (Ferguson, 1968). Both English and Scottish parliaments were abolished and a new unified Parliament established on the basis of the Act of Union. Public law was to be common throughout the state but matters of Scots private law were to be altered only for the 'evident utility of the subjects within Scotland', a vague formula with no mechanism for determining its meaning in any given case. In the event, the new Parliament of Great Britain took on all the practices and the inheritance of the English Parliament, even celebrating its 'seven hundredth anniversary' in 1954. More importantly, it assumed absolute sovereignty, to the extent of overriding the provisions of the Act of Union on several occasions, thus showing up the absence of any mechanism for making the terms of the union effective.

For most of the eighteenth and nineteenth centuries there was little opposition in Scotland to the union. Such as there was tended to come from Jacobites, supporters of the exiled Stuart dynasty, who while seeking a return to the British throne, offered repeal of the parliamentary union as part of their platform. In practice, Jacobitism gained most of its support among the Celtic and Gaelic-speaking Highland clans of Scotland's periphery and struck fear into the hearts of Lowlanders. The final defeat of Jacobitism at Culloden in 1746 and the subsequent destruction of most of the Gaelic culture was less of a triumph of England over Scotland than of Lowland Scotland over Highland Scotland but was critical in allowing a modern, more unified Scottish identity to emerge.

Between 1746 and the expansion of the franchise in the nineteenth century, Scotland was run as a political dependency of the British oligarchy. In return for securing a majority of Scottish Members of Parliament for the government of the day, the Scottish 'manager' was given a free hand with local patronage. The extremely limited franchise in Scotland (Harvie, 1977), together with the existence of separate Scottish offices and institutions, thus enabled the manager to establish a clientele, while the parliamentary union enabled him to deliver votes to the British government. So Scotland was contained politically while keeping its own identity and institutions and, over much of 'low politics', continuing to be governed by its native elites. As long as the union safeguarded the position of the separate Scots legal profession and of the ministers of the church, with their control over education, these were unlikely to challenge it. The system was not only corrupt, though, it was also increasingly inefficient as the nineteenth century advanced. While management fell into disuse after the franchise expansion of 1832, demands for the reform of Scottish administration strengthened in mid-century to form part of the platform of the emerging Scottish nationalist movement.

The management of Scottish politics on behalf of the Westminster oligarchy did not mean that Scots occupied a subordinate role in the British state. This was far from the case. Union had open up trade in England and the colonies to Scottish entrepreneurs and the development of native capitalism in Glasgow, successively in tobacco, in cotton and in heavy industries, owed much to this. By the end of the nineteenth century, Glasgow boasted of being the 'second city of the British Empire' with industrial wage levels above those of London. Scots were prominent in imperial administration, the military and engineering and, far from being a colonised nation (Hechter, 1975), Scots were among the most active colonisers of the nineteenth century. Even the remnants of the old Highland culture, once their subversive potential had been destroyed, were pressed into the service of the Empire, with the creation of kilted Highland regiments and the adoption of a romanticised version of Scottish culture by the monarchy.

Ireland's accession to the United Kingdom took a different form again. The claims of the English Crown to Ireland went back to the Norman invasion of 1169, but for over three hundred years, however, the effective power of the monarchy was confined to an area around Dublin known as the Pale, while the Norman settlers, through intermarriage and alliances with the Gaelic tribes, became indistinguishable from the native Irish (Kee, 1976). In contrast to Scotland there was no successful effort to create an independent Irish state, though an Irish Parliament had developed in the Middle Ages. In the sixteenth century, as part of their programme for strengthening royal power, the Tudors determined to subdue Ireland. The Irish Parliament was subjected, under Poyning's law, to the supremacy of that of England while in 1541 Henry VIII had himself proclaimed in Dublin 'King of this realm of Ireland as united, annexed and knit for ever to the Imperial Crown of the Realm of England' (Kee, 1976).

Ireland's effective colonial status was reinforced by the Reformation. As most of the Irish remained Catholic, they were perpetually regarded as potentially disloyal to the national Protestant order of England and a danger in England's conflict with the Catholic powers of Europe. Resistance by the Gaelic nobility to the centralising policies of the Tudors was finally crushed at the battle of Kinsale in 1607 and a policy of 'plantation' by Scottish Protestants was started in the north of Ireland. Thereafter, land and religion provided a powerful focus for resentment among the Catholic Irish. It was a rebellion in Ireland in 1640 which, forcing Charles I to reconvene the English Parliament to collect taxes, led to the English Civil War. The victory of the extreme Protestant party on the parliamentary side led to further suppression under Cromwell. In the late seventeenth and early eighteenth centuries, Jacobitism gained in Ireland, as in the Highlands of Scotland, the support of traditional, anti-centralist and Catholic elements. This not only reinforced suspicion of Ireland among the English Whig elite but deepened the division within Ireland between Catholics and Protestant settlers who, unlike previous generations of settlers, were to remain unintegrated into Irish society.

The government of Ireland, too, developed in a colonial mode, with a separate administration under a Lord Lieutenant who, in contrast to Scottish practice, was invariably English. The Irish Parliament, being entirely Protestant, excluded not only the middle and lower classes, as did those of England and Scotland, but also the Catholic gentry. Penal laws persecuted those of the Catholic religion while land was held in large estates by Protestant families, the Anglo-Irish 'ascendancy' who identified with the English regime. Regular rebellions reinforced England's view of Ireland as a danger to Britain's back-door, but without succeeding in forging a strong sense of Irish national identity before the nineteenth century. The Enlightenment of the late eighteenth century did produce some relaxation and reform. Catholics were permitted to buy land and under Grattan the Irish Parliament recovered some of its independence, though remaining exclusively Protestant. The French Revolution held out the promise of further liberation for some enlightened middle-class Protestants who launched the rebellion of the United Irishmen, in alliance with Catholic malcontents and land-hungry peasants.

Its defeat led to a policy of increased integration. In 1800, with fears of a French invasion, the Irish Parliament was suppressed and Ireland given representation in the British Parliament at Westminster. Executive government was shared by the Lord Lieutenant and the Chief Secretary, a member of the British Cabinet. The franchise remained tightly restricted and Catholics excluded until 1829 but this was equally true of England and Scotland. What distinguished Ireland was the absence of powerful local collaborators for the regime. In a rural Irish community, the landowner was regarded as a usurper, the Protestant minister of the established Church of Ireland as a heretic (Dangerfield, 1979) and the relations of deference and duty found in the English 'squirearchical' system were largely absent (Macdonagh, 1977). Local administration and justice remained in the hands of the resident magistrate, a centrally-appointed figure more familiar in continental states. So large sections of Irish society were alienated from the state, denying it the sort of legitimacy it might command in England and regarding the periodic attacks on landlords and the symbols of state power if not with enthusiasm then with passive tolerance. Of course, Irishmen up until and during the First World War enlisted in the British Army but this in itself is no proof of commitment to the established state. It merely indicates that Irish nationalism had not yet taken hold as a competing and exclusive focus of loyalty, excluding the British connection; the phenomenon is found in many colonial situations. Despite Ireland's membership of the United Kingdom, there was limited cultural assimilation over the centuries. The Irish language did retreat to the western periphery but speaking English did not cause the Irish to think like Englishmen.

The Irish economy developed in a dependent mode. Union was followed in 1825 by free trade with Britain and in 1826 an assimilation of the currencies (Lyons, 1971). Previously protected industries collapsed though in the north-east, strong industries developed in linen, shipbuilding and engineering, geared to export markets and thriving in free-trade conditions. For the country as a whole, there developed a 'dual economy' reminiscent of colonial situations. The 'maritime economy' of the east coast was commercialised and geared to trade with England; the 'internal economy' of the interior was largely based on subsistence agriculture. The great famine of 1849 was an indictment of this unbalanced pattern of development, an indictment which was in due course turned on the union itself.

This is not to say, though, that England's presence in Ireland was dictated by economic considerations. In fact, Ireland was regarded by British governments until the late nineteenth century largely in security terms. It presented a threat to internal order, with its outbreaks of peasant violence and secret societies, and an invitation to external enemies.

Pacification was pursued by alternating periods of reform and repression. Its ruling classes were part of the wider British and imperial political society. The masses were not part of this political society, any more than their counterparts in England, Scotland and Wales, but not until the national and industrial revolutions of the nineteenth century did this become the key issue and the ambiguous status of Ireland—colony, integrated territory or federal unit—within the realm have to be faced.

France—the myth of the nation-state

France is often seen as the archetypal example of the formation of a nation-state through the process of diffusion and assimilation in which political, economic and cultural values were unified within a set of 'natural boundaries', the Alps, the Pyrenees, the Atlantic, the North Sea and the Rhine. In practice, matters were a great deal more complicated than this. Hayward (1983) claims that France should be regarded as a 'state-nation' rather than a 'nation-state', a unitary state imposed upon a multinational society in which 'the peoples which make up France may have been swallowed up but are not wholly digested' (Hayward, 1983, p. 21). Braudel (1986), warning against geographical determinism, insists that the creation of France was the work of men and that the idea of natural boundaries, too, was something which was invented after the event to legitimise the state rather than a driving force in its creation.

France was in fact a dynastic creation of the Middle Ages. At the death of the Holy Roman Emperor Charlemagne, his kingdom was divided into three. With the elimination of the 'Middle Kingdom' (the Lotharingian empire) by the Oath of Verdun in 843, two kingdoms were created which romantics like to see as the basis of contemporary France and Germany. In fact the Capetian monarchy established in Paris in 987 controlled a small territory around the Île de France. The southern territories of Occitania (about 40 per cent of present-day France) were beyond its control until the thirteenth century while the rise of English and Burgundian power in the fourteenth century hemmed it in to the west, north and east. In Occitania a separate language had evolved with its own literature and the rich culture of the troubadors. Political power was in the hands of local magnates who were sometimes unsure whether their nominal feudal superior was the King of France or the King of Aragon (Armengaud and Lafont, 1979). A separate state might have developed, independently or as part of a greater Catalonia, were it not for a series of political and religious events. By the thirteenth century, the spread of the Cathar heresy, abetted by some of the local nobles who had their eyes on church lands, was exercising the Pope greatly. A pastoral approach having failed, the Pope decided on a military crusade which, rooting out heresy, would inevitably mean a conflict with the nobles who protected it. At one time, he considered entrusting the task to the King of Aragon but preferred to leave him the task of fighting the Moors in Spain; he was also fearful that the creation of a greater Catalonia could destabilise papal influence in the Mediterranean (Armengaud and Lafont, 1979). The King of France, to whom he next turned, proved unwilling, engaged as he was against England. So the Pope was reduced to announcing a crusade, encouraging French nobles led by Simon de Montfort to flock to Occitania in hopes of conquest. Only after the death of de Montfort fifteen years later and well after the subjugation of the local aristocracy, did the French King take advantage of a power vacuum to intervene and annex Occitania to France.

Burgundian and English power was not destroyed until the fifteenth century and, with the annexation of Brittany by dynastic marriage in 1536, France attained very approximately its present boundaries, though it was later to acquire Roussillon, Alsace, Nice and Savoy. The establishment of a unified monarchy was a far cry from the building of a uniform state, culturally, economically and politically integrated. Rather the French monarchy inserted itself into the institutions and customs which it found, concluding a series of 'historic compromises' with its new subjects (Braudel, 1986) and leaving them to run their own affairs as long as it was guaranteed peace, a supply of grain and a reasonably steady flow of taxes. Some provinces retained their medieval representative institutions, the *états*, with their three orders of nobles, clergy and townsfolk, though some of these just faded into disuse, like the *états* of Normandy (1655) and Auvergne (1651) (Braudel, 1986). Local *parlements* functioned as judicial/administrative bodies and generally saw to 'defence of local and provincial privileges and liberties and adaptation of French law to local and provincial customs and usages' (Mousnier, 1984). Holders of bought offices regarded themselves by their purchase as independent of royal power, while tax farming, though it assured the monarchy of its funds, made control of abuse virtually impossible. Internal customs barriers persisted up to the Revolution and territorial privileges abounded (Braudel, 1986).

There were major language differences not only between the *langue d'oïl* of the north and the *langue d'oc* of the south but also within these categories, while substantial numbers spoke Breton, Catalan and Flemish. The *langue d'oc* was the first vernacular to be used in official documents at a time when Latin was still used in the limited territories of the King of France but after the Albigensian conquest the Occitan nobility went over to French (the *langue d'oïl*) which was henceforth used in official transactions. This was a measure of cultural assimilation for the upper classes but had little impact on the illiterate masses; in the long run, though, it was to prevent the development of a written standard for Occitan and help reduce it to a series of peasant *patois*.

Some moves to unification and integration were made after the wars of religion (1562 to 1598) and the consolidation of the monarchy under Henry IV and again after the Frondes (1648 to 1653). The territorial nobility were subdued and brought to Paris where they kept their privileges but lost their power. Richelieu limited the powers of the *parlements* and removed the fiscal privileges of Burgundy, Dauphiné and Provence but left the other special *pays d'état* to keep theirs (Green, 1964). Colbert established a customs union covering about half of France. Gradually, a system of *intendants* was established to act as the king's direct representatives in the provinces and their *généralités* came to supersede the provinces as the main unit of administration but the system remained haphazard and *ad hoc*. The powers of the absolute monarchy were extended in other dimensions. Monarchical control of the church, first attempted in the Pragmatic Sanction of Bourges (1438) was consolidated and the national parliament, the States General, having long conceded the king the power to raise money for a standing army, was not summoned for a hundred and seventy-five years. It was left to the Revolution, though, to create a French nation and with it a nation-state.

Spain and the Empire

Spanish unity came about through a mixture of conquest and dynastic expansion and, as in the United Kingdom, the extension of the national territory immediately preceded the creation of empire, with important implications for the development of the Spanish state. There is no dispute that the political core of the state was the Kingdom of Castile, expanding in the Middle Ages to conquer the Moorish territories of the south in a process later glorified as the *Reconquista*, the 'restoration' of lands to Spain and Christianity. Dynastic marriages united the Christian kingdoms of Leon, Navarre, Aragon and Portugal to Castile by the end of the fifteenth century but not to create a unitary state on the English model. Instead, the various territories of the Spanish Crown retained an extraordinary variety of feudal privileges and institutions. Castile was the nearest to a unitary monarchical state, with a weak Cortes (parliament) and a uniform tax system but in their other territories the powers of the monarchs were severely circumscribed. In Navarre and the Basque provinces, ancient *fueros* provided for separate customs duties and the payment of a lump sum of taxation by the provinces to the Crown, each province being free to determine how this should be raised (Vasquez, 1981). The Kingdom of Aragon was itself a confederation of four territories, Aragon, Catalonia, Valencia and the Balearic islands, each with its own parliamentary institutions, laws and taxes. In the Middle Ages, the Aragonese kings had been in the habit of dividing their kingdoms among their sons, giving rise to such ephemeral entities as the Kingdom of

Montpellier and Majorca (Suarez, 1981).

Under the Spanish kings from the sixteenth century, there was little attempt at assimilation. Four languages remained: Castilian, Catalan, Gallego-Portuguese and Basque. There were royal councils for Castile (including the Basque provinces and Navarre) and for Aragon (including all the territories of the Aragonese Crown) but local customs and institutions severely limited their scope. In practice, Castile was ruled directly from Madrid while in the Aragonese territories there was a Castilian viceroy who could do little without the consent of the local Cortes or its executive body, the *Diputación*. None of the non-Castilian territories was obliged to raise taxes except for its own administration and defence. On the other hand, the new possessions in America were attached to the Crown of Castile and Castilians had an effective monopoly on their colonisation. The structure was further complicated by the accession of the Bourbon Charles V to the Holy Roman Empire, creating a multinational European empire within which was a multinational Spain, its component units themselves internally divided. With Spanish kings looking outwards, there was little incentive to nation-building at home (Linz, 1973).

While the immediate effect of the American connection was to enrich Castile so that it overtook the old medieval trading economy of Catalonia, the longer-term effects of empire were disastrous. American gold caused inflation and a loss of competitiveness in Castile, while emigration and harvest failures drained its population in the course of the seventeenth century (Vasquez, 1981). European wars imposed heavy taxation burdens which the non-Castilian territories refused to share. Divergent economic interests were a further centrifugal factor, with Catalonia continuing to look to its trading interests in the Mediterranean but fearing increased French competition and already in the sixteenth century formulating the protectionist demands which were to be such a prominent feature of later history (Vasquez, 1981). Navarre favoured free trade while the Basques enjoyed their privileged position which allowed them their own customs regime and also access to the Castilian market.

This all seems to present major problems for a simple

centre–periphery diffusionist model of nation-building. Certainly, we can identify a political core, the Castilian Crown which, by military conquest and dynastic marriages contrived to create a Spanish kingdom. At the same time, however, the central political elite was pulled into overseas ventures in Europe and America, bypassing its own peripheral territories. In the absence of political and administrative unity, there was little cultural diffusion. Separate languages remained in Catalonia, Galicia and the Basque country with the major unifying factor at the cultural level being provided by the Catholic religion, itself an ambiguous factor in national integration since it was based on allegiance to an external power, the Papacy. The pull of external forces on Spain also makes it difficult to speak of an economic core, with the economic advantage lying with Castile or the Catalan and Basque peripheries at various times.

There were attempts to convert Spain into a unitary state. In 1624, for example, Philip IV's minister Olivares showed a keen understanding of the needs of state-building in a secret memorandum (Linz, 1973). This set out three ways to build a unitary state. The first, 'the most difficult to achieve but the best if it can be managed' was to integrate the people of the kingdoms, 'introducing them to Castile, marrying them to Castilians' and 'by admitting them to the offices and dignities of Castile, to prepare a union'. The second was to negotiate, but from a position of strength, when the army and fleet were otherwise unoccupied. The third, 'not so justified but most effective', was to provoke a popular tumult as a pretext for military intervention. In 1635, with French troops threatening the frontier, Olivares' opportunity came and he demanded a financial contribution from the non-Castilian territories. Navarre and Aragon paid up but Portugal and Catalonia rose in revolt. Portugal's rebellion succeeded but in Catalonia the outcome was the division of the territory, with France, on which the Catalans had counted for support, taking possession of a part of Catalonia which it has held ever since.

The continued weakness of the monarchy, however, prevented the complete assimilation of Catalonia and, with the fall of Olivares, the attempt to establish a unitary state was abandoned until after the war of Spanish succession. Then support for the Hapsburg Carlos by the Aragonese territories sealed the fate of their representative institutions and in 1714 the victorious Bourbon Philip v set about creating a unitary state on the lines of Louis XIV's France (Vasquez, 1981)—or at least what France was thought to be. Foral rights and the local *diputaciones* were suppressed in Aragon, Valencia and the Balearic islands, together with the Cortes and Generalitat of Catalonia. Local customs duties were abolished, municipal privileges suppressed, the four Catalan universities replaced with a new one, the laws unified and, by the decrees of the *Nueva Planta*, modern administrative units created which ignored traditional boundaries. Posts in the Aragonese territories were opened up to Castilians and the American trade to Catalans and others. On the other hand, in the Basque provinces and Navarre, which had supported the Bourbon side, the old foral regime was left intact for another century.

The *Nueva Planta* programme marked a major step forward in nation-building but did not destroy territorial politics. Historians are generally agreed that union helped the economic take-off of Catalonia. Destruction of archaic local and municipal privileges aided trade while the mercantilist policies pursued by Spanish governments gave the nascent Catalan industries advantages in Castilian markets, and with the abolition of the colonial monopoly of Seville and Cadiz those of America. The economic core of Spain began to shift decisively to the periphery. Yet the political core remained in Madrid and the abolition of the Generalitat, like that of the Scottish Parliament, would present a potent symbol of lost identity to future generations of nationalists. Failure to tackle the privileges of Navarre and the Basque country indicates that the programme, like the incorporation of Scotland and Ireland into the United Kingdom, was more a pragmatic step to consolidate the dynastic regime against an obvious threat than a determined effort at national unification.

The Unification of Italy

If the creation of Britain, Spain and France is conceded to be the work of dynasties, wars and politics, Italy is still sometimes cited as a case in which the 'nation' preceded the state. Indeed, the very description given to the process, the 'unification' of Italy suggests the consolidation of an existing entity rather than the creation of a new one. In practice, the creation of an Italian state was not so different from that of our other cases, but the climate was very different, for Italy was born into a world where the nation-state not only existed as a model but had been given ideological expression following the French Revolution. So the creation of the Italian state was accompanied by the intellectual movement of the *Risorgimento*, legitimating it as a means of unifying a single people—but the influence of the movement on the actual process of state-building was limited, and the ideology of nationalism never penetrated more than a tiny fraction of the population until well after the establishment of the state. Then, the influence of nationalist propaganda and historiography presented the whole process as a popular movement based on a surge of national consciousness (Grew, 1963; Mack Smith, 1968a). In fact, the most glorious expression of the *Risorgimento* was the failed revolutionary movement of 1848, crushed by domestic reaction and foreign intervention and its greatest success, the political unification of Italy in 1870, was the fruit of cynical manipulation by ruling elites.

Mid-nineteenth-century Italy remained a mere 'geographical expression'. Though medieval and Renaissance scholars had an idea of 'Italy' as some sort of community, there was no agreement on what its boundaries were (Mack Smith, 1968a) and it had not been seen in terms of a unified state on the French model. It remained profoundly divided economically, culturally and politically. Economically, the north was beginning to industrialise and look towards northern and central Europe. In the south a backward agriculture prevailed, with a few small industries; feudalism had been abolished during the Napoleonic occupation but social relations remained semi-feudal. There was a 'standard' Italian based on the dialect of educated Florentines but few people spoke it, most of them as an 'artificial' second language. Apart from the myriad of local dialects, French was widely used in Turin, Latin in Rome and Castilian and Catalan in Naples, Sicily and Sardinia. Politically, Italy was divided into four main spheres, the possessions and dependencies of the Austrian Empire, the Papal States in the centre of the peninsula, the Kingdom of Piedmont and Sardinia in the north-west and the Kingdom of Naples and Sicily in the south. In addition, a number of small territories maintained a degree of independence among the rival powers. Localist sentiment was strong, though as it attached to small territories, towns and villages rather than to the states and dynasties, it eventually served to make the political unification of the peninsula easier, albeit doing nothing to promote national integration. With a history of centuries of invasion and occupation, politics in the peninsula remained critically dependent on the attitudes of foreign powers, while the support among many groups for the Napoleonic regime showed that sectional, class and individual interests were stronger than any nationalist ideology.

The three fathers of Italian unity are cited in nationalist historiography as Mazzini the philosopher, Garibaldi the soldier and Cavour the statesman. It is true that each brought a major contribution to the outcome and that Garibaldi did cooperate at times with Mazzini and, less willingly, Cavour but their perspectives and objectives were very different. Mazzini was to die under sentence of exile, officially banished from the new united Italy while Garibaldi never forgave Cavour for ceding his native city of Nice to the French as the price for their help in his acquisition of central Italy. For his part, Cavour seems to have abandoned his scheme for the creation of a north Italian state in favour of unification of the peninsula only when the opportunity for the larger goal presented itself around 1860 (Mack Smith, 1969).

Mazzini, the philosopher of the *Risorgimento*, was the product of the French Revolution and its doctrines of popular sovereignty and national self-determination (Romano, 1977), and believed in the necessity of popular insurrection to establish liberty and national unity. In practice his life was a history of plots and risings, often ill-prepared and all unsuccessful but despite this and his eventual disillusionment with the lack of enthusiasm on the part of the masses for Italian nationalism, he remained the inspiration for groups of intellectual and middle-class nationalists for many years. To the established governments of the peninsula, he represented a double subversion, for his republicanism and his belief in the dissolution of the existing state system. These fears were fully shared by the Kingdom of Piedmont and those who were eventually to unite Italy and, despite being elected to Parliament several times, he was never allowed legally to return from exile.

Garibaldi was the nationalist pure and simple. For him, Italian unity was the overriding goal, for which all other considerations must be sacrificed. Starting out in alliance with Mazzini and his popular nationalism, he later sided with the King of Piedmont, and having raised expectations of reform on his arrival in Naples and Sicily proceeded to put down peasant rebellions in the name of established authority.

In the event, it was not Mazzini's popular idealism or Garibaldi's nationalism which triumphed but Cavour's political manœuvring in a lucky combination of circumstances. Becoming Prime Minister of Piedmont in 1852, Cavour appears to have set the aim of building a north Italian state, politically conservative but economically advanced, to rival and emulate Britain and France. To this end, he conspired with Napoleon III of France and, with the benevolent neutrality of Britain, engineered a war with Austria, gaining the reward of Lombardy and Tuscany in 1860. Nice and Savoy were ceded to the French in return and, if respect for the principle of self-determination led to a referendum in Nice, it was agreed only on condition that the French could run it themselves so as to guarantee the correct result (Mack Smith, 1968a). Venice was to be acquired similarly in 1866 in alliance with Prussia despite another poor Italian performance in arms against the Austrians. The acquisition of the Papal States (except Rome) also occurred in 1860 when Cavour saw the opportunity to provoke incidents to justify an invasion on the pretext of preserving the conservative social order against the danger of revolution.

The annexation of the Kingdom of Naples and Sicily was

the work of Garibaldi who, taking advantage of a popular uprising in Sicily, embarked with his Thousand, landing at Marsala in May 1860. It seems clear that Cavour was opposed to this venture, distrusting Garibaldi's popular nationalism and suspicious of the whole idea of supporting revolutions, though the King may have given some private encouragement. Although Cavour had been unable to stop Garibaldi leaving Genoa, the Piedmontese government did confiscate his rifles and sent the navy to try and intercept him, only claiming credit for the expedition after its unexpected success (Mack Smith, 1968a). In fact, Garibaldi and his volunteers found a kingdom seething with discontent and a decrepit royal administration and army which soon collapsed before his forces, swollen as these soon were by local volunteers. After five months as dictator, he handed the new possessions over to King Victor Emmanuel of Piedmont and the unification of Italy was virtually over.

The enthusiasm which greeted Garibaldi's arrival in the south was no reflection of a popular desire on the part of the population for Italian unity, an idea regarded with indifference by those few who could understand it. Though to justify incorporation into the new state, a plebiscite was held, the 99% 'yes' vote invites suspicion. Voting was in public and southern peasants were disinclined to snub the new authorities so openly. Many peasants thought they were voting for Garibaldi and some Sicilians were said to be convinced that *L'Italia* or, rather *La Talia*, was King Victor Emmanuel's wife (Mack Smith, 1968a). The peasants had initially seen in Garibaldi's revolution the hope of land reform but their land seizures were firmly put down during his dictatorship as a threat to the state while the landowners for their part began to see in the new order a more effective safeguard for their interests than the defeated Bourbon monarchy. In this they were following an age-old tradition, persisting to the present day, of dominant elites in the south throwing their lot in with the prevailing power in return for retaining their own privileges. There followed a prolonged period of unrest characterised by the government as 'brigandage' but which some left-wing writers have described as more like civil war. Subduing the Mezzogiorno eventually required 250,000 troops, carabinieri and police, together with naval forces. Seven thousand were killed in battle, 2,000 executed and 20,000 sentenced to jail or forced labour (Salvadori, 1976). Just as it would be wrong to see the initial support for Garibaldi as evidence of popular enthusiam for Italian unity, so it would be a mistake to see the unrest as a protest against this. Certainly, a variety of political elements sought to exploit it, including elements of the old nobility, the clergy and officials of the old regime. Peasant revolts even took place under the old Bourbon flag with shouts for the exiled king but observers remarked that they would have shouted for the devil if he had promised them bread (Salvadori, 1976).

Cavour and his colleagues were profoundly ignorant of the ways of the Mezzogiorno and the government had no clear idea as to how to handle the administration of the territories so unexpectedly acquired. There were Jacobins, aiming for a centralised state on French lines to cement national unity. There were federalists who were aware of the great differences among the component parts of Italy and wanted to build unity from below. Most ministers, however, were indifferent to forms of government and merely wanted to consolidate their position as quickly as possible. The civil unrest called forth a strong response, the position of the landowners was buttressed and northerners sent into the south to organise the new administration. The result was less the creation of a new state than the annexation of the Mezzogiorno by Piedmont whose constitution, one of the few lasting fruits of 1848, was extended to the whole of Italy, remaining in force until 1946. Piedmontese laws, administration, tariffs and foreign obligations were extended to the whole country, the King retained his title of Victor Emmanuel II and internal customs barriers were abolished.

Most commentators are agreed that the abrupt merger of two such differing political and economic systems worked to the disadvantage of the south. Naples and Sicily under the Bourbons had maintained a system of industrial protection which was now overturned, allowing northern goods to wipe out the nascent industries of the south. Piedmont's high public debt became a charge on the whole country and the resulting higher taxation in the Mezzogiorno was compounded by the pattern of taxes while public expenditure was notably higher in the north (Salvadori, 1976). Not surprisingly, despite the conviction of many northerners that they were conferring great benefits on the backward south (Mack Smith, 1968b), all this caused great resentment in the Mezzogiorno and a periodic resurgence of autonomist and separatist sentiment, especially in Sicily. The old ruling classes were mollified when the dispossessed state and church lands were disposed of to them rather than the peasantry and their ranks were swollen by some middle-class elements which had made good in this way but the liberal middle classes remained alienated, as did the mass of the peasants.

So a unified Italian kingdom had been created but not as a result of the upsurge of Italian national feeling. Rather, unification suited the often short-term interests of key politicians and the nationalism of the romantics was used, as most, as a common language enabling elites to coordinate their actions (Breuilly, 1985). The absence of a popular basis for nationalism was one of the major problems in the way of the creation of an integrated nation after 1870 so that that task, too, had to be organised from above.

3
The National Revolution

Nationalism and the State

Nationalism, according to Kedourie (1966, p. 9), is 'a doctrine invented in Europe at the beginning of the nineteenth century', tracing its origins to the eighteenth-century Enlightenment and receiving democratic sanction in the French Revolution. Although there are earlier examples of nationalist feeling and a type of nationalist ideology in Europe, the modern doctrine was to be critical in the transformation of states into nations. The revolutionary doctrine of nationalism had both 'internal' and an 'external' dimensions. Internally it vested sovereignty in the people rather than the monarchy and was thus intimately bound up with the idea of liberty and the breaking of traditional structures of authority in the monarchy, feudalism, the aristocracy and the church. An extension of the principle of individual liberty was the 'external' aspect of national self-determination, according to which each people had the right to regulate its own affairs, free from external interference. Despite its appearance of elegance and simplicity, the doctrine is full of contradictions and problems. The peoples of most European countries in the nineteenth century failed to feel the spontaneous urge of nationalism and national feeling had to be created through education and socialisation. The units to which self-determination was to be conceded were not in any sense 'natural' or their boundaries obvious. Mazzini, for example, thought that Germany and Holland should be a single nation, that Hungary should be joined with Rumania and Greece with Bulgaria.

He also thought that all Scandinavia was a single nation but that Ireland was not a nation at all (Mack Smith, 1968a).

Another problem with the principle of self-determination, is that the nation could have no recourse against any subgroup within it which might decide to constitute itself a nation and secede. Yet the idea of secession was anathema to the Jacobin revolutionaries of France, as to their later imitators elsewhere. Mazzini was looked to for nationalist inspiration by elements of the emerging nationalism of Wales, despite the fact that, as a Jacobin centralist, he could be expected to have little sympathy with the sub-nationalisms of peripheral territories and had, as we have noted, explicitly denied Ireland's nationality. There was a further problem in accommodating the demands of sub-groups falling short of secession, for nationalism could recognise no intermediate institutions between the citizen and the nation-state, nor could it recognise that the content of citizenship could differ from one part of the state to another. So there was a tendency for extreme nationalists to insist on the centralisation of state power and uniformity of administration to the point that the term 'Jacobinism' itself came to refer to support for centralised government. Perhaps the basic problem here was the difficulty in bridging the gap beween individual liberty for the citizen and collective self-determination for the group, whether this be the nation, the sub-group or whatever. As Kedourie (1966, p. 32) puts it 'a society of autonomous individuals could not be that collection of individuals possessed of inalienable natural rights which, to the French revolutionaries, constituted the sovereign nation'. The problem was resolved by Fichte and the 'German' nationalists by denying that the primary unit was the individual at all and insisting that he derives his identity from the larger unit of which he forms part. In this way, nationalism was stripped of its liberal and individualist elements and became a doctrine justifying the subordination of the individual to the state. Although not all nationalisms have followed this train of development, Kedourie is no doubt right that this is the logical consequence of the pure doctrine of nationalism and it is not surprising that such exclusive claims of loyalty, even in their more moderate forms, have produced a reaction among groups seeking to maintain a degree of autonomy within the modern state. It is somewhat confusing that the territorial reaction against Jacobin nationalism has itself so often been described as 'nationalism', albeit sometimes with the prefix 'peripheral' or 'ethnic'. Though this reaction has often drawn on the same liberal and autonomist premisses as the Jacobin nationalism of the French Revolution, only in exceptional cases has it taken the form of the aspiration to create a new 'nation-state' on the lines of the old one. It has, though, given rise to a wide range of political programmes and coalitions.

Breuilly (1985) identifies the key feature of nationalism, not as a spontaneous eruption of mass feeling nor as a product of social and economic change—though these may help or hinder its development—but as a form of politics. It is about the organisation and distribution of power in the state and, despite all its intellectual and practical problems, Jacobin nationalism was an instrument of state-building elites, progressives and modernisers in nineteenth-century France, Italy and Spain. These sought, with varied degrees of success. to construct a politically and economically unified, modern, centralised and secular state, not necessarily democratic but based nevertheless on a popular sense of national identity, even if that sense had first to be created. With the social change and franchise extensions of the late nineteenth century, the state was forced to accommodate the aspirations of new social groups not previously part of the political nation, though sharing the same assumed national identity, producing territorial as well as social tensions within the four polities. At the same time, nation-building was conditioned by the external environment. This was critical in the case of the United Kingdom where nation-building was overtaken by imperialism, and in Spain where the loss of the external support system of empire caused a severe economic and political crisis for the regime. We must now examine the political basis of state-building in these four cases before going on to consider the economic, social and cultural basis for nation-building and the resistance which it encountered.

France—The Consolidation of the Jacobin State

As the French model of nation-building was to be so influential in nineteenth-century Europe, it makes sense to discuss French experience first in this chapter. Some writers (Avril, 1969; Tilley, 1964) have noted that the Revolution merely carried forward ideas about authority and power which had been developing in the eighteenth-century Enlightenment. The Revolution, by destroying intermediate forms of authority more effectively than the monarchy had been able to do and by investing sovereignty in the people, not only unified but also reinforced the state (Birnbaum, 1982). It abolished the old *parlements* and aristocratic and clerical privileges and established the *départements* and communes as the basic units of territorial administration. Thus it was hoped to suppress 'the provincial spirit, which was opposed to the national spirit, that is, to reform and progress' (quoted in Bernard, 1983, p. 30). Under Napoleon, prefects were appointed to represent the authority of government in the provinces and ensure the smooth administration of the unitary state, seen as an unbroken hierarchy from Paris to ground level (Machin, 1977). The autonomy of the state from competing pressures, whether territorial or corporate, was a constant theme of nineteenth-century French politicians, especially under the Third Republic. So Waldeck-Rousseau insisted that while there should be free debate in advance of decisions, 'after such discussions, the whole nation is the judge; it decides and its will must be obeyed by everyone' (quoted in Avril, 1969, p. 135), while Gambetta complained in 1881 about improper pressures on the prerogatives of the state (Avril, 1969). This ideology of the 'one and indivisible republic' has remained a powerful influence in French public life ever since, moulding the development of the bureaucracy, with its conception of the 'general interest' above squabbling factions and recurring in successive attempts at reform, down to the Fifth Republic. Recent scholarship showing that this is a poor description of reality does not detract from its influence as a prescriptive model for government in France and, often in exaggerated form, other countries. In particular, the association of centralisation with democracy and progress was to have a lasting impact on liberal and left-wing thought.

In practice, the attempt to impose a uniform and centralised system of government in nineteenth-century France encountered a host of difficulties, giving rise to a tension between the Cartesian clarity of the 'official' view of France and the untidy reality, which has formed a point of contention to this day. The various ministries spawned field offices which escaped prefectoral control, while the prefects themselves were engaged in a struggle for influence with local politicians. Though the prefects had a role in managing elections to secure the return of deputies favourable to the government, over time the relationship was reversed and by the end of the Second Empire in 1870, the deputies were in control. Under the Third Republic the role of the deputy in controlling local patronage, including prefectoral appointments, was consolidated while the power of the prefect was further reduced by the laws of 1871 and 1884 on direct elections and reform of the communes and *départements* (Machin, 1977). In practice then, the unity of the state gave way to a variety of devices for managing its diversity through the intermediation of territorial administrators and politicans, or *notables*.

Recognising that the 'one and indivisible republic' is a myth should not blind us to the considerable progress made in nation-building in nineteenth-century France, especially under the Third Republic after 1870. Weber (1977) stresses the importance of universal education, military service and improved communications. Jacobinism which at the Revolution had been a universalist ideology of liberation and democracy, came to be associated with French nationalism and support for the state against its enemies, both internal and external. Education was consciously used as an instrument for nation-building as well as dissemination of secular and republican values. The celebrated laws of Jules Ferry brought into being free, compulsory and secular education while deepening the gulf between the republic and the church; centralised state control over the curriculum was seen as an essential part of state-building. Regional languages were to be stamped out as barbaric and backward, for French was the language of progress. At the end of the Second Empire, some 70–90 per cent of the population of Languedoc, according to locality, were monolingual in Occitan (Armengaud and Lafont, 1979). In twenty-four of the eighty-nine *départements*, more than half the communes were non-French speaking (Weber, 1977). After 1870, state education and the need for a common languge for communication in a more mobile society rapidly reduced these figures. Patriotism became quite obsessive after 1870, with all French children taught the sacred duty of struggle to recover from Germany the lost provinces of Alsace and Lorraine and by 1914 France had largely succeeded in forging a nation, if not in eradicating local and provincial identities.

Spain—The Failure of the National Project

In Spain, state formation had left deep cultural, economic and political differences among its component parts and much of the nineteenth century was occupied by attempts to overcome these. The process was hampered, though, by the context of national decline, the loss of overseas empire and deep divisions of ideology, religion and class. The struggles against the Napoleonic invasion, the so-called 'War of Independence', do seem to have tapped a vein of Spanish national sentiment in the early nineteenth century (Olabarri, 1981) and the Constitution of Cadiz, forced on a reluctant king by liberal reformers, laid the basis for a unitary state on the French model. Regional, ecclesiastical and aristocratic privileges and guilds were to be swept away and a uniform system of local government established under a series of centrally-appointed *jefes* (Carr, 1975). Although the constitution was never implemented, it had a profound influence on later thinking. In 1833, the country was divided into artificial provinces, ignoring traditional boundaries, on explicitly 'Jacobin' grounds, to destroy old loyalties and allow no intermediaries between the state and the citizen (Olabarri, 1981). A civil governor, modelled on the French prefect, was appointed for each province and the elected *Diputación* was subordinated to him. In the Basque provinces, the *fueros* were abolished though, under pressure, the special taxation arrangements of the *conciertos económicos* were restored in 1878. Similar arrangements had earlier been made for Navarre. Reforms such as the 1857 Education Act, the Civil Procedure Code of 1855 and the Mortgage and Property Registration Law of 1863 ignored regional differences and destroyed the last traces of distinct Catalan law and administration (Linz, 1973).

Despite these importations from France, the Spanish state remained weak and archaic. While power for much of the century alternated between the parties of liberal conservatism, the limits to reform were set by the continued influence of the monarchy, the church and the army (Solé Tura, 1985). In a period of national decline, these were the bearers of a vision of Spanish national identity rooted in the past. The construction of a modern state was also inhibited by a series of Carlist revolts. Like Jacobitism in eighteenth-century Britain, Carlism had no consistent ideology but, drawing support from traditionalist and rural areas, tended to include in its programme the restoration of the traditional institutions of regional government, including the Basque *fueros*. This in turn reinforced the support of liberals and progressives for Jacobin centralisation but did not enhance their capacity to achieve it. Following the defeat by the United States in 1898 and the loss of the last of the Empire, a vision of Spanish nationalism was also taken up by the *regeneracionistas*, groups of intellectuals aiming to revitalise Spanish society, and to modernise and reform its institutions. Yet another vision of the nation was the federalist one, which had some influence within the republican fold and which saw national unity being created through decentralisation. It appealed neither to Jacobin unitarists nor to those seeking recognition of the peculiar status of Catalonia and the Basque Country, since federalists wanted decentralised but uniform institutions. Following the experience of the First Republic in the 1870s, federalism lost influence except among small groups of intellectuals. A sense of national identity had also begun to develop from the spread of universal education, modern communication, military service and the development of the state (Fusi, 1985). Yet none of the competing visions of Spanish nationalism, the old, military–clerical–monarchical one, the modernising Jacobin one, or the republican–federalist one, was able to create a state which could manage the deep ideological, religious and regional tensions within the country.

As in France and Italy, the superimposition of a unitary and uniform system of government on a diverse country with little tradition of political participation gave rise to a layer of intermediaries able to manage the relationship between the local society and the state, the *caciques* (Carabana, 1977). Although its origins lay in the mid-nineteenth century, *caciquismo* enjoyed its heyday during the Restoration regime of parliamentary monarchy from 1875 to 1923. A classic form of machine politics, it operated by trading the votes of the locality for governmental favours, allowing the *cacique* to establish extensive networks of patronage and clientilism (Carr, 1975). Like the French prefect, the civil governor was part of the system and had to help organise elections for the party in power while keeping in with the local *notables*. Again as in France, centralisation reinforced the power of the latter since, to get a favourable decision on any matter, it was necessary to exercise influence in Madrid, which only the *cacique* could do. Even the theoretical devolution of power to local government was largely illusory since the centre constantly intervened in response to pressure (Anderson and Anderson, 1967). Although both parties, Conservatives and Liberals, claimed to be against the system and many reform proposals were brought forward, the vested interests in *caciquismo* were too strong and, at the end of the day, central politicians feared a truly independent local government system which might encourage regionalism or federalist tendencies.

The Making of Italy

In Italy, the unified state was created very rapidly, not by the liberal visionary followers of Mazzini but by the Piedmontese monarchy and the activities of Garibaldi. As Cavour had hardly contemplated the idea of unified Italy before it happened, it is not surprising that he had few fixed ideas on its constitution. Instead, Piedmontese institutions and laws, themselves based on the French model, were extended to the whole country. Although Cavour had made promises of autonomy for Sicily at least (Mack Smith, 1968b), these were put aside in the turbulent aftermath of unification for fear of encouraging separatist forces, which might be exploited and encouraged by clerical and Bourbon elements. Liberals and progressives continued to preach Jacobin centralisation, fearing the reactionary potential of the south and jurists in the early years of the state looked to France for models and theories (Flogaitis, 1979). The non-recognition of the new state by the Catholic Church, while depriving it of legitimacy in the eyes of a large section of the population, also weakened those who might have argued within it against the secular, Jacobin trend. There was in the late nineteenth century a federalist movement comparable to that of Spain, arguing for federalism, not as a means of weakening unity but of strengthening it by recognising a degree of diversity but maintaining uniform institutions (Good, 1976), but it was largely confined to intellectuals and had little political impact. Parliamentarians continued to profess at least a verbal Jacobinism and proposals for regional government presented by the Minister of the Interior Minghetti were rejected by Parliament in 1861 (Rotelli, 1973).

Despite the French inheritance, the politicians of monarchical Italy never succeeded in building a modern state machine on Jacobin lines. Prefects were appointed, uniform local government instituted and laws and the administration unified. The education system and military service were used to spread national consciousness, and as illiteracy declined from 78 per cent in 1861 (Romano, 1977) the standard Italian language spread. The social basis of the regime, however, prevented the construction of a modern, efficient state. Politics in Rome came to be characterised by a pattern of alliances known as *trasformismo* in which potentially disruptive elements were absorbed into the governing coalition. So, while the interests of northern industrialists and southern landowners might seem in conflict, they were reconciled in an effective alliance to the exclusion of the northern industrial proletariat and the southern peasantry. This prevented a social revolution in the south which might have created a popular constituency for the unified state. Instead, the social and economic system of the south was left largely undisturbed apart from the incorporation of the layer of new bourgeois who had profited from unification by acquiring church and Bourbon state lands.

The territorial expression of *trasformismo* was a clientilistic system. By delivering a solid block of parliamentary votes to the government of the day which might change its complexion from time to time but was never supplanted, southern deputies were able to secure prominent positions in government and were allowed control over patronage within their constituencies (Anderson and Anderson, 1967). The local government system, by placing impossible demands upon councils, reinforced centralisation and, consequently, the role of the deputy as the man who could get things done in Rome. At the same time, by reducing political questions to individuals' problems, the system inhibited the aggregation of demands on a territorial basis.

The phenomenon was taken furthest in the Mezzogiorno and particularly in Sicily. Sicilian deputies, usually from the landlord class, including those who had enriched themselves with dispossessed church and state lands after unification, would rarely speak in Parliament but always vote with the government, meeting in private to concert their policy and protect Sicilian affairs from parliamentary scrutiny (Mack Smith, 1968b). Prefects who refused to go along with the local bosses could be removed, revenues were diverted into private pockets and corruption and intimidation were so rife that it was known for juries to protest at not being bribed. By the end of the nineteenth century, the Mafia, drawing on old Sicilian traditions but reinforced by American repatriates, was thriving, using the machinery of the state for its own ends and those of its landed allies but posing as heroic defenders of Sicily against the 'foreigners' of the north (Mack Smith, 1968b). So Sicily and the south of Italy adapted to unification as they had adapted to changes of rulers over the centuries, with local political and economic elites making an accommodation with the new regime. This is not to say that the south did not change, but rather that the mechanisms of accommodation to the sovereign power of the day remained in place, to be adapted and exploited by successive ruling elites. The Italian national revolution had not been achieved.

The United Kingdom—A Multinational State

The United Kingdom stands apart for its lack of an official nationalist ideology. The explanation of this lies in constitutional and historical experience. In the absence of a British revolution, no doctrine of popular sovereignty comparable to that of France emerged. Rather, sovereignty remained vested in the institution of the Monarch-in-Parliament as in pre-modern continental regimes, while the parliamentary franchise was successively extended to accommodate new social interests. So, although the oligarchic constitution was gradually reformed, the basic rules of the political game remained the same. Imperialism was also a crucial factor. The construction of the United Kingdom coincided with that of the Empire and it was the latter which was the focus of loyalty and the target of socialising measures through education and public ceremonials. That parliamentary sovereignty was really the only constitutional principle which the country possessed provided a considerable degree of flexibility in governmental arrangements, yet, in the twentieth century, was to pose serious problems for efforts to reform the state. The parliamentary regime was itself maintained partly by the pattern of territorial government beneath it.

'Anglo-Saxon' self-government was regarded with considerable admiration by nineteenth-century continental observers brought up in centralist regimes with their accompanying clientilism and other distortions of local politics. Yet the phrase 'Anglo-Saxon' is misleading not only in confounding England with the Celtic periphery but also in lumping Britain in with the United States. In the USA, local self-government rests upon traditions of pluralism and self-help. In the United Kingdom, local government derives its power and authority from Parliament and exists as its creature. As Bulpitt (1983) has shown, local government represented not so much the ability of local elites to wrest power from the centre but the convenience for the centre in handing over 'low politics' to trusted local collaborators, freeing itself to concentrate on the 'high politics' of empire, foreign affairs and finance. The 'dual polity' was thus less about local autonomy from the centre than about central autonomy from the local pressures, something not achievable in the centralist–clientilist systems of France, Spain and Italy. The resultant exclusion of territorial politics from Westminster allowed the development of an alternating two-party system at the centre and, in due course, the replacement of the Liberals by Labour as one half of this, once the latter had learnt the rules of the parliamentary game (Jones and Keating, 1985).

Territorial politics was further contained by varieties of administrative devolution to the various constituent countries of the UK. Ireland continued to be governed in a quasi-colonial mode, with a Chief Secretary, a member of the Cabinet and usually an English MP, heading a separate administration. From early days of the Union, little faith was placed in local collaborators since the local elites were alienated culturally, religiously and politically from the mass of the population even before the democratic upsurge of the late nineteenth century. Instead, an administration more akin to the ideal Napoleonic model was created, with resident magistrates sent into the country from London and a centralised police force, an invention which, on the mainland, was still regarded as a dangerous threat to local liberties (Dangerfield, 1979).

In Scotland considerable leeway was given to local elites as long as these did not challenge the union. Though the Secretaryship had been abolished in 1746 precisely because of doubts about its loyalty, a separate legal system continued to exist, as did a separate established church and educational system. In the course of the nineteenth century there had been some creeping integration but after 1870 this was halted with the establishment of the Scotch (sic) Education Department and, in 1885, the Scottish Office. Only in Wales was there no concession to territorial distinctiveness though here, as in the English shires, the local gentry class maintained order, dispensed justice and provided what administration was felt necessary.

This degree of flexibility in governmental arrangements was possible precisely because of the absence of a project for the creation of a modern nation-state. Economic expansion, imperialism and British world dominance, what Bulpitt (1983) calls the 'external support system', in turn allowed the system to remain intact until the end of the nineteenth century when, in reaction to the threat from Germany and the United States, the social imperialist and national efficiency movements began (Barker, 1978), the nearest the United Kingdom has come to a national revolution. At the same time the British state was coming under a severe challenge from within which was forcing it to consider seriously the basis of its constitution.

The Economic Revolution

Late nineteenth–century states presided in each case over societies undergoing rapid economic and social change. The opening of markets and communications and the development of capitalist industry profoundly altered the internal economic balance, while in the agricultural sector population growth, and changes in technology and markets resulted in serious problems about land ownership and tenure. Land agitation was to be particularly closely associated with the development of territorial political movements but was by no means their only source. While it is often assumed that industrial development in itself and capitalism in particular will serve to break down territorial distinctiveness and reduce political issues to purely class or sectoral ones, in practice matters are not so simple. In fact, economic and industrial change, by altering the balance of class and territorial relations, brought a series of territorial issues onto the political agenda. The resulting conflicts involved the impact of national policies such as tariffs and central economic management as well as specifically regional policies and fed into the emerging regionalist and autonomist movements.

In France capitalist development and internal free trade favoured the north and the Paris region. While the advantages of the former may be explained largely in terms of natural resources, Paris owed its pre-eminence to the presence of the state, attracting banks and finance houses as well as making it the nodal point for transport routes. In the south, on the other hand, locally-based industries went into decline while few of the new or the heavy industries developed (Trempé,

1980). Lafont (1967) sees the consequent dependence of Occitania on extractive industry and agriculture whose products had to be sold to the north on unfavourable terms, as evidence of internal colonialism. This theme has recurred over the years, though it is not necessary to buy the whole internal colonialism thesis to accept that capitalism develops unevenly. Cultural as well as economic and political factors are important. The southern middle classes had little of the entrepreneurial spirit, preferring to place their money in land and buildings, railway development, government bonds or conspicuous consumption (Cholvy, 1980), resulting in a capital outflow from the region.

In the agricultural sector, while France did not have the same problem of landless labourers as Italy or Spain, there was a serious problem of small peasant proprietors, especially in the west and south. Unable to raise the capital to modernise and without control over access to national markets, these had great difficulty in surviving. Many of the Languedoc peasants turned to the easiest solution, the cultivation of the grape. The cooperative wineries eased the problem of distribution of the product while the viability of the industry was assured by protectionist and subsidy policies on the part of the state. These in turn were maintained through the intermediation of the local political *notables*. Periodic crises of disease and overproduction led to peasant unrest and the beginnings of a cross-class regional alignment uniting large landowners, small peasant producers and even labourers and the sense of regional solidarity which this engendered was a factor in the developing regionalist movement of the turn of the century.

Brittany, too, suffered from some of the effects of the economic revolution. As a maritime economy, it had traditionally looked outwards rather than to the interior of France, where communication was more difficult. The creation of a national market with external tariffs thus had the effect of increasing the peripheralisation of the province. Industry was slow to develop and the marketing of agricultural produce was a constant problem away from the railway lines.

In Spain industrialisation was most marked in Catalonia and the Basque Country, though the presence of the state machinery had encouraged some activity in Madrid. The rise of Catalonia represented a return to its economic dominance of the Middle Ages and here and in the Basque Country living standards moved decisively ahead. Industrialisation also created a capitalist middle class and a working class as well as producing large-scale immigration into Catalonia and the Basque Country from other parts of Spain. The resulting divorce between the centre of political power in Madrid and the centres of economic power in Catalonia and the Basque Country, gave rise to a complex pattern of territorial interests. While the Catalan middle classes regarded their region as subsidising the rest of Spain and might appear to have an interest in separatism or at least a high degree of home rule, their industry was dependent on a protected Spanish market. While in Spanish terms Catalan industry was advanced and competitive, compared with that of Britain and France and even northern Italy it was backward (Giner, 1984). So the Catalan middle classes developed an ambiguous attitude to the state, which they needed yet constantly attacked for its backwardness and lack of sympathy for industrial values. Basque capitalism, on the other hand, was much more integrated into the Spanish power structure (Solé Tura, 1985), particularly in the finance sector where the Basque houses dominated the Madrid banking system.

Within both regions, industrialisation had deepened class, sectoral and cultural divisions. In Catalonia the regionalism of the middle classes was attenuated not only by the desire for Spanish trade protection but also by the need to call on the Spanish state to suppress working-class discontent in the early years of the twentieth century. In Catalonia and, more markedly, the Basque Country, tensions between native and immigrant workers both fed Catalan nationalism and limited its appeal to the working class and, particularly, the socialist movement which came to regard it as a divisive force. Rural–urban divisions also deepened and the mediating role of the *caciques*, a marked feature of rural society, became more difficult in the urban context.

In the southern regions of Andalusia and Extremadura, industrial development was limited and small–scale. The loss of colonial trade together with Spanish protectionism deprived

Andalusia of the overseas markets which it needed and reduced it to a supplier of raw materials for industry in the north (Sevilla, 1986). Andalusian capital was diverted to the purchase of disentailed church lands, government bonds and speculative investments in Madrid. The result has been described as 'internal colonialism' in the terms familiar from analyses of southern France and Italy (Alburquerque, 1977). The principal social problem of Andalusia, though, was land, the predominance of *latifundia* and the army of landless labourers dependent on seasonal work. The dominant landowners, both traditional aristocracy and the newly-enriched, were part of the governing alliance in Madrid and, like their counterparts in southern Italy, had a vested interest in preserving the economic, political and social order including protectionist tariffs. In the countryside, the peasantry were scattered, insecure and disorganised while in the small towns, *caciques*, allied to the dominant classes, held sway, controlling access to state resources but not providing a dynamic productive bourgeoisie as in Catalonia and the Basque Country.

Galicia presents yet another pattern. In the absence of industrial development, the economy was dominated by small farms, *minifundia*, with a largely illiterate and deferential peasantry. The middle classes were well connected to the Spanish state and military, in which they often held important positions (Linz, 1973). Local politics were controlled by an alliance of lawyers and small landowners who had purchased church lands (Carr, 1975) and had access to Madrid. Wider political issues were reduced again to the distribution of state resources on a personalised basis.

Arguments over protectionism and free trade continued throughout the nineteenth century. In the 1880s, a National League of Producers embraced Catalan textile-producers, Basque steel-makers and Castilian wheat interests in an unusual alliance to press for protection. Under the Conservative government of 1891, tariffs were increased (Carr, 1975) but it was defeat in the Spanish–American war of 1898 and the loss of the last colonial markets which was to push tariff levels up to the highest in Europe. While this met one of the principal Catalan demands, the autonomist movement had now developed a momentum of its own and broken the old system of territorial representation (see below). In any case, the Catalan middle classes continued to regard Madrid as backward and unsympathetic to industrial values.

In Italy the main territorial problems continued to stem from the north–south division, the 'failed unification'. In the north, notably in Piedmont and Lombardy, a modern advanced industry had developed under a market-oriented, free-trade regime. In the south the economy remained predominantly agricultural, based on *latifundia* and an army of landless labourers, though under the protectionist regime of the Bourbons, a weak capitalism tied to the state had produced some industrial development (Davis, 1979). The immediate effect of unity, so drastically imposed in the 1860s, was to wipe out this nascent industry and with it the development of an industrial middle class or proletariat. Most liberals believed that the south was a naturally rich country ruined by Bourbon bad government and that, with free trade and unity, levels of development and living standards within the new state would be evened out by the operation of market forces. Yet the effect of the terms upon which unity was consolidated was to inhibit any such development, to immobilise southern economic and social development and to deepen the north–south divide. Taxation and expenditure policies had the same effect. As a result of the expansionist policies of its pre-unification governments, Piedmont–Sardinia had a public debt four times that of Naples and Sicily (Salvadori, 1976) while the latter had a full treasury, reflecting the Bourbons' lack of interest in public works (Galasso, 1978) but interpreted by northerners as further evidence of the natural riches of the south. The new state not only assumed the total debt of its constituent parts but brought in an inequitable form of taxation, which bore more heavily on land (where it was passed on in rents) than on movable goods.

Unification, with its promise of a national revolution, was not accompanied by a social and economic revolution, an attack on the social and economic power of the landed classes in the south. By and large, these made their peace with the new order, realising that the new regime was probably a more effective guarantor of their interests than the old. The suppression of the peasant disturbances in the 1860s amply confirmed this judgement. It was not that there was no change at all. The old landowning aristocracy was joined by a rising middle class made rich on the purchase of disentailed church and state lands and together they provided the economic and social basis for the regime of *trasformismo* in the late nineteenth and early twentieth centuries.

Observers came to recognise four social-territorial groups, the industrial middle classes of the north, the urban proletariat of the north, the landowners of the south and the peasantry of the south, which were the basis for the conflicts within the Italian liberal regime until its extinction by Fascism in the 1920s. The policies of the united state came to be geared to the alliance of northern industrialists and southern landowners. By the late nineteenth century, their representatives, faced with industrial and agricultural competition from Britain and France, had agreed on a policy of protectionism. While the sudden imposition of free trade had had a devastating effect on the south in the 1860s, protectionism within an Italian market produced equally severe distortions. Given the high protection for grain, its production was expanded at the expense of a diversified agriculture tailored to the climate and geography. In turn, this suited the interests of the large landowners but exacerbated the problem of the landless peasantry in the south. For their part, the representatives of the northern industrial workers in the emerging union and socialist movement were torn between support for free trade as an instrument against the industrial bourgeoisie and its allies in the southern *blocco agrario*, and an interclass protectionism to safeguard Italian industry against foreign competition.

In the United Kingdom the battle between agrarian protectionists and industrial free-traders was resolved by the middle of the nineteenth century. As the first and most advanced industrial country, the UK then preserved a vested interest in world free trade until the end of the century when, like other states, it experienced protectionist pressures. Industrial development was strongest in parts of the periphery, central Scotland, south Wales, northern Ireland and northern

England, near to sources of raw materials but, given the interest of British industrialists in *laissez-faire* and free trade, this did not give rise to territorial demands on the political system. Some of the spatial effects of industrialisation, though, were politically significant. In Ireland, industry was largely concentrated in the north-east, which was also the area of greatest Protestant settlement, giving the dominant groups within Ulster and a section of the working class a material interest in the British link. The effect was to increase the division within Ireland while not, however, reducing the political impact of religious differences within the north. Indeed, by increasing competition in the labour market, industrialisation reinforced sectarian differences in the north of Ireland and in western Scotland, where Scots and Irish workers vied for position.

In Ireland and the Highlands of Scotland, agrarian and land reform issues inspired strong territorial movements. Indeed, it was the peasantry of Ireland and Scotland who, well before the British industrial working class, first learnt to use parliamentary institutions as a means of furthering popular demands against entrenched economic interests. In Ireland, the struggle for the land was soon identified with the 'national' question, given that landlords tended to be Anglo-Irish and Protestant. Certainly, this is a simplification, for there were some Catholic landlords in the nineteenth century and some of the most prominent nationalists were to be Protestants, but this did not essentially qualify the contemporary perception of the problem. The history of land agitation goes back to the eighteenth century, when secret societies emerged to mete out rough community justice (Garvin, 1981) and a tradition of social solidarity against the landlords developed. In the north, however, the 'Ulster custom' provided greater security of tenure and, with a much lower level of land agitation, inhibited solidarity with the Catholic peasantry of the south. The historic disaster of the famine of the 1840s created a legacy of bitterness and distrust of British government, most marked among exiles and their descendants in the United States. The callousness of contemporary politicians to social distress may have been no more pronounced in Ireland than elsewhere in the UK and in Ireland the Malthusian crisis would have taxed the most caring government; but in Ireland the memory of the famine encountered a developing national consciousness. In the longer term, by reducing the population, the famine made viable a system of peasant proprietorship which could not possibly have supported a population of over eight milliion and this in turn was a factor in the developing national movement.

With falling agricultural prices and rising expectations from the late 1870s, evictions of defaulting tenants resumed and the most significant phase of land agitation began. The Land League blended the traditions of solidarity and anti-landlordism with the methods of the boycott into a disciplined mass organisation, the first of its kind in the United Kingdom. The expansion of the franchise and the institution of the ballot gave tenants a formidable weapon which convinced them that parliamentary activity was the means of their emancipation. Suppressed in 1882, the League was reconstituted as the Irish National League closely tied to the Irish Parliamentary Party and assuming the role of 'local law-giver, unofficial parliament, government, police and supreme court' (Garvin, 1981, p. 82). Land agitation was to provide the mainspring of Irish politics up to the end of the century.

In Scotland, land agitation was tied to the reform of the Highland crofting system. This had developed following the assumption of proprietory landlord rights by the Highland chiefs and the commercialisation of the estates, notably for sheep-rearing and later for sport. Evictions, known as 'clearances', reduced the numbers of peasant farmers, while the periodic raising of rents forced the crofters into the wage economy part-time in order to pay them. The 1840s potato failure did not lead to famine on the Irish scale but did produce large-scale emigration and further clearances. Then, as in Ireland, a brief period of stability was broken by the depression of the 1870s. With the support of southern Gaelic revivalist societies (see below), the Highland Land Law Reform Association was formed in 1883, in imitation of the Irish movement. Like the Irish, under middle-class leadership, they broke the hold of the Tory and Whig lairds in the crofting constituencies with five crofters' MPs elected in

1885, the first mass popular breakthrough in politics on the British mainland, and a precedent taken to heart by the early industrial Labour movement. By 1887, encouraged by the Irish example and the assumption that an English-dominated Parliament would never give a sympathetic ear to the crofting demands, crofters' leaders were calling for Home Rule for Scotland (Hunter, 1975). This was no mere sectional demand by the Highlanders for land reform had wide support among radicals and leaders of the industrial working class and fitted easily into the programme of the early labour movement (Keating and Bleiman, 1979). Land agitation died down in the late nineteenth century but when a new Highland Land League was formed in 1909 its commitment to Home Rule was firm for, as it reported in 1916, 'the experience of government by Westminster has been a sad one for the Gaelic race' (HLL, 1916).

The Cultural Revolution and the Assertion of Identity

Diffusionist theory would predict a homogenisation of culture with the expansion of capitalism and the modern state, though without excluding the possibility of short-term resistance from the periphery. It is true that the nineteenth century did witness the extension of 'national' languages within each state, together with a growth in secular values and a breakdown of ascriptive value-systems. Accompanying this was the ideology of nationalism promoted by the state. Yet countervailing trends were also visible. Despite the advance of secularism, religious revivals occurred in many parts of late nineteenth-century Europe. Cultural revivals followed the rediscovery, or invention, of tradition and renewed interest in vernacular languages and literature, often on the part of intellectuals but still helping provide a focus for loyalty and identity other than the nation-state. The relationship of culture to other more explicitly political values, is problematical. Cultural revivalism could represent a nostalgia for a real or imagined past and align itself with the reaction against modernity, or it could present in itself a different path to modernity and development. Rokkan and Urwin (1983) claim that a periphery is more likely to lose its language where there is economic integration before the periphery has had a chance to develop its own written standard. On the other hand, language survival could be achieved despite this where the language was seen by important elites as a symbol of identity, where there was a drive to establish a common standard, where this common standard was diffused through important religious ceremonies or education. Particularly important for the last issue is the use of the language by the church against dominant central, secularising elites and the establishment of vernacular schools. So linguistic and cultural questions became caught up in the religious–secular struggles and the consolidation of the modern state. In some peripheries the cultural revival was able to present an alternative focus of identity to the state-nation, a different image of the territory and its people. In other cases, this failed to happen and in others again cultural revivalism proved divisive and failed to cement an alternative territorial identity.

France
In France the national education system served as a vehicle of national socialisation, with children taught that the creation of France was an inexorable process of the pre-existing nation consolidating itself within its natural frontiers. Clerical and religious influences were progressively removed while teaching was only through the medium of French. Breton children were punished for speaking their native tongue and ministers repeatedly insisted that the unity of France required its extinction (Weber, 1977; Guiral, 1977). Lebesque (1970) recalls that in his childhood the middle classes of Nantes described themselves as 'of the west' or the 'fifth region' while the 'Bretons' were the poor folk on the edge of the city. The language survived largely through the agency of the church, with priests continuing to preach in Breton well into the twentieth century, though this served, in the eyes of republicans, further to identify the Breton cause with clericalist reaction. Occitan, too, came under attack and, from the high literary language of the troubadors, a language

of law and administration, descended into a series of *patois*, regarded with contempt in schools and by the upwardly mobile, in rapid retreat in the larger towns and cities of the plains though widely used among the peasantry of the interior.

The nineteenth century saw literary and linguistic revivals in both territories. The Breton revival focused on the rediscovery of traditional song and poetry, put at the service of an idealised past of hierarchy and social harmony and supported by the clergy and traditional landed elites (Guillorel, 1981). There was some success in achieving common standards but some later left-wing Breton campaigners have accused the church of preserving the parochial variants as a means of keeping the masses in subjection (Lebesque, 1970). Under pressure from the competing agencies of state schools and church, the language was helped to survive by the continued isolation of the province and the absence of large-scale immigration. Occitania, too, saw a literary revival in the late nineteenth century under the inspiration of the *Félibrige*, a romantic movement whose most prominent figure was the poet Mistral. Although it had been estimated by the Ministry of Education at the end of the Second Empire that some 70–90 per cent of the region, according to area, was monolingual in Occitan, the literary revival was an affair of intellectuals with little attempt at a popular appeal. As in Brittany, the literary revivalists tended, where they were not entirely apolitical, to traditionalist social and economic views and opposition to the secular, centralising republic, but in contrast to Brittany, piety was not strongly entrenched among the peasantry. In some rural areas, indeed, there were strong traditions of anti-clericalism, militating against an identification of linguistic and religious distinctiveness. So while the literary revivalists tended to the anti-revolutionary camp, among the Occitan peasantry and town-dwellers there was widespread support for the republic.

Spain

In Spain, linguistic uniformity was an important element in nation-building both for Jacobin liberals and for the *españolista* monarchical and military elites but the weakness and inefficiency of the state made the imposition of cultural homogeneity on the French model, as envisaged by the Public Education Law of 1859, impossible (Vives, 1986). While, under the impact of unified markets and administration, Castilian had come into general use in the course of the nineteenth century, Catalans and Gallegos still spoke among themselves in their own languages—Basque was more clearly in retreat. In each case, monolingualism survived only in the rural areas, along with high levels of illiteracy. In Catalonia and more especially the Basque Country, high rates of immigration from other parts of Spain, the result of industrialisation, had reduced the number of native speakers. In Galicia, the language was preserved by an isolation and lack of immigration comparable to the experience of Brittany. In all three regions Catholicism was strong, with a consequent suspicion of republicanism and indeed of the liberal monarchy which, while not as overtly anti-clerical as the French radicals, was never forgiven for the failure to restore church lands seized under Napoleon (Carr, 1975). In the rural areas this led to sympathy for Carlism, though in the city of Barcelona Carlism had little appeal and there was some anti-clerical sentiment.

Catalonia, the Basque Country and Galicia all experienced cultural revivals in the nineteenth century but of different types, with differing political consequences. The Catalan *Renaixenca* can be traced back to 1833, with the publication of Aribau's *Ode a la Patria* (Mercadé et al., 1981). In 1859 the *Juegos Florales* were instituted and became the focus for a romantic-literary movement which flourished after the Restoration of 1874. Initially devoid of political content, the romantic movement in time developed an idealised vision of Catalan history and of a future devoid of class conflict. The implications of much of this were conservative, rooted in traditional values and there was considerable contact with the similarly-minded writers of the Occitan *Félibrige*. After the Restoration of 1872, religious orders flourished in Catalonia and the abbey of Montserrat became the centre of an intense Catalan cult (Vives, 1986). In the Catholic thinker Torras i Bages, bishop of Vic, the traditionalist element in Catalanism was taken a stage further, to a vision of an ordered, hierarchical society based on tradition, family, religion and language and opposed to revolution, liberalism, universal suffrage and political parties (Mercadé et al., 1981). While this type of thinking might seem antithetical to the commercial and individualistic values of industrial middle classes, these were often steeped in Catholic values, and Catalanists sought to reconcile traditionalism with industrial society by presenting a vision of powerful but paternalistic employers who would treat their workers well. So, far from industrialisation producing secularisation and the dominance of purely commercial values, there was a revival of piety. Among the Barcelona middle classes, too, cultural associations of all sorts flourished. The Liceo opera house attracted wide support, while the Ataneo club and reading room brought together the worlds of culture and business (Vives, 1986).

The cultural and religious revivals had little impact on the industrial working class who tended to support the anarchist or socialist movements. These in turn often saw linguistic issues as divisive of the interests of native Catalan and immigrant workers. Catalan speaking was nevertheless widespread among the native and some of the immigrant working class and, shorn of the 'floralism' of the romantic movement, was to provide a basis for the nationalism of the left which emerged in the twentieth century.

The Basque cultural revival dates from the late nineteenth century, with the formation of the Society for Basque Studies and the Academy of the Basque Language but its impact was weakened by the lack of a written literary tradition in Basque or common standard for the language. While Basque was widely spoken in the countryside, it was a divisive force among the industrial workers and the various Basque territories. Great Basque writers and thinkers like Unamuno were, in the absence of a Basque university, educated in Castile and wrote in Castilian (Olábarri, 1981) leaving Basque revivalism to the traditionalist and backward-looking elements. It was linked to the rural clergy in a manner reminiscent of Brittany and presented visions of a Basque Country cut off entirely from Spanish influences along with secularism, liberalism and bourgeois individualism.

In Galicia the literary revival was influenced by pan-Celtic themes, reflecting the racial origins of the people, though the

Gallego language is a Romance and not a Celtic tongue. Widespread illiteracy necessarily limited its appeal in the countryside while in the towns the middle classes were 'Castilianised', looking to opportunities in the military and the state (Linz, 1973).

The United Kingdom
In the United Kingdom the absence of a missionary nation-building ideology meant that central elites were less concerned with political socialisation than in France, Italy or Spain, though in the late nineteenth century the imperialist ideology made considerable headway at all levels of society. For the languages and culture of the Celtic periphery, governments and administrators adopted an attitude of haughty contempt and a policy of practical neglect, rather than active suppression. In contrast to other European countries, where education has been such a vital part of nation-building that it must be rigidly centralised, there has never been a single department of education for the whole of the United Kingdom, while the administration of schools and the syllabus have been the responsibility of local authorities.

The disparaging comments of the Commissioners sent to investigate Welsh education in 1846–7 still rankle with Welsh nationalists (Stephens, 1976) and the landmark Education Act of 1870, introducing the principle of universal schooling, ignored the Welsh language altogether, as did the 1899 Act for secondary education. Yet in 1901 half the population of the Principality were still Welsh-speaking and, though the proportion of Welsh-speakers was falling, their absolute numbers continued to rise until 1911 (Morgan, 1981). The reasons for the resilience of Welsh appear twofold. First, the sixteenth-century Welsh translation of the Bible set a standard for written Welsh and prevented its fragmentation into local dialects, while the nineteenth-century religious revival carried it through the country. Second, there were economic factors. Immigration into the industrial areas of Wales, particularly the mining valleys, came initially from rural Wales so that in 1851 Merthyr Tydfil, the largest town in Wales, was 90 per cent Welsh-speaking (Stephens, 1976). A Welsh-language press thrived. In time, though, the influx of English and

Irish workers together with the effects of English-language education eroded the language which, in the first half of the twentieth century, went into rapid decline, especially in South Wales, creating a cultural divide and weakening the sense of collective territorial identity.

The nineteenth-century Welsh cultural revival was more than just an elite affair, for the anglicisation of the Welsh gentry meant that Welsh language and culture were inherently a popular matter. The *eisteddfod* had been revived as early as 1701 and during the eighteenth century a whole mythology of Welshness was invented, claiming descent from the ancient Druids and Welsh heroes. As in other parts of Europe, nineteenth-century romanticism provided further embellishment, such as Welsh 'national dress', but also helped to develop and standardise the language (Morgan, 1986) and create a sense of common identity. From 1880 the National Eisteddfod Association gave wide prominence to Welsh cultural achievement, though it remained true, as Morgan (1981, p. 112) notes, that 'the leading figures in the cultural movement were scarcely political, certainly not separatist.'

Along with language and culture, religion provided the third great mark of Welsh identity in the nineteenth century. A serious of religious revivals had weaned the mass of the population away from the established Anglican Church, deepening social divisions between the gentry—wealthy, English-speaking and Anglican—and the masses in both town and country. In turn, this provoked conflict over the payment of tithes to clergy of the established church, over the temperance issue and over the control of the education system following the education acts of the late nineteenth and early twentieth centuries. The 1870 Education Act had given control of schools to local school boards, allowing the nonconformists to dominate, but an abortive Conservative proposal of 1896, followed by the Education Act of 1902 provided for rate support for Anglican Church schools, sparking off a massive revolt in Wales. Already by 1886 demands for disestablishment of the church had become a major issue.

A common theme of the developing Welsh identity was democracy, the assertion of the rights of the *Gwerin*, the popular masses, against the landed aristocracy and their privileges. In contrast with some of the romantic cultural movements on the Continent, this took the Welsh sense of identity beyond the pseudo-archaism of the Druidic rituals, into the political sphere and gave it a popular and progressive basis, counterposing the politically 'advanced' periphery to the archaic social order supported from the centre.

Scotland entered the nineteenth century divided culturally. Gaelic predominated in the Highlands and Western Isles but had been in retreat over much of Scotland since the Reformation. The first measures against Gaelic had been taken by pre-Union Scottish governments and the Society for the Propagation of Christian Knowledge in its missionary work in the eighteenth and nineteenth centuries strove hard to displace it through education (Stephens, 1976). After the 1745 Jacobite rebellion, measures were taken to suppress Gaelic culture, including both the language and Highland dress. Though such measures were scarcely enforceable, the Highland chiefs did become anglicised, sending their sons to 'public' schools in England and Scotland and assimilating into the Anglo-Scots upper classes. Gaelic hung on among the masses in the Highlands, fostered by the free churches which broke away from the Church of Scotland in 1843. The Education Act of 1872, however, made no reference to Gaelic and in the schools taken over under it the use of the language was frowned upon. In the Lowlands, the Scots tongue gave way to English among the elite following the Union of 1707 and, despite the contribution of poets such as Burns, never developed a standard written form. Indeed, by the twentieth century, there was controversy over whether such a language, as opposed to a series of dialects of English, ever existed.

Scotland's nineteenth-century cultural revival was weak and fragmented. A romantic movement was sparked off from the 1760s by MacPherson's *Ossian* whose doubtful provenance and authenticity did not prevent it gaining a large following. The romantic movement had no link with politics, nor were there immediate political implications in the works of Sir Walter Scott. Although, as Harvie (1977, p. 132) notes, Scott was the 'acknowledged precursor of those reconstructions of historic identity which were to dominate European nationalism in the nineteenth century', his work had little relevance to the problems of contemporary industrialising and urbanising society. By the end of the nineteenth century, the Scottish novel had largely lapsed into the escapist sentimentality of the 'kailyard school', presenting a picture of a wholesome small-town and rural Scotland untainted by the economic and social problems of industrialism. Only in the interwar years of the twentieth century was this seriously challenged. Meanwhile, symbols of a depoliticised Scottishness had flourished under the influence of the romantics. In 1782 the Disarming Acts banning Highland dress were repealed and a stylised form of kilt came into use, receiving official recognition when Scott persuaded King George III to wear it on his visit to Edinburgh in 1830. Highland regalia was pressed into the service of the British Army and Empire with the raising of Highland regiments and the symbols of kilt and bagpipes came to represent Scotland in the world—but a Scotland which was essentially British.

A Gaelic cultural revival was promoted by Gaelic societies and, from 1891, by *An Commun Gaidhealach* which organises an annual *Mod* on the lines of the poetic and musical festivals in other European peripheries. Though Gaelic revivalism made little impact on the mass of Scots in the Lowlands, politics and popular culture were not entirely separate. Some nineteenth-century radicals and Labour leaders were fired with a vision of Scottish history as a struggle against papal, English and landlord oppression, whose heroes ranged from Bruce through the seventeenth-century Covenanters to early-nineteenth-century revolutionaries. Border ballads and the poetry of Burns helped provide the inspiration and gave an emotive strand to politics which mingled uneasily with the concern with bread-and-butter issues. While this was an element in the nationalism of the early Labour movement, the anti-Catholic undertones of the Scottish dissenting tradition cut it off from the large Irish Catholic working-class community in the west of Scotland. More improbably, the aristocratic Erskine of Mar had visions of a Gaelic Scotland based on what he saw as the primitive communism of the old clan system, a theme also touched upon by the socialist leader John Maclean.

In Ireland, the language, in gradual retreat since Tudor times, declined dramatically after the famine until by 1891 only 14.5 per cent of the population spoke it. From 1831 the National Schools had banned it and, with the expansion of secondary education after 1878, channels of upward mobility were opened to the poorer classes, but only if they spoke English. It was the economic recovery of the late nineteenth century which produced the major cultural revival both in Irish and in the English language. In 1893 the Gaelic League was founded, largely by professional people and civil servants, many of them returning to Ireland from abroad (Garvin, 1981). Although initially it was non-political, the mythical view of Irish history which it cultivated had obvious political implications given the Repeal and Home Rule agitations of the century and a generation of nationalist leaders emerged steeped in the values of self-sacrifice and violence with which the Celtic heroes of old were credited. In 1884, the Gaelic Athletic Association was formed to promote indigenous Irish sports and resist 'foreign' influences, soon becoming a recruiting ground for extreme nationalism.

At the same time, an Irish literature in English was thriving, often from the pens of members of the old Anglo-Irish Protestant ascendancy (Dangerfield, 1979). In rescuing the Irish peasant from the contempt and ridicule in which he had been held not only in the music-halls of England but also among the Irish middle classes, the literary movement helped develop a new sense of national identity and, while the Gaelic revival could by its essence appeal only to a minority of the population, the English-language movement could appeal to the whole nation. Writing about the condition of contemporary Ireland could not avoid politics, while such was the mythical power of Yeats' *Caitlin ni Houlihan* that many years later the author was to ask, 'Did that play of mine send out certain men the English shot?'

Post-famine Ireland also saw a remarkable religious revival among the majority Catholic population, with an extraordinary increase in the number of priests and nuns, a trend which Garvin (1981) attributes to the adaptation of peasant society to post-famine needs through sexual abstinence, puritanism and social regimentation. Being close to their flocks, the parochial priests often sympathised with land agitation and nationalism, even where these were frowned upon by the hierarchy, and generally provided social and political leadership in the rural areas. The church sought, too, to control education and protect Catholic youth from unwholesome influences. It was church insistence that higher education should be Catholic, which delayed the establishment of the national university in the late nineteenth century (Hepburn, 1980)—it was not until 1970 that the ban on Catholics entering Trinity College Dublin was lifted.

The association of Catholicism with Irish identity had long been cemented by religious persecution and the new romantic nationalism fitted into the same constellation of values. As Garvin (1981, p. 104) puts it, 'neo-Gaelic nationalism retained the values of self-sacrifice for the group, religious communalism, purity, respect for women, fear of external evils and idealism which were taught by the Irish Catholicism of the period.' This remained true despite the anathema heaped by the hierarchy upon extreme nationalists in their secret societies. Though some progressive attitudes were found amongst the nationalist intelligentsia, the neo-Gaelic movement was not a liberal-democratic one seeking the fulfilment of the individual through self-government or even a class one seeking social justice. Its objective was rather the attainment of an Ireland purified of corrupting influences and its legacy a narrowing of the definition of the Irish nation (O'Brien, 1972) from which the Protestants were excluded (Cronin, 1980) and an intransigence and intolerance which has plagued Irish nationalism to this day.

Italy

In Italy, linguistic unification was achieved after 1860 through education, though there were non-Italian-speaking minorities in the border areas and local dialects continued in daily use. Nor were there interreligious conflicts in a society which, nominally at least, was almost unanimously Catholic. There was, of course, a clerical–anticlerical conflict exacerbated by the Vatican's long refusal to recognise the unified state and not until 1919 was a Catholic party, the *Partito Popolare* of Sturzo able to function.

As for the Mezzogiorno, a striking feature of nineteenth-century Italy is the presence of so many writers from the south combined with the absence of a real southern literature (Galasso, 1978). The great southern writers tended to be Italian figures, men of the *Risorgimento*, and when they wrote about the south, it was to regret its failure to integrate with the north and realise the dream of Italian unity. Images of the Mezzogiorno projected in the region itself through myths and folk-tales and, for those who could read, through literature, were such as to discourage regional self-assertion. In Sicily the myth of the Sicilian Vespers was sometimes invoked as the foundation of an independent identity but the literature of the eighteenth and nineteenth centuries portrayed a romanticised view of an unchanging land resistant to the successive 'foreign' invasions of the island (Ganci, 1978). On the southern mainland, the notion of *meridionalità* conveyed the same idea. This was, of course, in the interest of the dominant classes, especially the new bourgeoisie who had made their accommodation with the new regime and wanted to resist social and economic change. Lampedusa's novel *The Leopard* and, in more biting form, the work of Sciascia portray the way in which successive regime changes managed to leave the basis of the social structure intact, merely replacing one set of elites with another, but these came much later. In the late nineteenth century, there was no realistic literary *genre* to present the condition of the south as a problem, still less a literature of protests, presenting an alternative and better future.

The Survival of the Periphery

The peripheries of the four states thus emerged from the nineteenth century with a marked degree of economic, cultural and political distinctiveness, in some cases enhanced rather than eroded by the processes of state-building and modernisation. Indeed, it is in some cases possible to turn the traditional modernisation/diffusion argument on its head and argue that the effects of social and economic change helped create a common identity in Wales or Catalonia, where little such sense had previously existed and to relate it to contemporary issues. The confrontation between these regional identities and the expanding state were the basis for the first peripheral revival, examined in the next chapter. In southern Italy, on the other hand, the lack of social modernisation not only inhibited the spread of notions of Italian nationality and citizenship but also discouraged the development of a common sense of regional identity.

4
The Revolt of the Periphery

The Mobilisation of the Periphery

Late nineteenth-century western Europe saw an upsurge of territorial movements challenging the nationalism of the big states. The elements of this have been traced above: an incomplete nation-building, often resting less upon universal norms and behaviour patterns than upon complex mechanisms for territorial representation, accommodation and management; the development of distinct economic interests among key social groups in the peripheries; and the sense of identity stimulated by cultural revivals. The three elements of political/administrative institutions, culture and economic differentiation did not automatically produce territorial political movements. That required organisations to integrate the complex of territorial demands and needs into programmes with a more or less coherent ideological framework with a social base. For their part, state-level elites showed varied degrees of skill and good fortune in managing the new territorial politics.

For the sake of thematic continuity, it makes sense to discuss first the two countries, the UK and Spain, in which territorial strains were most severe, causing variously violence, secession and the breakdown of the regime. In France and Italy, territorial politics, though an important element of political life, was managed within the institutions of the state.

The Crisis of the United Kingdom

Social and economic change in the peripheries of the United Kingdom provided the basis for territorial political movements in Ireland, Scotland and Wales which presented the regime with serious problems of adjustment from the mid-nineteenth century to the 1920s. State responses were conditioned by the immediate needs of the major parties at Westminster, with their primary interest in stable government and by the lack of clear constitutional guidelines or theory, with a still unclear boundary between the metropolitan homeland and the Empire. It would be impossible in the space here to do justice to all these movements, particularly Irish nationalism, which is the subject of an enormous literature, so attention will be confined to those aspects which are directly relevant to the main theme of the book.

Although an Irish nationalist tradition, with a project for independent statehood, can be traced back at least to the United Irishmen of the late eighteenth century and the mass of Irish people had never thought of themselves as British, the formation of a national consciousness dates from the nineteenth century (Kee, 1976) and the growth of the modern state. This emphasised the social gulf between Anglo-Irish gentry and the mass of the peasantry and raised a series of new issues not resolvable by the quasi-colonial administration. The first organised mass nationalism was the work of Daniel O'Connell who, in the 1820s, challenged the British state to live up to the implied promise of the Union and allow Catholics to sit in Parliament and enjoy full civil rights. While emancipation was won for the whole United Kingdom, the issue was most critical in Ireland where the Catholic preponderance was to produce a massive shift of political power as the franchise was extended in the course of the century. O'Connell's next movement for repeal of the union itself, while more explicitly nationalist, was consistent as the next step toward political power for the rural Catholic majority. Although finally killed off by the great famine, it suffered all along from an ambiguity of aims and methods which was to plague Irish nationalism for generations. O'Connell was a constitutionalist and no separatist, believing in a reconstituted United Kingdom, but when he failed to get allies among the British parties and constitutional pressure was spurned, he had nowhere to turn. The movement, however, set the tone for Irish politics for the rest of the century.

With the franchise and reforms of 1867–72, Charles Stewart Parnell was able to draw the strands of land reform, Irish Catholic identity and Home Rule together in another mass movement which was also parliamentary and constitutional. While the aim of the Irish Party up to 1918 remained that of finding a new accommodation for Ireland within the parliamentary regime of the United Kingdom, constant tensions arose with other elements of the coalition, the land agitators in the countryside given to direct action along the boundaries of legality; and the Catholic hierarchy, sympathetic to the plight of the peasantry but opposed to direct action and suspicious of the secular/Protestant leadership of Parnell. Further problems arose in the north, for the more progress the Home Rule movement made, the more anxieties it aroused among Protestant Ulstermen fearful of a rural, peasant, Catholic-dominated Ireland in which they would be a besieged minority.

The mainland parties had lost their electoral base in Ireland and could look upon it only as a 'colonial' issue outside the mainstream of British politics. Yet, as long as Irish members remained a permanent, dissident minority in the Commons, obstructing business and reducing the likelihood of stable majority government, Ireland remained an internal problem with a capacity to destabilise the whole regime. Their policies were confused and inconsistent, alternating between repression and conciliation, both based on an exceptionalism more likely to nurture than to kill the Irish sense of collective identity. Coercion legislation of 1881, 1882, 1887, while not without effect in quelling unrest, amounted to British recognition that Ireland was different from the rest of the UK and fanned nationalist resentment. Along with repression, though, went conciliation, notably legislation to give the Irish peasantry ownership of the land. The most extensive reforms, the Balfour and Wyndham Acts of 1891–1903, put through ironically by a Conservative administration, were consciously seen as 'killing Home Rule by kindness'. While undermining the old Anglo-Irish landed ascendancy, the reforms put in place an essentially conservative peasant class but this was not to stabilise the regime, for these peasant proprietors, and especially their younger sons, were to be a more fertile and stable recruiting-ground for Irish nationalism than their insecure and repressed forbears. Nationalism remained strongly embedded in the population, albeit below the surface, waiting for the spark to ignite it (Lyons, 1971).

Also in the conciliatory mode were the administrative reforms of 1898 establishing elected district and county councils dominated by members of the Irish Party. This was a factor for stability, giving nationalist politicians a source of patronage and bolstering the constitutional nationalist position but it was a fragile basis for re-establishing consent to the government of Ireland. The collaborative elite thus brought into being was in a weak position between the popular nationalist consciousness and rise of militant nationalism on the one hand and the intransigent unionism of British governments on the other. Conservatives remained adamantly opposed to their main demand for Home Rule, while even their Westminster allies, the Liberals, had other priorities.

Home Rule itself, offered first by Gladstone in 1886, was the greatest concession offered before the First World War. Gladstone's bill provided for a devolved Irish parliament within the United Kingdom, with limited powers and, at least in the initial form, the end of Irish representation at Westminster. Whether this would have satisfied Irish opinion in the long run is a much-debated but necessarily speculative point. It certainly could not command a consensus amongst British parliamentary opinion. The Liberal Party was split and thrust into opposition for most of the next twenty years and, even when a Commons majority could be mustered for Home Rule, it was frustrated by the House of Lords.

It may be difficult to understand the uproar which these modest proposals caused (Lyons, 1971), yet Irish Home Rule forced British unionists to consider the meaning of the union and its intellectual justification in a way which they never had before and this was a distinctly uncomfortable experience. In defending the union, they were able to draw on no existing theory of the state or what it meant to be British. Certainly Dicey (1886) formulated a powerful intellectual case for English rejection of Home Rule but his classic unionist case was itself rejected by unionists with their long history of treating Ireland differently from England. There was no obvious constitutional ground on which to object to Home Rule, since parliamentary sovereignty, the only immutable principle of the constitution, was unaffected by the proposals. Nor were there vital social or political interests at stake. Landlordism, and with it the social position of the Anglo-Irish ascendancy, had already been dealt a death blow by Tory land reforms. The Conservatives retained a modest political stake in Ireland, in the shape of the Ulster unionists but any diminution in Irish parliamentary representation would be to their benefit. In fact, the vehemence of Conservative reaction which, on the eve of the First World War, went as far as condoning treason and armed rebellion, seemed to stem from a fear that not only the territorial regime but the whole social and economic order was in danger from the advance of democracy. While social and economic interests could be sacrificed through policy concessions in Ireland, constitutional change was more threatening, with implications for the mainland and the position of a Conservative Party still coming to terms with mass suffrage. So in order to guarantee the territorial and social order, the Conservative Party seemed at times prepared to abandon the constitution and system of law which until then had protected their interests.

The political vacuum created by the failure of the Home Rule bill and the fall of Parnell—the victim of clerical censure—allowed new political movements to develop, drawing on the traditions of armed revolt, Fenianism, secret societies and the Gaelic revival. The disparate elements of this alternative nationalism were by no means all committed to physical-force solutions. Sinn Fein, founded in 1905, initially favoured a duel monarchy on Austro-Hungarian lines, to be obtained through elected Irish MPs abstaining from attendance at the British Parliament. The physical-force element was concentrated in the secret Irish Republican Brotherhood which was able in due course to infiltrate the

Irish Volunteers organised in response to the Ulster Volunteers in 1913. This allowed a revolutionary minority to spark off the chain of events which was to lead to war and independence, but only because a politically alienated population and public acceptance of the counter-legitimacy of Irish nationalism provided the authority for the revolution in the country.

The resulting contest between the legal/parliamentary and physical-force traditions continues to this day. By the early twentieth century, with the Irish Party reunited under Redmond, the parliamentary tradition appeared to have regained the ascendancy; but the failure to deliver Home Rule undermined their role as collaborators of the Westminster Liberals. This failure in turn stemmed from the resistance of Ulster Protestants and the dynamics of party politics at Westminster. The earliest suggestions of armed resistance to Home Rule in Ulster, building on traditions of militia organisation in the north and the earlier resistance to the disestablishment of the Church of Ireland, had come with the 1886 Bill, when Lord Randolph Churchill had sought to make political capital by playing the 'Orange card'. In 1912, with Home Rule on the statute book and bound to come into effect under the terms of the Parliament Act which had limited the Lords' veto, the Ulster Volunteers, a paramilitary organisation, were formed. Conservative leader Bonar Law openly endorsed the use of force to resist the legislation while treason was plotted in the armed forces. Faced with this rebellion, the Liberal government temporised, unable to proceed and unable to turn back.

Meanwhile, the growth of nationalist and unionist politics, together with the weakness of industrial development and trade unionism outside Belfast and Dublin, had sidelined the Irish Labour movement. The British Labour Party at first seemed disposed to organise throughout the United Kingdom and even held its conference in Belfast in 1905, but its attitude to Irish questions was conditioned by its Liberal allies and Gladstonian traditions and, supporting Home Rule, it withdrew from the field. So class politics which could have served an integrating role, on a UK or an all-Ireland basis, failed to develop as it did in Scotland and Wales and the workers of Ireland were divided by religion and nationality.

Catholic workers were expelled from the shipyards by their Protestant fellow-workers in 1912 (Hachey, 1977). In the south, James Connolly, one of Ireland's greatest Labour leaders, putting the national revolution before the class one, to the bewilderment of his friends in Scotland, committed himself to the 1916 Rising.

The final failure of management on the part of British government was the reaction to the 1916 Rising, itself staged by the IRB's inner leadership, using the Irish Volunteer organisation but without the knowledge of the Volunteer leadership. The Rising was far from a popular revolution. On the outbreak of war most of the Volunteers had followed Redmond into support of the war effort, many of them joining the thousands of Irish Catholics who volunteered for the British Army. Of the minority under Eoin McNeill who stood aside, few contemplated armed resistance to British rule and McNeill himself believed that a rising could be justified only if it had popular support and a chance of success. Neither of these conditions was present when the General Post Office was seized in 1916 and the defeated rebels were even jeered in the streets of Dublin. Yet the British reaction, in treating the Rising as criminal treason and executing its leaders, offended deeply-held feelings among the Irish population and ensured the dead a place in the pantheon of Irish heroes.

The victory of Sinn Fein in the 1918 election and the guerrilla war which followed afforded opportunity for further miscalculation. Armed repression merely sowed further hatred but even a successful military pacification could not have saved the United Kingdom in the sense of creating an integrated political entity. Armed groups would have remained in the country and Irish politicians outside the political and party mainstream, a troublesome presence if they chose to attend Westminster, a challenge to its authority if they did not. The solution embodied in the 1922 Treaty was a compromise but of vital importance in saving the UK territorial regime and the parliamentary system of which it was part. Effective independence without representation at Westminster was given to the larger part of Ireland; Home Rule and parliamentary under-representation to the smaller part. Politics on the mainland could continue to evolve towards the alternating two-party model with governments normally able to count on a stable majority and no need to negotiate with territorial parties. What was not resolved was the problem of nationality in Ireland. For republicans the national revolution was incomplete since a republic had not been achieved and north-east Ulster remained outside the Irish state. In practice the two aims of unity and the republic were never compatible since the very concept of the Irish Republic developed since the late nineteenth century and insisted upon by the anti-Treaty forces, excluded the Ulster Protestants—or simply defined them out of existence. In the north, a similar view of ascriptive group identity as fixed and exclusive prevailed, under the management of the Ulster Unionist Party. With the Irish problem thus out of the way, British politics on the mainland continued unhindered by these questions and only decades later was the relationship of the Northern Ireland enclave to the modern liberal British polity seriously questioned.

The cultural dimension to nationalism in nineteenth-century Scotland was weak. Campaigns against the threat to Scottish banknotes or heraldry may have played some part in keeping alive Scottish identity but their romantic/Tory sponsors were not economically or socially at odds with the Union settlement. The grievances leading up to the most intense Home Rule agitation were more mundane and concerned, firstly, the inability of the system of semi-assimilation to meet the needs of an expanding state and, secondly, the rise of new economic and political interests in Scotland and their struggle for recognition. In the event, British statecraft was able to defuse Scottish agitation by tactical concessions on a range of specific issues and the cooption of key Scottish elites into a new system of territorial management. Scottish industrial capitalists were in favour of the Union from the earliest days of industrialisation and by the late nineteenth century were highly dependent on export markets, especially in the Empire. While they favoured administrative reform to improve the efficiency of Scottish administration, they were highly suspicious of constitutional change or anything hinting at separatism. The accommodation of labour into the political system proved more difficult but in time, the growth of a strong Labour movement proved an integrating factor.

The threat posed to Scotland's informal system of devolution by the growth of the late nineteenth-century state was first clearly revealed by the 1870 Education Act, initially intended to cover the whole of Britain. After a campaign to protect Scotland's educational traditions, a separate Scottish Act was brought in, administered by a Scotch (sic) Education Department. This was the beginning of the modern phase of administrative devolution and was followed in 1885 by the appointment of a Secretary for Scotland. While the agitation for a Secretary of State was described as 'nationalist' by analogy with Ireland, this seems to be stretching the term too far altogether for its mainspring was a mundane concern by businessmen about the inefficiency of the ramshackle system of boards which ran most Scottish administration. Indeed, in some respects the appointment of the Secretary for Scotland was an integrating device, placing Scottish government in the hands of an appointee of the ruling party at Westminster (Harvie, 1977). A firm convention was soon established, though, that the appointee be a Scottish parliamentarian and that he articulate distinctively Scottish concerns within their government. Such practical concerns continued to inspire Scottish demands for more devolution during the expansion of state activity in the First World War and in the 1940s (Keating and Bleiman, 1979). In each case, the response was administrative concession to satisfy immediate demands without the need for constitutional change.

The main political interest pressing Home Rule in the late nineteenth century was the radical wing of the Liberal Party, especially following the franchise reforms of 1867 and 1884. In 1876 a radical West and South of Scotland Liberal Association was formed, followed in 1885 by a National Liberal Federation of Scotland modelled on Joseph Chamberlain's ideas. Their reform agenda encompassed parliamentary procedure, the House of Lords, land, local government, temperance and disestablishment of the Church of Scotland. This was no reactionary cry against modernity but the latest in democratic and progressive thinking, which the Scottish radicals saw as obstructed by the entrenched interests of a Tory-dominated England and the House of Lords. Scotland's separate educational tradition, seen, with some justice, as more meritocratic than that of England, was particularly precious to radicals while the campaign for land reform tapped myths of revolt against alien oppression. Following the Disruption of 1843, the Church of Scotland was widely seen on the left as a bastion of privileged interests propped up by its status as the established church.

It was the Home Rule campaign in Ireland and, above all, Gladstone's conversion in 1886, which crystallised radical sentiment in Scotland in favour of Home Rule. A Scottish Home Rule Association was founded in that year and in 1889 the crofters' MP, G.B. Clark, introduced the first Home Rule motion in the Commons. Successful motions were carried in 1894, 1895, 1912 and 1919, while first readings of bills were obtained in 1908, 1911, 1912 and 1913—the last even received a second reading. While this might indicate Liberal acquiescence in the idea of Home Rule for Scotland, it equally showed that Liberal governments had no intention of pressing the issue, at least while the question of Ireland was unresolved. Proposals for Home Rule All Round were floated as a means of accommodating the Irish question within a general reform of the state but no government was prepared to upset the constitutional structure of the whole kingdom merely to settle Ireland. Instead, the problems of each part of the UK were looked at separately. For their part, while they made some very nationalistic noises, the Scottish radicals were unwilling to break with the national Liberal Party and form a party of their own on Parnellite lines.

There were two distinct phases of Home Rule agitation. The first was in the 1880s, parallel to the Irish debate and revolved around questions of land reform and the radical agenda. The second occurred around the First World War and was inspired not only by the new legislation for Ireland but also by powerful interests within the Scottish Labour movement. Labour in Scotland had separate local origins and was in its early days profoundly influenced by its radical inheritance which presented Home Rule as an article of faith.

Trade unions, too, developed separately in Scotland and at the turn of the century there was a large number of purely Scottish unions as well as a separate Scottish Trades Union Congress (STUC), to which were affiliated both Scottish and British unions. Although the foundation of the STUC stemmed from an argument about trades council representation in the British TUC and had nothing to do with Scottish nationalism, the existence of the organisation provided a focus for Home Rule agitation. While this had largely died down at the turn of the century, it began to revive again in the years leading up to the First World War, to climax around 1920–22. There were several reasons for this new outburst, led largely by Labour interests.

One was a renewed land campaign. In 1909 a new Highland Land League had been formed in Glasgow by Tom Johnston and other Labour figures, in an effort to wean the crofters away from the Liberals and attach them to the Labour coalition. This involved reaching out to the Gaelic societies and a firm commitment to Home Rule. The Irish example was again important, as the election of the Liberal government of 1906 and its return as a minority in 1910 presaged a renewed effort at Irish Home Rule. During the war itself, the rhetoric about the rights of small nations was not lost on Scottish Labour leaders who had become increasingly frustrated with the conduct of politics and administration in Scotland. Some of these frustrations were on the practical level and concerned the inconvenience and expense of travelling to London to deal with the myriad of regulations and orders required by the wartime economy. Others were more strictly political. With the wartime boom of the heavy industries of the Clyde came a confidence in the capacity of the Scottish economy and an outbreak of industrial militancy which created the belief that Scotland was economically and politically in advance of England and, left to its own devices, would proceed rapidly to social and economic reforms which could take a generation in the south. Election results before the war had given little credence to this view, a variant on the nineteenth-century myth of Scottish radicalism, but in 1922 came a dramatic breakthrough, with the return of twenty-nine Labour MPs in Scotland. In 1923 Labour came within two seats of an overall Scottish majority, prompting claims at Labour's Scottish conference that, with Home Rule, there would be a Labour Government in power north of the Border (LPSC, 1923). As early as 1915 the newly-formed Scottish Advisory Council of the Labour Party passed a Home Rule resolution and continued to pass similar resolutions up to 1923. In 1919 a draft bill, whose emotive preamble rejected the 'corrupt' Union of 1707, was presented to its conference (LPSC, 1919). At the STUC, Home Rule resolutions were carried unanimously or with large majorities every year from 1914 to 1923 and at meetings with the Prime Minister and Secretary for Scotland in 1918 and 1919 Home Rule was at the top of the agenda. The STUC even at one stage demanded Scottish representation at the Peace Conference and in 1923 voted for 'Dominion Self-Government' (Keating and Bleiman, 1979). In 1918, a new Scottish Home Rule Association was formed, dominated by Labour figures.

It is easy, in the light of Scottish Labour's later steadfast unionism, to dismiss all this as empty rhetoric but there is no doubt that, at the end of the First World War, the movement was at a crucial turning-point. Labour was emerging into political maturity with, for the first time, a mass working-class electorate provided by the franchise reform of 1918, and a role in the state presaged by the collaborative arrangements of the war. In the event, it opted for incorporation in the institutions of the British state, rejecting the road of territorial separatism just as, with rather less effort, Labour had rejected the road of revolutionary politics (Jones and Keating, 1985); but this was not preordained or the inevitable product of industrial society.

The fissures in the Labour–Home Rule coalition emerged after the war, first on the land question. An electoral pact between Labour and the Highland Land League had caused divisions between supporters of the crofting movement (and the HLL) and those who saw the promotion of peasant proprietorship merely a 'bulwark of reaction', echoing the fears of urban socialists in continental Europe (Keating and Bleiman, 1979). In the event, the joint Labour–HLL candidatures were a failure and, with the decline of land agitation, Labour retreated to its urban strongholds.

For the industrial wing of the movement, the crucial event was the post-war slump in Scotland's heavy industries, which followed the boom in 1921. This knocked the self-confidence out of the Scottish Labour movement at a critical moment in its development and directed attention to seeking help from the south (Keating and Bleiman, 1979). In the longer run, the separate Scottish trade unions were absorbed by amalgamations with British unions, in parallel with the decline in Scottish-owned industry. Thereafter, Scottish union leaders have strenuously insisted that legislation on industrial matters and working conditions should be the same in England and Scotland even where a separate Scottish regime might have promised more favourable treatment. This is not a matter of seeking a global uniformity in economic and industrial conditions, for Scottish trade unionists have been among the strongest opponents of membership of the European Economic Community. Rather, it seems to reflect a preference for settling issues in those forums in which the trade unions have, not without struggle, gained some place, for preserving the existing networks of influence.

On the political side of the movement, there was tension as early as 1919 when the Scottish Council of the Labour Party declared that, as Labour was committed to Home Rule, Labour members had no need of the Scottish Home Rule Association. This was partly inspired by organisational jealousy rather than ideological antipathy, for the SHRA was dominated by Labour people, but it also betrayed a fear that concentration on Home Rule could damage Labour's prior commitments which involved maximising its impact at Westminster. The critical break in the Labour–Home Rule alliance came at the time of its peak, in 1922–3. Labour's very success in Scotland, while confirming the tactical case for Home Rule, opened up new vistas of influence at Westminster. These prospects were confirmed by the installation of a Labour government in 1924, marking the party's integration into the Westminster regime. A Home Rule bill was introduced in 1924 and supported by the Secretary for Scotland, but the Cabinet, though it discussed the matter, had other priorities and took no action. The last bill of the series was introduced in 1927 but, in the face of Labour apathy, was easily talked out by the Conservatives.

This experience finally convinced Roland Muirhead, leader of the SHRA, of the futility of working through the British parties, who would always have greater priorities. In 1928 he announced his independent candidature for West Renfrewshire and, with others, founded the Scottish National Party. This may have been of great long-term significance as the first party in Scottish history dedicated single-mindedly to the goal of self-government, but it reflected a major setback for the Home Rule movement for it was to be nearly fifty years before the party could make a significant electoral impact. Meanwhile, Labour and, to some degree, the Liberals, were forced on the defensive and adopted an increasingly anti-nationalist stance.

What did not occur from the 1920s was an assimilation of Scottish political and social institutions with those of England. There was a marked increase in economic integration to the point at which it became difficult to talk of a 'Scottish economy' but there still remained distinctive Scottish economic problems stemming from the impact of British and international developments upon industry in Scotland—the decline of the traditional industries and the 'drift south' are examples. Administratively, Scotland was left with much of the infrastructure of government—the Scottish office was consolidated during the interwar years and there was no threat to Scotland's local government or distinctive education system. Rather, Scotland's dominant political forces had decided that these issues could be resolved at Westminster and through the limited administrative devolution available in the Scottish Office and that schemes of Home Rule, by putting at risk Scottish access to London largesse, was a very dangerous idea. Labour did not abandon the Home Rule policy until 1958 but from 1923 it ceased to be taken seriously or, at best, was treated as a political luxury to be indulged when Scotland's economy was in a better shape. The resulting Scottish regime, its successes and failures, are discussed below (Chapter 5).

Social, economic and political changes in late nineteenth-century Wales produced the 'rebirth of the nation' (Morgan, 1981). The cultural revival, with its popular base, reinforced

Welsh identity, though cutting out the English-speaking population of the south. The religious revival brought to the fore a series of political issues, notably the payment of tithes to the Anglican Church and state support for Anglican schools and after the disestablishment of the Church of Ireland in 1867, the possibilities of a separate Welsh solution began to be canvassed. The temperance issue produced the first recognition of Wales as a distinct legislative entity in the 1881 Welsh Sunday Closing Act.

More widely, the late nineteenth century saw an assertion of a new middle-class Wales as a 'yawning gap opened up between the anglicised gentry and the largely nonconformist, Welsh-speaking majority, comprehending industrial and rural Wales alike' (Morgan, 1981, p. 27). With the franchise and ballot reforms of 1867–1884, middle-class Wales found the means for its political expression, no revolt against modernity but, for its time, a democratic and progressive movement associated with the radical wing of the Liberal Party. Its targets were the antiquated Anglo-Welsh state with its established church and the landed-gentry class which sustained it.

The early Labour movement too had distinct Welsh roots, drawing on intensely local traditions of solidarity (Morgan, 1980) and faithful for longer than its English counterpart to 'Lib-Labism', the securing of Liberal parliamentary nominations for working-class candidates rather than support for a separate Labour Party. It was thus close to Welsh radicalism, and when socialism began to appear in South Wales it often took the form of anarcho-syndicalism rather than the statism of the English Fabians (Jones and Keating, 1982). This was fertile ground for the developing Welsh consciousness, particularly in the coalfields where nonconformist ministers sought to unite 'the red dragon and the red flag' (Morgan, 1980).

Politically the Welsh revival was channelled into massive support for the Liberal Party which, by 1885, held 30 of the 34 seats. The Chamberlain schism had little effect and in 1892 no less than 31 Gladstonians were returned in Wales. There thus arrived in Parliament a number of fiery young activists, imbued with the politics of the new Wales. Men like Tom Ellis and David Lloyd George faced a choice—to throw in their lot with the national Liberal Party and hope for high office in London, or to place themselves at the head of a Welsh national movement and press for Home Rule. Their first inclination was to the latter and some younger members formed a Welsh Parliamentary Party in 1888. Although this was seen by some firebrands as the equivalent of the Parnellites, an instrument to force Westminster to concede Welsh demands, not everyone took it so seriously and it never came close to the point of seceding from British Liberalism. Indeed, at this stage, the Welsh programme was focused on gaining priority for measures to which the Liberals were already largely committed and Home Rule was only beginning to be mentioned as a distant possibility. More serious was the *Cymru Fydd* organisation. Founded originally in 1886 in London as a cultural and literary movement, this spread into Wales itself from 1891 and Liberals in its ranks began to call for Welsh Home Rule and the transformation of the movement into a campaign for self-government (Morgan, 1981). In the North Wales Liberal Federation, Lloyd George and his associates sought to bring *Cymru Fydd* into politics and make Home Rule part of the Liberal platform. The Chamberlain secession had deprived the Liberals of much support in England where they were only once again—in 1906—to win a majority, and left them dependent on Scottish and Welsh support. This gave the Welsh campaigners great leverage and in the Newcastle Programme of 1891 Welsh Disestablishment was placed second only to Irish Home Rule.

Within a few years, however, the movement was in ruins. The first indication of fission came in 1892 when, to the consternation of many of his Welsh supporters, Tom Ellis accepted office in the new Liberal government, becoming Chief Whip in 1894. Lloyd George, for his part, played the Welsh card all the harder but a national *Cymru Fydd League* established in 1896 as the basis of a national movement foundered soon after in South Wales, ostensibly on the question of the division of church revenues after disestablishment but more fundamentally on what Morgan (1981, p. 118) describes as the 'gulf between north and mid-Wales on the one hand and mercantile, industrial south Wales on the other'. Subsequent attempts to revive an all-Wales Liberal body proved impossible to sell in the south. For all the fervour of the Welsh revival, the movement had failed to create a new sense of identity for the principality which could express itself politically in competition with other calls on loyalties. *Cymru Fydd* collapsed and with it the Home Rule campaign. Lloyd George abandoned his career as a Welsh nationalist and instead went to the top in British politics.

There was to be one more outbreak of Welsh feeling before the First World War, provoked by the 1902 Education Act's provisions for Anglican schools to be supported from the rates. With the last of the great religious revivals still sweeping the principality, this was a grave affront to the nonconformist conscience. Welsh councils, firmly under Liberal, nonconformist control, sought to evade or defy the Act and Lloyd George placed himself at the head of the revolt. A serious crisis was developing by the time the Unionist government fell in 1905 but it is noteworthy that the revolt, though it touched the heart of the Welsh nonconformist radical tradition, did not produce a united nationalist movement. Home Rule continued to be canvassed in a rather half-hearted way, notably in the context of the Home Rule All Round proposals of 1910-20 but the issues which inspired the Welsh revolt had either been accommodated by the Liberal government or were no longer urgent. The gap between the old radical agenda and those of the rising Labour movement was only confirmed by Lloyd George in 1906, when he urged that temperance, education, disestablishment and Welsh self-government were essential for the working man (Morgan, 1980). It was not that Labour leaders opposed these measures. On the contrary, they regarded them as part of their inheritance, but they were no longer the main priority and, with the extension of the franchise in 1918, they ceased to be the great vote winners. In contrast to Scotland, there was no resurgence of nationalism within the industrial Labour movement during and after the First World War.

The Welsh revival had, none the less, produced a permanent legacy in the form of a Welsh identity and a series of administrative and legislative concessions marking off Wales as a distinct entity within the British polity. This did not go as far as in Scotland, and Welsh society continued to be divided between north and south, English-speakers and Welsh-speakers, supporters of the old radical politics and unionist socialists, but the process of assimilation to England, in progress since Tudor times, had suffered a reverse.

We have traced the territorial movements of the late nineteenth-century United Kingdom as a response to the growth of the state and the mobilisation of new social and economic interests at a time of franchise expansion. The issues involved were diverse—peasant land hunger, middle-class concern with education, religion and culture, industrial working-class grievances—and some of these issues burnt themselves out. Others were accommodated by concessions on policy. Some elements of the territorial revival represented remnants of the old society faced with modernity. Others represented modernity in the face of an archaic British state. Some general points, though, are worth emphasising.

In the first place, there is the relative weakness of the territorial revolt. Nowhere did it succeed in creating a mass separatist movement with a consensus on a political order divorced from the British state. The most powerful movement, in Ireland, retained its force only by confining its appeal to the majority community and coexisted with an equally passionate rival dedicated to the opposite view. Even among nationalists, disputes on the meaning of the creed spawned conflict. Elsewhere in the United Kingdom, the meaning of the much-canvassed idea of Home Rule was obscure. At various times it was presented as federalism, as dominion self-government and as mere regional devolution. Federalism was never a serious proposition, since, as Dicey (1886) pointed out, it would have upset the central tenets of the constitution such as parliamentary sovereignty, unified government and ministerial responsibility for the sake of what British elites saw as a marginal issue. Advocates of dominion self-government saw the UK not as a nation-state but as the centre of an evolving commonwealth in which Scotland, Wales and Ireland could as easily operate as separate components as could Canada or Australia but the evolution of the old dominions into independent states eliminated this half-way house to sovereignty. This might have stimulated debate about the constitutional status of the mother-country itself, but after the shelving of the Irish problem, it did not. Regional devolution and how it might work was given little serious thought.

Yet, except in the case of southern Ireland, territorial management had succeeded. Local elites were found to replace those swept aside in the mobilisation of the late nineteenth century, and given secure niches within the Westminster system. This 'success', however, was achieved only at the cost of an almost total failure to examine the basis of the United Kingdom and the meaning of unity. A thoughtful unionist like Dicey was able to criticise the existing union for failing to live up to its promises while special legislation was applied in Ireland:

> It were the strangest anomaly for the law to sanction a mode of procedure which convicts a dynamiter in Dublin and not to give the Government the same means for the conviction of the same criminal for the same offence if he has crossed to Liverpool. (Dicey, 1886, p. 116)

After 1921 Northern Ireland was entrusted to 'loyalist' elites whose mode of governing could by no stretch of the imagination be reconciled with liberal-democratic principles upon which the United Kingdom supposedly rested. Thus the unionists ironically confirmed one of Dicey's criticisms of Home Rule, the lack of protection for minorities and the differentiation of law.

In Scotland and Wales a politics of dependence developed, with a sense of territorial identity jealously guarded by the local elites, including MPs and administrators, combined with the doctrine that all progress and wealth came via Westminster. Neither self-government nor assimilation, this compromise was to be very vulnerable in later years.

The Disintegration of Spain

The weakness of the nineteenth-century Spanish state, growing self-identification in the peripheral territories and political mobilisation posed a serious threat of fragmentation. Cultural and linguistic distinctiveness was an element in this fragmentation but this in itself was not sufficient to spark off territorial political movements, as the case of Galicia shows. Despite its distinct language and the Celtic cultural connection, regionalism was defeated by the strength of *caciquismo* in the rural areas and the connections of the professional middle classes in the towns to the Spanish state. Local politics were firmly in the hands of an alliance of lawyers and small landowners who had purchased church lands (Carr, 1975) and wider political issues were reduced to personal linkages characteristic of machine politics.

In Catalonia, by contrast, a combination of cultural, economic and political factors served to create a regionalism or 'nationalism' which was to be one of the major issues of Spanish politics in the early twentieth century. Catalanism has complex roots and, like other territorial political movements, contains both traditionalist, backward-looking and progressive, modernising elements, both romantic, literary elements and practical elements concerned with immediate economic matters. Like Wales, Catalonia was first effectively unified in the nineteenth century with the migration of country-dwellers to the cities, absorbing industrial/urban values but at the same time bringing their own spiritual values to the urban centres (Vives, 1986). Industrial Catalonia continued to be closely tied to the countryside in which industry had its origins and on which it relied for labour and materials (Oltra *et al.*, 1981). At the same time, the end of Carlism as a political force removed a source of internal division comparable to Jacobitism in eighteenth-century Scotland and lifted the suspicion of reaction from Catalanist ideas. Among the middle classes, the cultural revival (Chapter 3) emphasised Catalan themes and brought together the worlds of culture, religion and economics. Protectionism began to be projected not merely as an economic device but as an ethical principle, an assertion of Catalan identity and its defence (Lores, 1985).

It was because of their distinct economic interests, especially in the free-trade period of 1869–1900, and their frustration with the unresponsive Spanish state that the Catalan middle classes turned to political regionalism. In 1892 the *Lliga*

Catalana was born from earlier movements, formulating its demands in the *Bases de Manresa* for self-government and wider use of the Catalan language, and in 1901 this gave way to the *Lliga Regionalista* under the leadership of Prat de la Riba with the aim of establishing a 'great Catalonia within a great Spain'. In 1901, following the political bankruptcy of the Spanish state revealed by the 1898 defeat and the loss of the Cuban textile market, the *Lliga Regionalista* broke the pattern of *caciquismo* at local and national elections in Catalonia, establishing a pattern of separate Catalan parties which has persisted since. At the elections of 1907 the alliance *Solidaridad Catalana* was able to win forty-one of the forty-four seats in Catalonia. Francesc Cambó led the block of Catalan deputies with the ambivalent aims of gaining a degree of self-government while seeking the 'catalanisation of Spain' (Oltra *et al.*, 1981).

Despite the modernising aims of the *Lliga*, much of its Catalanism was based on the traditionalist and Catholic precepts of Torres and Balmes, which accorded with the social conservatism of the Catalan middle classes and gave them an identity but sometimes jarred with their commitment to liberal, commercial values. Prat de la Riba himself sought to reconcile the various strands of Catalanism through an ideology which subordinated social and political questions to the 'national' one (Oltra *et al.*, 1981) but social tensions within the Catalan coalition were none the less real. The tension between autonomy and dependence on the Spanish state, already apparent in the arguments over protectionism, was starkly brought home in the early twentieth century when the Barcelona bourgeoisie had to call on the authority of the state and its forces to put down unrest among their own workers. With its combination of traditionalism and dynamic modernity, the middle-class Catalan movement was a powerful force but its internal contradictions were to be its undoing. The ultimate mistake of the *Lliga* was to be support for the coup of Primo de Rivera in 1923 in the fond belief that, while re-establishing order and authority, he would adopt a sympathetic attitude to Catalanism. It was this peculiar combination of distinctiveness with dependence which inhibited the development of separatism in Catalonia though regionalism developed rapidly in the late nineteenth century among the middle classes.

The ascendancy of the *Lliga*, particularly in the years in which it controlled the Mancomunitat (see below), was clearly important in consolidating a sense of Catalan identity but it never achieved total hegemony. The radical republican Alejandro Lerroux espoused an uncompromising Jacobinism, centralist, Spanish-nationalist and anti-clerical while the working-class movement after 1890 inclined to anarcho-syndicalism, as hostile to the idea of a Catalan government as to any other type. In 1914, it is true, the Catalan federation of the socialist party PSOE demanded a 'confederation of the small Iberian nationalities' (Oltra *et al.*, 1981), but this was a tactical compromise between the need to fight on the ground in a Catalonia where regionalism was in the ascendant and the centralist instincts of the party in Spain as a whole.

There were nevertheless radical-democratic and leftist varieties of Catalanism, appealing to the lower middle classes and artisans who associated it with the expansion of democracy and often republicanism, but not with Marxism or socialism. In Spain as a whole, it was this type of radical republicanism which was to dominate governments for much of the Second Republic—but this was the very political family of Lerroux and his Jacobin followers. In Catalonia the left-regionalist position was filled by a succession of groups breaking away from the *Lliga* or PSOE until the Primo dictatorship. With the fall of the dictatorship in 1931, the *Esquerra Republicana de Catalunya* (ERC) was formed as a left-of-centre movement calling for Catalan self-government in a federal Spain and drawing on the support of the lower middle classes and artisans. With the discrediting of the *Lliga* through its support for the Primo dictatorship, the ERC was to dominate politics in Catalonia from 1931 up to the Civil War, though the extent of its support and the collapse of the conservatives were exaggerated by the workings of a non-proportional electoral system.

The turbulent political events of the 1920s and 1930s pushed Catalanism a great deal further than it might otherwise have gone as politicians exploited or reacted to the needs of the moment. The Primo dictatorship, with its suppression of regional identities, not only disillusioned the Barcelona bourgeoisie. By providing the left and the regionalists with a common enemy, it served to unite them. PSOE's own ambiguous attitude to the dictatorship also increased support for the left-regionalist position in Catalonia. An invasion of Catalonia from France established Macià, founder of the ERC, as a popular hero (GEC, 1976). Tactical considerations pushed the Catalan cause still further in the confused politics of the Second Republic as various formations manoeuvred for position.

Basque nationalism, though also developing in the late nineteenth century, was a very different phenomenon, reflecting a different pattern of interests. Although the Basque country, like Catalonia, experienced rapid industrial expansion, Basque capitalists were much more integrated into the Spanish political and economic system. Basque nationalism certainly fed on economic grievances, particularly over the size of payments to the Spanish treasury under the *conciertos económicos*, but it should not be seen as the movement of an advanced periphery seeking to escape from a backward core. On the contrary, it drew its support from the most traditionalist sectors of Basque society and was strongly imbued with Catholicism and the Carlist legacy. Arana, founder of the Basque Nationalist Party, preached an uncompromising racial exclusiveness with none of the ambiguities of Catalan regionalism, a message appealing to those marginalised by the advance of industrial society and feeling threatened by the immigration of non-Basques. Its support was greatest among peasants, fishermen and artisans, with some appeal to the urban lower middle classes (Gispert and Prats, 1978) and Basque nationalism never established the ideological hegemony of Catalanism, gaining only around one-third of the vote at elections before the Civil War. Language was always a key element in the Basque movement but one which limited its appeal to the urban masses, while for the middle classes the absence of a written literature or vernacular cultural revival was important.

For its Catholicism, its racial exclusiveness and its social conservatism, Basque nationalism was regarded with hostility by progressive and left-wing forces in Spain. For its separatism it was also detested by the Spanish-nationalist right and the military. Only the advent of the Second Republic produced a tactical accommodation between republicans and Basque nationalists though this in itself was full of tensions.

Elsewhere in Spain the weakness of the state, together with the example of Catalonia and the small nations emerging from the First World War, produced regionalist stirrings in the early decades of the twentieth century. In Andalusia some left-wing writers (Sevilla, 1986) maintain that the latifundist aristocracy and bourgeoisie had reduced the region to the status of an internal colony comparable to the Italian Mezzogiorno, from which capital and raw materials were exported and in which industrial development had been inhibited. It is certainly true that the key issue was land reform and it is not surprising then that the first Andalusian movement under Blas Infante focused on this, seeing regional autonomy as a means of breaking the latifundist aristocracy whose economic power within the region was complemented by their political power in Madrid. This was not separatism but a form of regenerationism comparable to the Catalan with the slogan, *Andalusia for itself, for Spain and for Humanity*. Blas Infante's movement, though, made little progress. The peasantry were more attracted by anarchist or socialist ideas, and as in the Mezzogiorno, interspersed periods of violent unrest with periods of sullen resignation. In any case, Blas Infante's economic theories, based on Henry George, were never entirely realistic and Andalusianism tended to be limited to relatively small groups of intellectuals. In 1918 the *Congreso Andalucista de Ronda* adopted a flag and a hymn, demanded regional autonomy and launched a movement which continued into the Second Republic. Although without great influence at the time, this did create a legacy of Andalusianism identified with progressive and left-wing causes, which was to be important in later years.

The peripheral regionalist movements in Spain were opposed by the army, the church and the monarchy, the bastions of the regime, but also by progressive liberals committed to a Jacobin vision of the state. Early socialism, too, tended to see in the Basque and Catalan movements a resurgent Carlism and the danger of clerical reaction while a strong state was seen as a necessary instrument of modernisation and social advance (Solé Tura, 1984; Fusi, 1985). Federalism might have provided the means for reconciling the demands of the periphery with the maintenance of the state. The federalists' republicanism, however, cut them off from supporters of the Spanish monarchy, while their rationalist and uniform conception of the new Spanish state and their opposition to special treatment for Catalonia and the Basque Country was far removed from the mystic/romantic conception of the Catalan and Basque nationalist right or the demands for self-determination voiced by the separatist left. Federalism continued as an undercurrent within PSOE which in 1918 adopted a position in favour of a federal republic. While this allowed socialists right up to the 1970s to deflect regionalist criticism, it remained for most of the time a dead letter and PSOE leaders in the Second Republic never sought to press the issue, often dismissing it as a 'bourgeois' concern while their parliamentary group in 1931 went so far as to deny that they had ever been federalists (Granja, 1981).

For the Spanish state, the most pressing problem in the first third of the century was that of Catalonia. What Madrid really needed was a level of territorial collaborators within Catalonia but, while the *Lliga* was more than prepared to play this role, their price was the transformation of the Spanish state, a development blocked by the powerful interests at the centre. Lacking a political base in Catalonia, Madrid politicians could not understand the problem and feared the effect of any real devolution of power. So attempts were made to resolve the Catalan question in the context of local government reform, avoiding the issue of the reform of the state itself. After several false starts, a law of 1914 allowed groups of provinces to come together to form *mancomunidades*, pooling the powers of the individual provinces but receiving no devolved powers from the centre. The only one to be formed was the Mancomunitat of Catalonia, under Prat de la Riba. Despite its limited powers, it provided a voice for Catalanism and a platform for its leaders and was able to create or revive a number of cultural, educational and literary institutions (GEC, 1976). Far from assuaging Catalan demands, this merely focused them more clearly, adding an institutional dimension to the cultural and economic markers of Catalan identity.

The Primo de Rivera dictatorship in 1923 marked a return to strict centralisation and made regionalism an objective ally of the republican and radical opponents of the regime. Although this was helped by the eclipse of the *Lliga* by the more radical and republican ERC and a moderation of the intransigent and racist trappings of Basque nationalism, the alliance remained uneasy throughout the Second Republic which followed shortly after the fall of the dictatorship. It was sealed in the Pact of San Sebastian, in which representatives of the republican forces agreed on the basis of a new regime. Catalonia was still the vital issue and, though the *Lliga* was absent, not being republican, the Catalan republicans were able to persuade those present, including Lerroux, of the need for a Catalan statute of autonomy as part of a republican settlement. The Socialist Party PSOE was not represented though the Socialist Prieto, attending in a personal capacity, insisted on the absolute sovereignty of the future Spanish parliament (Hernández, 1980). Nor were the Basque nationalists present at San Sebastian, since they were not committed to the republic and were highly suspicious of the left—the extension of autonomy to the Basque Country was opposed by Prieto though the Pact was to leave open the possibility.

This confusion over the extent to which the republic could accommodate regional demands carried over into the debates on the new constitution. On the fall of the monarchy, republican leaders in Catalonia declared a Catalan republic as part of a non-existent Iberian federation, to the consternation of republicans and socialists in Madrid. A delegation from the provisional government had to be despatched to talk the Catalans into abandoning their unilateralism in favour of a legislated solution. Nevertheless, the Catalans produced their own Statue of Nuria in advance of the new constitution.

The constituent assembly of 1931 faced two principal tasks—to settle the form of the new republican state and to accommodate the autonomist pressures from Catalonia and the Basque Country. On the latter question, a wide variety of views presented themselves. The Catalan deputation was dominated by the ERC, supported, where Catalan autonomy was concerned, by the remnants of the *Lliga*. They denied Spanish sovereignty in principle and insisted on the need to negotiate an arrangement in which Catalonia would take its place in an Iberian confederation. In practice they took their stand on the statute of Nuria, submitting reluctantly to the modifications imposed by the constituent assembly. The Basques were divided between the nationalist majority, itself flanked on the right by the extreme clericalist traditionalist group, and the republican/socialist minority (Hernández, 1980). The Basque Nationalists accepted the republic only because of the autonomy promised at San Sebastian, though they themselves had not been party to the Pact. They too had framed their own scheme, the Statute of Estella, regarded as reactionary by the left both within the Basque Country and in Spain as a whole because of its clerical bias. A provision for a Basque government to maintain direct links with the Holy See in Rome (Gispert and Prats, 1978) was condemned as establishing a 'Vatican Gibraltar' (Granja, 1981). By 1932, another division had opened up, when the town councils of Navarre decided to opt out of the Basque autonomy process. Navarre was to be a Francoist stronghold during the Civil War.

The traditional, unitarist right was poorly represented in the assembly since the electoral system, while abandoning the single-constituency mode of election in order to break the *caciques*, had not introduced anything like full proportionality. This, together with the end of the monarchy, broke up the old territorial power network in many parts of Spain and removed much of the old intransigent opposition to regionalism. Intellectuals like Unamuno and Ortega y Gasset who insisted on the principle of Spanish national sovereignty and put the case for unity (Granja, 1981) were few in number and carried little weight.

PSOE, the socialist party, comprised the largest single grouping in the constituent assembly. Its ambivalence on the territorial question reflected its unitarist bias combined with the need to accommodate regionalism and its embarrassment at its weakness in Catalonia, Spain's major industrial region, where it should have been at its strongest. While insisting that they were not bound by the San Sebastian Pact (Granja, 1981), the PSOE deputies had to work with the radicals and republicans who were. At the same time they were extremely suspicious of the clerical/reactionary potential of the Basque movement and worried about their own base in the Basque Country, where they depended heavily on the votes of immigrant workers. So they supported autonomy but surrounded it with qualifications. A 1931 special congress declared support for autonomy but demanded referendums to ensure that there was a popular demand (Hernández, 1980). Radical and republican groups comprised the next largest element and included Jacobin centralists, federalists and autonomists. Needing to win the support of regionalist groups for the republic but to sustain the central state, they took a pragmatic line on the territorial question, avoiding federalism but acceding to autonomist pressures.

Of the two peripheral territories, Catalonia was the primary issue and one which proved easier of resolution given the ideological affinity (on non-territorial issues) between the ERC and the parliamentary majority and the weakness of anti-republican, clerical, racial or separatist elements in the Catalanism of 1931. A Catalan statute approved by Madrid and by local referendum, went into operation in 1932 and the Generalitat was restored. In the Basque Country, the clerical issue slowed progress and the process was incomplete when a centralising rightist government came into office in 1934. The victory of the Popular Front in 1936 allowed progress to be resumed but Basque autonomy was conceded only at the onset of the Civil War, a move which committed the Basques to the republican side—and to Franco's vengeance. By this time the expectations raised by the republic, the leftist opposition to the government elected in 1934 and the disintegration of central authority had spawned regionalist demands not only in Galicia where an autonomy statute was conceded in 1936 but in Andalusia, Aragon, Mallorca, Valencia and Asturias (Gispert and Prats, 1978). These tended to be left-wing and republican, confirming the identification of regional autonomy with the left.

This rush to autonomy was what the republican and leftist parties in the constituent assembly had feared and had sought to avoid in their constitutional formula. This was named the *Estado Integral*, an ill-defined term but which indicated that it was neither federal nor unitary. At the time the only relevant precedent was the German Weimar Republic, though in later years a similar principle was to be tried in Italy and post-Franco Spain. From unitary theory, the *Estado Integral* took the sovereignty of the Spanish people as a whole and the need for autonomy statutes to be passed by the national parliament. From federalist and contractual theory, it took the principle of the framing of autonomy statutes in the regions themselves, their negotiation with the centre and the need for approval in a local referendum. In line with the principles of national sovereignty and uniformity, the autonomy provisions were of general application and, except in the case of the Basque statute, excluded reference to the *fueros*, traditional rights immune to state power and entrenching territorial and social interests (Clavero, 1981). Yet, to keep as much power as possible at the centre, provisions were inserted intended to limit autonomy to the historic regions of Catalonia, the Basque Country and possibly Galicia. Regions could gain a statute of autonomy only if a majority of the town councils requested it, two-thirds of the entire regional electorate approved it in a referendum and the national Cortes (parliament) accepted it. Certain matters were reserved to the exclusive competence of the centre; in others the state would legislate but regions could execute; all other matters could be devolved to regions by their individual statutes of autonomy (Olábarri, 1981).

It is impossible to say how the autonomy provisions would have operated in a peaceful Spain for the whole process was caught up in the strife and political disintegration which led up to the Civil War. The return of the right in the elections of 1934 brought a halt to the autonomy process and a serious conflict in Catalonia, where the Generalitat was attempting to introduce a major land reform. The landowners who had previously argued that foral land law should be devolved on the assumption that they would be favourably treated, now turned to the central government (Clavero, 1981), starting a process which rapidly led to the suspension of the Generalitat. This in turn pushed the Catalan left towards separatism, not as a principle but as a tactic. The restoration of the Generalitat by the Popular Front government in 1936 was rapidly followed by the Franco rebellion. In conditions of Civil War, Catalonia effectively functioned independently, at least until the republican government itself moved to Barcelona. In the Basque Country, autonomy was rapidly conceded to ensure Basque support for the republic.

Franco's victory closed the chapter in the history of Spanish regionalism with the triumph of the most intransigent, *españolista*, militarist elements in the country. In the Francoist 'crusade', regionalism ranked alongside communism and atheism as the deadly enemies of Spain and all traces of regional identity were wiped out. Regionalist leaders like Companys, President of the Generalitat, and the veteran Andalusian Blas Infante were executed, and speaking Basque or Catalan in public became a crime. Such was the Francoist paranoia about regionalism that no attempt was made to gain regime collaborators among the Basque or Catalan-speaking communities, despite the presence, especially in the former, of rightist, clericalist elements. Franco's persecution certainly crushed the Basque and Catalan movements but, in so doing, created an enhanced sense of anti-regime solidarity in those regions and ensure that any return to democracy would need to have a regional dimension.

France

The relative weakness of territorial agitation in Third Republic France is attributable both to external and to internal forces. On the external front, defeat by Germany in 1870 led to a policy of cultural and national indoctrination more extensive and efficient than elsewhere in Europe. The insecurity of the frontiers confused movements for regional autonomy with irredentism, particularly in the case of Alsace–Lorraine, lost to Germany in 1870, recovered in 1918 and lost again from 1940 to 1945. The sacred duty to recover the lost provinces was instilled into French schoolchildren after 1870 and agitation for autonomy in Alsace between the wars was seen as a threat to national security. After 1922, Fascist Italy was suspected of expansionist designs, particularly on Corsica. All this poisoned the atmosphere for regionalism throughout France. Internally the regionalist movements which developed tended to be of the reactionary right and cut off from rising democratic expectations. They failed to integrate the economic, cultural and political elements of regionalism and were prone to doctrinal and organisational schisms.

In Brittany three *emsavs* or phases of the regionalist movement are recognised: that before the First World War; that between the wars; and that following the Second World War (O'Connor, 1983). The first *emsav* represented not, as in some other European peripheries, an assertion of new social groups against an archaic state structure and an existing pattern of territorial representation, but a reaction by the existing territorial elites against the threat to their position posed by the modern, democratic and secular republic and its inroads into Brittany. Reece (1977) illustrates the grip of the old aristocracy on representation under the Third Republic, noting that in 1870 nobles held 40 per cent of the seats on the councils of the Breton *départements* while another 40 per cent were held by their professional and middle-class dependants. By 1910 noble representation was still at 30 per cent. In the countryside power was wielded by the clergy, financially independent of the nobility but pressing the same conservative interests. As industry began to grow and military service and emigration stimulated the circulation of ideas, this power structure was progressively threatened. Having failed in 1870 with the monarchist card, the aristocracy counted on religion to maintain order but, with the acceptance of the republic by the Pope in 1890, this card too was lost—so they turned to regionalism (Reece, 1977).

A regionalist ideology was available in the historical writings of Pitre-Chevalier and in Borderie's history of Brittany, which appeared between 1897 and 1901. Correcting French distortions of history with distortions of their own, these contrasted French nationalism with an alternative Breton identity. Borderie insisted that 'Brittany is better than a province, it is a people, a real nation' (O'Connor, 1983). Yet the *Union régionaliste breton*, founded in 1898 by conservatives including the Marquis d'Estourbeillon, deputy for Morbihan from 1902 to 1946 (Mayo, 1974), was far from nationalist in this sense. Under aristocratic control, it was monarchist and reactionary and profoundly committed to France, albeit a decentralised, conservative, Catholic and monarchical France. Its aristocratic and clerical basis provoked a series of schisms by moderate elements and prevented any serious attempt at mass mobilisation. Indeed, by its very definition, such a movement could not lend itself to the sort of peasant risings which elsewhere in Europe were sustaining regionalist revivals. In 1914 it threw itself into the *union sacrée* in the defence of France. After the war, taking the Wilson doctrine of the rights of small nations literally, it presented a petition to the Peace Conference (Beer, 1980) but French government influence ensured that this was ignored. Some evidence of support, at least verbal, for the Breton idea is provided by the growing number of deputies who included reference to Brittany in their election manifestos (Reece, 1977) but this seems to reflect the use of Breton symbolism by the old elites rather than a challenge to the system.

Splinter groups from the *union régionaliste* fared even worse and an explicitly separatist *parti nationaliste breton*, founded in 1911, disappeared with the war. After the war the second *emsav* was equally ineffectual, spawning a variety of groups perpetually in conflict over separatism v regionalism, clericalism v anticlericalism, left v right and Breton-speakers v Francophones. Attempts by elements of the clergy to merge Catholicism and Breton identity in a political form were stamped out by the hierarchy who were fearful of separatism and more concerned with maintaining the position of the church in France as a whole (O'Connor, 1983). Finally the strongest element in the Breton movement veered to the extreme right and adopted an explicitly Fascist policy. The numbers involved in these groups were tiny and interventions by independent candidates in elections proved disastrous. By this time the old ruling classes were no longer the mainspring of the movement, though the usefulness of the rhetoric of territorial solidarity was still recognised by Brittany's representatives in Paris. In 1936 a Breton Front was organised on a moderate platform, circulating proposals for electoral reform, regional decentralisation and Breton teaching in school to parliamentary candidates in Brittany. Forty-one signed, three-quarters of these on the political right, though including a few communists and socialists (Reece, 1977). Despite the success of these candidates in harvesting 43 per cent of the second ballot vote, this was no revolution. It merely showed that support for regionalism was a considered a safe cause by Brittany's representatives, particularly in the conservative quarter, without committing them to anything specific. Breton regional demands made no impression in the new Parliament, nor did the right, largely integrated into French parties while still cultivating their home bases, react to the Popular Front victory by pressing for Breton autonomy.

The association of elements of the Breton movement with fascism in the late 1930s, together with some bombing incidents (in which no one was killed) brought official harassment of the small groups of campaigners. The final blow was delivered during the war when a group of Breton nationalists collaborated with Nazi Germany, leaving a taint on the movement which was to take decades to erase.

In Occitania the elitist and literary basis of the *Félibrige* distanced it from the immediate economic and political concerns of the masses while its Catholic, right-wing bias was at odds with the anti-clericalism of a large part of the male population (women did not have the vote before 1946). The economic discontent which broke out in the viticultural crisis of 1909 did at one point take on a regional dimension and echoes were even evoked of the ancient Occitan tradition of revolt back to the Cathars—an association of ancient and modern comparable to the Scottish radicals' harking back to the Covenanters. This tradition was, of course, far removed from the monarchist and traditionalist bias of most of the *Félibrige* and, when asked to support the wine-growers, the economic basis of Occitania, Mistral refused. The organisation of the protest was essentially non-political until Marcellin Albert and Ferroul, the mayor of Narbonne turned it into a mass, interclass organisation, uniting landowners and small-scale peasant cultivators. A large number of municipal councils were persuaded to resign in protest at government inaction. A demonstration at Narbonne was dispersed by soldiers, leaving five dead, and was followed by the sacking of the prefecture at Perpignan in retaliation (Cholvy, 1980). There was, though, no political strategy here and certainly no project for regional autonomy. The demands were essentially couched in terms of the French state and concerned protection and the need for state support and intervention. The central authorities nevertheless claimed that reactionary monarchist elements were behind the unrest and were able to outmanoeuvre a leadership unprepared to defy the state. With some legal regulations and a rise in prices, the territorial representatives were able to recoup the position before the critical point of political mobilisation was reached.

The advance of socialism was not accompanied by a complete assimilation of regional politics with national norms. Rather, the Socialist SFIO, gradually displacing the nineteenth-century radicals, took over the management of Languedoc's relations with the state. In the wine-growing areas, the cooperative movement allowed the small peasant holdings to survive by providing a guaranteed outlet for their produce, under the tutelage of well-fed leaders whose purely verbal radicalism allowed them to attack the old targets of church and state without questioning property rights (Lerner, 1980). In the city of Toulouse an urban political machine developed, with its own social organisations (Nevers, 1983). Power resided in the party section, not the mayor, and patronage took the form of distribution of low-cost housing and jobs in the large direct-works department. With the steady decline of local industry after the First World War, especially locally-owned and controlled industry, attention was more and more focused on the state. The policy of the state, in turn, followed no overall strategy but was rather the product of the more or less successful manipulations of the *notables* (Trempe, 1980). So a system was established which could combine intense localism with support for the centralised state. Intense ideological conflicts were fought out between the *rouges* and the *blancs*, corresponding to the republican/anticlerical and the Catholic/rightist factions in French politics but, as this division bore only the faintest relationship to class divisions, bread-and-butter issues were resolved through the client system centred on the *notables*. This regime was to survive in its essentials until the Fifth Republic.

The French state thus weathered the territorial upheavals of the late nineteenth and early twentieth centuries more successfully than the British or the Spanish and even the defeat of 1940 provoked little territorial reaction. A strong sense of national identity had been deliberately cultivated under the Third Republic, while the potential of territorially-based social and economic grievances to touch off political movements was restrained through a system of territorial management which disaggregated demands and focused them on a centralised system of territorial representation. The development of this system under the Fourth and Fifth Republics is covered in the next chapter.

Italy and the *questione meridionale*

In Italy regionalism and the problem of the Mezzogiorno were constant themes of political debate in the late nineteenth and early twentieth centuries but among intellectuals concerned not to react to existing political movements but to stimulate regional consciousness in the south and use regionalism to strengthen Italian national unity by reforming the state. The forces wanting to reverse unification were forcibly suppressed in the 1860s and their links with political reaction tainted regionalism in the eyes of progressives and liberals for many years. This attitude was confirmed by growth in the south of the *garantista* tradition (Zagarrio, 1981) defending the social and economic order and, when this was threatened, falling back upon regionalism to defend it, notably in Sicily in the 1920s and 1940s. Around the turn of the century there were popular movements, notably the Sicilian *Fasci* who organised sporadic land seizures and strikes and were a component of the early Socialist Party but in general peasant unrest was barely politicised and never developed a regional perspective.

The first serious consideration of the social and economic conditions and political corruption of the south was given by the northern intellectuals, Franchetti and Sonino (Galasso, 1978). They were followed by Guistino Fortunato who, after a careful survey of conditions in the Mezzogiorno, concluded that its problems were due to natural handicaps combined with bad government. This was a break with the conventional wisdom that the south was a naturally rich place ruined by Bourbon misgovernment which would automatically thrive after unification or the often-expressed view that southerners were racially inferior. Fortunato's conclusion was that new policies were needed to make unity a reality but that self-government would merely hand power to the local elites who were themselves part of the problem. Instead, investment was needed to develop the southern economy while military service could create a unitary spirit and break the cultural particularism of the south. In similar vein, Nitti argued that the invisible hand of the market alone would not build a national economy without purposive public policies. By the 1880s the theme of the 'incomplete unification' had entered political debate, a realisation that nation-building was more than formal unity and required the construction of a national economy and a greater equality of living standards.

Fortunato and Nitti soon came under criticism for neglecting the political dimension of policy-making, ignoring the obstacles which the existing system posed to governments pursuing their recommendations. Whether these obstacles would be removed or reinforced by the concession of regional autonomy became one of the major items of contention in the debate on the Mezzogiorno. The need for a political solution focused on the middle classes and autonomism was stressed by Napoleone Colajanni in his journal *Isola* in the 1890s (Zagarrio, 1981). The Socialist Gaetano Salvemini stressed the role of the masses, arguing that only through popular mobilisation in the south could the alliance of southern landowners and northern capitalists be broken. This required universal suffrage and an alliance of southern peasants with northern industrialists to overturn the political order and break the politics of *trasformismo* (Salvemini, 1978; Galasso, 1978). If this were done, protectionist policies could be reversed and land reform with peasant proprietorship introduced. He was opposed by the Socialist Turati and the majority of the party in the north, who, like their counterparts elsewhere in Europe, feared the reactionary potential of peasant proprietors. While it would have been difficult for socialists to oppose universal suffrage on principle, the northerners in practice defended the electoral provisions of 1882, based on literacy, which were gradually enfranchising the industrial workers of the north while largely excluding the southern peasantry.

Salvemini's plea for universal suffrage received a hostile reception at the Congress of 1908 where priority was given to payment for deputies to allow northern working men to serve in Parliament (Salvadori, 1976). Turati insisted that before getting the vote the southern masses must be educated and weaned away from clerical and reactionary influence. Meanwhile electoral reforms should increase the parliamentary weight of the north and, with the help of social legislation, allow the northern workers to lead the south out of thralldom. To weaken the power of southern landowners, agricultural protection would be lifted but industrial protection should remain. In 1900 he stated what was to be a standard doctrine of the Italian left for many years, advocating a 'temporary hegemony of the more advanced part of the country over the more backward, not to oppress it but to emancipate it' (quoted, Salvadori, 1976, p. 110). This was both special pleading for a territorial section of the country—the north—and an implicit endorsement of a class alliance there, an alliance cemented by the commitment to protectionism. The breach caused in the Italian left by the territorial issue prevented it for many years from serving as a national integrating force. For his part Salvemini left the Socialist Party though he continued to campaign both for autonomy for the south and for reform of the Italian state as a whole.

Like other socialists the Marxist intellectual Gramsci could see in the unaided efforts of the southern peasants only a potential *Vendée*, a rural counter-revolution. The northern proletariat alone had the potential to liberate them by first establishing its own dictatorship; then it would help the south since it would be in its own interest to keep up agricultural production (Gramsci, 1978b). More to the point, perhaps, Gramsci identified the weaknesses in the simple slogans of land reform, noting that to maintain any real economic or political independence, peasant cultivators would need assured sources of credit and machinery and a marketing system.

Having written off the south in this manner, it is not surprising that in the years before Fascism the left made little progress there. In 1919 the Socialist vote ranged from 60 per cent in the central region of Emilia down to 2.2 per cent in southern Calabria (Farneti, 1985).

A more exclusively 'meridionalist' analysis was that of Guido Dorso whose *La Rivoluzione Meridionale* appeared in 1925. Dorso placed little faith in the alliance of southern peasants and northern workers since the latter were hopelessly given to reformism and collusion with a parasitic and protected capitalism (Caronna, 1970). Instead, the Mezzogiorno should be the instrument of its own liberation. Just how this was to be achieved posed a serious problem, given the lack of political awareness in the south and the fact, as Dorso himself recognised, that the mass movements which had sprung up there were ephemeral and unpoliticised and only vaguely directed at the unitary state. Dorso's answer was a *Partito Meridionale Rivoluzionario*, an elite of perhaps just a hundred men who would form the core of a new southern middle class. The proposal harked back to Garibaldi's Thousand who overthrew the Kingdom of Naples but Dorso was to search in vain in the 1920s and again in the 1940s for his revolutionary southern elite.

Very different in inspiration was the meridionalism of Luigi Sturzo, a southern Catholic priest who founded Italy's first Catholic party, the *Partito Popolare*. Sturzo's belief in autonomy was based upon an organic conception of society in which class conflict was stilled by community solidarity. This conservative conception of society was infused with Catholic social thinking but was democratic and reformist. Sturzo believed strongly in land reform and the creation of a class of peasant proprietors which he, like his opponents the northern socialists, saw as a Catholic, conservative and stabilizing force. For the same reason he favoured universal suffrage, with proportional representation to break the local client networks, and an end to the industrial protection in which the northern socialists colluded with industrial capital. For all its populist appeal, however, the *Partito Popolare* made little impact on the south where in all regions except Calabria its vote was under 15 per cent (Farneti, 1985).

After the First World War Sturzo himself became more interested in the promotion of political Catholicism in Italy as a whole and played down the issue of southern autonomy (Zagarrio, 1981).

Given the economic grievances, uneven development, exploitation, agrarian discontent, the cultural gap between north and south, and traditions of separatism and localism, the question we need to face is why the Mezzogiorno failed to produce an autonomist movement comparable to those found in other European peripheries. One reason lies in the process of state creation itself. It would have taken a bold leader to raise the separatist banner in the years following the harsh suppression of the 1860s. At the same time southern liberal intellectuals were mostly committed to the united state and the values of the *Risorgimento*—their complaint was with the failure of the Italian state to live up to its promises. At the popular level, mobilisation was inhibited by the restricted franchise up to 1919 and peasant discontents were channelled into the short-lived but often violent outbreaks characteristic of southern Spain without the disciplined parliamentary action with which agrarian unrest was accompanied in Ireland and Scotland. A quasi-feudal social and economic structure in the south kept the peasants in subjection and the influence of the church was exercised in favour of the social and economic order and against participation in the institutions of the state. In the absence of mass political, social and economic organisation, issues were reduced to personal grievances and resolved through the extensive network of patronage and corruption which connected local politicians to the state institutions in Rome, disaggregating social and economic grievances and inhibiting territorial mobilisation.

Social scientists have seen this type of patronage and clientilism as a feature of transitional societies, a mechanism whereby a pre-modern society used to personalised relationships and traditional hierarchy can relate to a modern state based on impartial bureaucratic principles. The territorial representative able to move in both worlds is the mediator. In pre-Fascist Italy, however, this was more than a traditional phase in the inevitable move to modernisation and full liberal democracy. It was the very basis upon which Italian unity was built, with its underlying social alliance between northern industrial and southern agrarian elites. Modernising policies, which could undermine this power structure, were therefore opposed by politicians in the Parliament in Rome. *Trasformismo*, under which the mainly Liberal southern deputies would support whoever was in power in exchange for a free hand in the south, was the political expression of this bargain. Franchise expansion and the collapse of the Liberals from 48 per cent of the national vote in 1913 to 9 per cent in 1919 (Farneti, 1985) threatened this system, despite the partial recovery in 1921. The persistence of southern habits of clinging to the office-holders of the day, though, was emphasised in 1924 when the new Fascist regime polled from 70 per cent to 86 per cent of the Mezzogiorno regions' vote outside Sardinia—in Italy as a whole they managed just 65 per cent (Farneti, 1985). The political legacy of *trasformismo* and clientilism was to persist long after Italy should by rights have completed the transition to 'modernity'. The workings of the system and its success in meeting autonomist challenges can be most clearly seen in the cases of Sicily and Sardinia.

In Sicily autonomist sentiment never died out completely among various social groups (Mack Smith, 1968b) and the agricultural crisis from 1885 provoked the popular discontents of the *Fasci* (Salvadori, 1976), which in turn provoked government repression. Urged on by Sicilian politicians and landowners who claimed there was a plot to sever Sicily from Italy, the government in 1893 despatched 30,000 soldiers and a fleet (Mack Smith, 1968b). Reform proposals were defeated by parliamentary machinations made possible by the southern deputies' hold on successive governments. Tentative land reform efforts in the 1890s were again defeated by southern parliamentarians, and when a reforming commissioner, Codronchi, floated the idea of autonomy, he 'regretfully . . . had to admit that nine tenths of the Sicilian deputies were opposed to his experiment' (Mack Smith, 1968b, p. 489).

So the system of clientilism and patronage prospered while under Giolitti corruption became rampant. The Mafia, strengthened by the return of criminal elements from the United States, extended its power and, while essentially serving the purpose of oppressing the peasantry on behalf of the landowners, tapped traditions of insular solidarity and alienation from the mainland to present themselves as local heroes defending Sicilians from the depredations of the northern 'foreigners'. In individual cases, indeed, they did help individuals and there was no popular trust in the Italian state bureaucracy—but in taking Mafia 'protection' Sicilians were helping forge their own chains.

There was a crisis of representation comparable to those of other European peripheries but it developed late and its effects were overtaken by the installation of the Fascist regime. The franchise reform of 1913 began to erode the domination of the Liberal notables whose representation was halved while seven socialists were elected. In 1919, with further franchise reforms and the return of ex-soldiers, the Liberals were routed, returning just six of the fifty-two Sicilian deputies on 8.6 per cent of the vote and the new members, mostly republicans and radicals, promised agrarian reform, the nationalisation of large estates and Sicilian autonomy (Mack Smith, 1968b). Whether they in turn would be absorbed by the practices of *trasformiso* or effect a permanent change in Sicilian politics we will never know, for within three years democracy had been crushed by the Fascists. The ambiguity of the concept of autonomy was revealed in 1920, meanwhile, when a meeting of Sicilian estate-owners at Palmermo sent an ultimatum to the government, threatening that if it did not put an end to the land occupation by former soldiers, *they* would organise a secession (Ganci, 1978). They were spared the trouble by the Fascists. While Fascism had been weak in Sicily before 1922, the landowners and their political representatives lost no time in jumping on the bandwagon to preserve their crumbling position—although Fascism had an anti-landlord, populist streak, no serious attack was made on the large estates. The Mafia declined under the offensive of a government unwilling to tolerate a rival source of organised violence but also because the landlords no longer needed it (Ganci, 1978). The habits of thought and social customs which underlay the old system, however, persisted right through the life of the regime and were to reappear at the Liberation (Mack Smith, 1968b).

Although Sardinia had not been conquered in the 1860s but annexed by Piedmont earlier it was part of the Mezzogiorno and suffered equally from inappropriate policies like protectionism dictated by the needs of northern industry. An undercurrent of autonomist feeling was always present, fed by a vague sense of a separate historic, ethnic, economic and geographic distinctiveness (Azzena and Palermo, 1981). As in Sicily, however, anti-state sentiment tended to be expressed through banditism, sabotage, killings of government tax-collectors and support for an informal system of authority and order. Sardinian deputies formed part of the southern block, trading votes in Rome for patronage at home. It was the return of soldiers after the First World War with the expanded franchise which broke the old pattern of territorial representation and produced a new political movement dedicated to Sardinian autonomy. The *Partito Sardo d'Azione* (PS d'A) made considerable headway among the island peasantry but, though there was some conscious imitation of the Irish movement, failed to generate a coherent ideology or conception of Sardinia's place within the Italian state. There was a vague anti-capitalism and commitment to free trade but positions on the constitutional issue ranged from separatism to mild reform. In the confusion leadership was assumed by members of the professional classes who developed an interclass regional ideology, excluding only the large landowners, rather than the class alliance between the southern peasantry and the northern proletariat advocated by Salvemini and others. The interclass base of the PS d'A, resisting attempts by Gramsci to split off its left wing, proved so remarkably resilient even in the face of Fascism (Zagarrio, 1981) that at the Liberation it was generally assumed that Sardinian autonomism would be a powerful force.

So territorial issues remained vital in Italian politics throughout the period of the liberal monarchy, albeit managed with some success. By the end of the First World War, this management system was experiencing considerable strain and movements of territorial assertion were growing but in the end, it was other strains which were to cause the collapse of the liberal regime and usher in two decades of Fascist authoritarianism accompanied by an aggressive Italian nationalism in which all expressions of regional identity were to be crushed. The *questione meridionale*, however, remained on the agenda to re-emerge with greater force in the 1940s.

5
Territorial Management in the Postwar Era

Territorial Integration in Postwar Europe

Theories of cultural diffusion and 'modernisation' predicting the end of territorial distinctiveness have been questioned by the survey of the previous chapter. Yet some would argue that the tensions of the late nineteenth and early twentieth centuries represented the clash of modernising forces with those of tradition, resulting in the victory of the former. This, as we have seen, is a gross simplification, since some of the peripheral revolts represented elements more dynamic and democratic than their respective state elites. Yet we can concede that after 1945 many of these conflicts were exhausted as land and religion had been displaced by the issues of industrial society. With rapid urbanisation and industrialisation it was to be expected that class issues would dominate national politics while the growth of big government and large-scale private industry would remove political choices, and hence political interest, to ever higher levels. Social and geographical mobility would be forces for integration, while national mass media, particularly radio and television, would provide all citizens with the same political stimuli. Political parties, increasingly concerned with programmatic policies and forging national majorities, would downplay divisive territorial questions.

To a large extent all this has happened, yet the 1960s and 1970s saw a powerful resurgence of territorial politics. This can be dismissed as yet another 'revolt against modernity' (Lipset, 1985) only by begging even more questions than in the case of the nineteenth century. In particular it assumes a universal standard of modernisation imposed by the logic of economic and political development, against which all other values are considered somehow deviant. The assumption, against all historical evidence, is that eventually, when 'development' takes its course, territorial politics will finally disappear. An alternative perspective is to see territorial politics as a perfectly rational way for citizens to frame their demands on the economic and political systems. From this perspective regionalism and territorial politics, far from being swept away by the process of modernisation, are encouraged by precisely those changes in economic, social and political systems which have marked the post-Second-World-War era. State political and administrative elites for their part, must manage the resulting demands and reconcile them with class and sectoral priorities. The mechanisms include political parties, local government, territorial administration, clientilism and distributive policies. In this chapter we shall examine these mechanisms as they emerged from the process of state consolidation following the first territorial challenges; but first we will consider the ambivalent impact of the rise of labour, the concentration of capital and the rise of the modern technocratic state committed to growth and welfare.

The relationship between labour and left-wing parties and the politics of territory is complex. There are several reasons why in principle these parties should favour centralised government. Traditions of labour and trade union solidarity are an important factor. Workers in depressed regions will seek equality of wages and conditions through national bargaining. Those in more prosperous areas equally have an interest in centralised bargaining to prevent undercutting of wage rates. There is a similar common interest in uniform taxation and regulation to prevent industry moving around in search of the most lax regime or playing off one jurisdiction against another. Since the Second World War, as labour and social democratic parties have approached government, they have become more committed to statist solutions to social and economic problems and consequently more centralist. Equalisation of welfare provision both accords with left-wing egalitarian provisions and discourages the mobility of capital in search of areas with lower welfare standards and thus lower taxation. In economic affairs social democracy has moved from a strategy of contesting the power of capital in the workplace to guiding the process of development through the institutions of the state. National economic planning is seen as the means by which the cyclical variations of capitalist output can be regulated and production tailored to social as well as individual need. This in turn requires the establishment of strong state administration, with little opportunity for local variation. On the electoral front, social democratic parties tend to mobilise on the basis of class interest as providing the largest available constituency with the minimum of internal division.

On the other hand, economic interests do not necessarily unite the working class of a state. Material interests may be seen in territorial as well as class terms and class appeals have rarely been sufficient to form a winning coalition so that social democratic parties must take on board other issues, including those rooted in specific territories. Nor are the parties of the left themselves constructed on purely class lines. The traditions of specific territories have left their mark on radical and left-wing movements even as they became integrated into larger national organisations. Strategies used by left-wing parties to deal with the territorial dimension in politics have varied from unyielding Jacobinism, through the provision of privileged access to central decision-makers for individual territories, to more or less qualified support for regional autonomy. Changing economic and political circumstances in the 1970s and 1980s have intensified the problem of reconciling these strands.

Concentration of capitalist industry has also been seen as a factor for increased national integration. In many of the peripheral territories, local ownership of industry has declined dramatically as mergers and take-overs have shifted control into the hands of conglomerates based in national capitals. There is thus no substantial local business class to articulate a distinct set of concerns on matters of economic policy or to provide middle-class leadership for territorial political movements. As major issues of economic policy are thrashed out at national level between leaders of economic interests and government, territorial politics is downgraded and proposals for regional autonomy are seen as, at best, irrelevant and, at worst, a means of isolating local political pressures, cutting them off from the central decision-making process. Yet from the 1960s, conflicting trends could be observed in the organisation of capital and labour. As industrial ownership became increasingly centralised at the level of the nation-state and then on a multinational basis, labour organisation became more decentralised. Local and shop-floor activity became more independent of national union leaders and labour federations and more responsive to conditions on the ground. While the main impact of this was felt in the difficulties of corporatist accommodation at national level in the large states, it also had territorial implications. The concentration of business ownership itself enhanced the importance of territory in some respects, since major business decisions could have very uneven territorial impacts, while labour interests were pushed into territorially-based struggles over wages and job opportunities. This created tensions within the parties of the left and was to be a factor in pushing them towards the politics of territorial defence.

From the 1950s the framework of territorial politics began to change as central state political and administrative elites became committed to economic and industrial modernisation policies and planning. The extension of these in space required new administrative forms and, for some, a new set of territorial collaborators. In the event centralised regional policies and the modernisation of the system of territorial representation and administration disturbed the old networks but, partly because of the very ambiguity of the goals of regional development policies, failed to install a new collaborative elite. At the same time exercises in regional planning raised the salience of regional issues and the territorial distribution of resources. Changing economic circumstances, notably the opening of national economies to foreign competition, further reduced the capacity of the old territorial representatives to deliver the goods. This coincided in some cases with a regime change or a party realignment to create a political opening into which territorial parties and movements could step. These movements themselves, however, faced immense problems in integrating the cultural, economic and political aspects of their appeal into a coherent ideology and in forging a stable constituency. Consequently the state-wide parties, particularly those on the left, were able to pick up some of their demands while leaving others. This gave them a degree of success in demobilising the territorial movements, but only at the cost of policy conflicts within their own ranks.

So, far from territorial conflicts disappearing under the influence of post-war trends, the next three chapters will seek to show that they have merely adopted a new form.

Territorial Management in Post-War Britain

By the 1920s the UK's territorial crisis had apparently been resolved. The secession of southern Ireland and the insulation of northern Ireland by devolution and parliamentary under-representation had removed a potentially disruptive influence in the development of the British parliamentary regime. The integration of Labour into the norms of the parliamentary state and the subordinate local government system ensured that a 'collaborative vacuum' did not develop at the local level in the transition to an urban and industrial society (Bulpitt, 1983; Jones and Keating, 1985). In the absence of a 'national revolution', though, the United Kingdom remained an untidy affair, its very citizenship undefined and with a confused boundary between the metropolitan state and wider Empire and Commonwealth.

A modernised 'dual polity' (Bulpitt, 1983) had been constructed on a number of key elements. Political life and decision-making continued to be centralised while the rigid separation of central and local political elites, with no accumulation of offices as in France and Italy, ensured that territorial bosses did not emerge as powerful figures in national politics. At the same time there was a very considerable devolution of the *administrative* responsibilities of the expanding state to local collaborative elites who in turn had a very restricted view of their political role. Only occasionally, as in the Clay Cross case in the 1970s, did local government leaders pick up the politicised, confrontational tradition which had died with Poplarism in the 1920s. It was this devolution of administrative responsibilities, including much of the business of dealing with individuals and allocating resources within the cities, which allowed the centre to retain that degree of freedom from territorial pressures which Bulpitt (1983) identifies as a key element of the 'dual polity'.

The Labour Party's contribution to this system was worked out under the post-war Attlee government. This imposed a strict centralisation of economic and industrial policy questions, keeping the newly nationalised industries and utilities out of the reach of territorial government. Cash benefits in the welfare state were similarly centralised in the interests of equity and economic unity. All this reflected the social democratic belief in using the centralised state machine to effect economic change and redistribute resources according to need, rather than economic or political power. At the same time urban Labour parties developed a 'municipal Labourism' (Gyford, 1985) focused on distribution through the expanding environmental and social programmes which the centre was encouraging and helping to finance. In many cases control over these resources, notably public housing, became an instrument of patronage and urban political machines developed, the power bases of local bosses. These remained *local* bosses, however, with no leverage over national politics.

Two other elements completed the post-war settlement, endorsed by both major parties in the consensus years of 1945–75. Keynesian economic policies allowed the centre a degree of macro-economic control without the need for detailed intervention in industrial sectors or territories, though Britain's poor relative economic performance created increasing pressures for intervention from the 1960s. Finally there was considerable functional devolution of areas of administration which central government wished to offload but which it was not prepared to entrust to elected territorial government. In many cases, such as the National Health Service or the University Grants Committee, this involved the cooption of professional elites into a process of self-government and regulation, easing the administrative and political burden on the centre but creating vested interests within the state apparatus and reducing the capacity of the centre to impose change.

For Scotland and Wales a special strategy was adopted in the expansion of the 'administrative devolution' begun in 1885, a formula which preserved some distinctiveness while satisfying the centralist preferences of both parties. Labour perhaps saw centralisation more in economic terms, the Conservatives in terms of unionist ideology but the contrast should not be exaggerated. Both shared a strong commitment to the unitary state based in considerations of principle and calculation. In 1926 the Secretary for Scotland had been raised to the rank of Secretary of State with a guaranteed seat in the Cabinet and by the 1930s the Gilmour Committee was describing him as 'Scotland's minister', with a general oversight of Scottish affairs and the task of promoting Scottish interests. Under wartime tenure of Tom Johnston, the capacity of a determined Secretary of state to bring home the goods was amply demonstrated.

In the post-war era the Scottish Office developed three roles (Keating and Midwinter, 1983). The first was to administer Scotland's distinctive administrative legacy, preserving the boundaries in areas such as education, law and the local government system. Secondly there was a limited capacity for policy differentiation, confined largely to social matters with a low partisan salience. Thirdly there was the task of lobbying for Scotland in Whitehall, in the Cabinet and in negotiations with the Treasury, which came to be the prime factor in assessing the performance of Secretaries of State. By convention the Secretary of State was supported in his lobbying role by all parties in Scotland, though this in no way attenuated partisan confrontation on general policy matters; nor did it prevent opposition parties criticising the inability of an incumbent Secretary of State to deliver enough. There is no doubt that this lobbying was effective. Scottish Office pressure played its part in strengthening regional development policies in the 1960s and well-publicised interventions by the Secretary of State brought major investments like the Linwood car plant, the Ravenscraig steel complex and the Post Office Savings Bank to Scotland in preference to other development areas. By the mid-1970s, Scottish expenditure levels were running some 20 per cent above the British average in domestic programmes (Heald, 1983).

This was centralised government with no political devolution, but it was government by Scots. The Secretary of State and his junior ministers may on occasions have been the representatives of the Scottish political minority but they were Scottish MPs and did, at least until 1987, have a political base within Scotland. The administration itself was from the 1930s located in Edinburgh where close contact was maintained with local government and interest groups and detailed issues resolved within a restricted elite. The existence of this administration provided a focal point for Scottish lobbying and sustained and even brought into existence Scottish interest groups which otherwise might have been absorbed into wider UK groupings. Taking their cue from ministers, Scottish Office civil servants saw their role in dual terms, governing Scotland on behalf of the centre while lobbying for Scotland at the centre (Keating, 1976).

In Parliament special arrangements were developed for dealing with Scottish legislation. To the Grand Committee which debated Scottish affairs generally, were added two standing committees to take Scottish bills and later an investigative select committee. Efforts were made to produce separate Scottish legislation rather than tacking Scottish clauses onto English or British bills and this increased the burden on the Scottish committees while progressively separating the treatment of English and Scottish affairs. The role of the Scottish MPs reflected the division of politics into an arena of 'Scottish affairs', corresponding to the responsibilities of the Scottish Office and Scottish legislation, and an arena of 'UK affairs'. The latter in turn divides into those matters impinging directly upon Scotland, notably in economic and industrial matters, and those without territorial implications. A detailed study of the attitudes and activities of the Scottish MPs in the period 1945–70 (Keating, 1975; 1978) showed that most of them confined themselves to the Scottish arena, entering the UK arena only where those matters with a direct territorial impact were involved. A minority of Scottish MPs were identified as 'UK-oriented', operating freely in the UK arena and often serving in UK ministries; these were also distinguished by their marked lack of involvement in the Scottish arena. Interviews confirmed that MPs saw their careers in UK or Scottish terms while the quantitative evidence showed that the differentiation of Scottish MPs' behaviour had increased over the period. Given the system of unitary party government in Britain, the amount of real policy discretion within the Scottish arena was largely limited to those matters, often involving 'conscience' questions like divorce and homosexuality, which governments leave to a free vote, but Scottish MPs none the less jealously guarded their prerogatives and would resent any interference by English members in Scottish affairs.

Kellas' (1986) description of all this as a 'Scottish political system' captures the separateness of Scottish politics but is perhaps misleading since the power to take authoritative decisions does not reside in Scotland but in the UK Cabinet and unitary Parliament. The Scottish Office is permitted to proceed with its own policy initiatives only in restricted circumstances and subject to Cabinet guidelines—indeed it is rare for the Scottish Office to take policy initiatives at all (Keating and Midwinter, 1983). Rather, its policies, where they are not identical to those being pursued in England, tend to be 'concurrent', designed to achieve the same ends by slightly different means (Rose 1982a; Ross, 1981).

Attitudes to the recurring issue of Scottish Home Rule were strongly conditioned by this system of territorial management and representation. Politicians were aware of the trade-off between autonomy at home and access to the centre, realising that if a devolved government were established, the Secretary of State and his administration, along with Scotland's overrepresentation in the House of Commons, would be brought into question. As the Scottish economy declined, access to the centre was seen as more important than a semi-independence for Scotland, even among Labour MPs when, after 1959, they formed the majority in Scotland but had to submit to Conservative government imposed from Westminster. Personal role considerations also played a part. Scottish MPs saw themselves as the representatives of Scotland and its privileged channel of access to the centre. A devolved assembly would deprive them of the role in Scottish legislation which occupied so much of their time and put in jeopardy their representational role. It is not surprising, then, that the 'Scottish-oriented' MPs tended to be more opposed to Scottish Home Rule than the UK-oriented ones whose role would be largely unaffected (Keating, 1975).

The success of the Scottish model prompted its extension to Wales despite complaints from centralists in the Welsh Labour Party, who saw it as a dangerous concession to Welsh nationalism. After experiments under the Conservatives with a 'minister for Wales' in a vague coordinating role, the 1964 Labour government established a Welsh Office with its own Secretary of State. It was never to attain the status of the Scottish Office, with fewer responsibilities and more dependence on leadership from Whitehall departments, but it was a major step in the recognition of Wales as a distinct political and administrative entity.

So centralised government did not result in the assimilation of Scotland and Wales to the centre. On the contrary, Scottish and Welsh distinctiveness increased with administrative devolution and the increased projection of ministers, administrators and MPs as territorial lobbyists. This was a style of territorial management which raised the salience of the old territorial units within the state and, instead of disaggregating territorial demands and demobilising territorial movements, positively encouraged people to formulate political demands in a territorial framework. It was thus a high-risk strategy, bringing rewards to parties, notably Labour, which could play up the importance of the territorial issue while denying its constitutional implications, but requiring a constant infusion of resources. Its high point was 1966 when Labour won thirty-two of the thirty-six Welsh and 46 of the 71 Scottish seats in Parliament (Jones and Keating, 1982). Within months the strategy was in a crisis fuelled by the failure to live up to Labour's great expectations.

The state's attitude to Northern Ireland in the post-war years can best be described as benign neglect. Unionists sat on the Conservative benches, providing a useful supplement to Tory majorities while the nationalists cooperated by declining to play a real role in politics either at Stormont or at Westminster. In order to maximise support from the British Treasury, Stormont governments followed closely the post-war welfare state legislation but supported a comprehensive system of discrimination which denied civil and political rights to the Catholic third of the population. As long as Ulster posed no threat to the stability of British politics, Whitehall and Westminster were content to leave it alone. In 1923 the Speaker ruled that matters coming within the competence of the Stormont Parliament could not be raised at Westminster (Rose, 1982b), so effectively barring discussion of the civil rights issue. Although some Labour backbenchers tried to raise the question, the Attlee government had other priorities and in 1949, in response to the declaration of the Irish Republic in the south, gave the Unionists a veto on constitutional change by enacting that Northern Ireland would not cease to be part of the United Kingdom without the consent of its Parliament and people. It is characteristic of British unwillingness to think about the state that there was no reciprocal requirement that citizenship should be equal in all parts of the kingdom. The exclusion of Northern Ireland from mainstream British politics was confirmed by the Labour Party's refusal to contest seats there. These policies no doubt helped the stability of politics on the mainland, where the two-party competitive system was in its heyday from 1950 to 1970, but at the cost of an eventual explosion of discontent.

France—The Survival of the Notables

In France the tension between the claims of the one and indivisible republic and the reality of political accommodation on the ground continued into the post-war state, assuming new forms. In a concession to right-wing and monarchist elements, the Vichy regime had given some encouragement to regionalism in the form of an archaic provincialism. By conscious contrast, the Fourth Republic was strictly Jacobin in conception. All traces of regionalism were to be swept away and only the approved republican institutions of commune and *département* were to exist between the citizen and Paris. In a democratic gesture, the *départements* were to have their own executives separate from the prefectoral administration, but fears about Communist councils after the break-up of the national coalition meant that this provision of the constitution was never implemented. In practice, regional forms of administration were not entirely eliminated and over the years new ones appeared—but these were never given political recognition.

The expansion of government, especially in the fields of welfare and economics, together with the growth of party politics gave territorial politics new shape. The *notable*, who in the past may have been an individual of independent social and economic standing, was now a professional politician and usually a party politician, drawing power from the state and his ability to manage its resources (Grémion, 1976). Multiple office-holding, the *cumul des mandats*, extended as the *notable* felt the need to exercise leverage at all points of the state apparatus while the parliamentary bias of the regime reduced the independence of the central executive. With the breakdown of the disciplined party system after 1948, this gave territorial representatives, especially the deputy/city mayor combination, great leverage in national politics. This phenomenon was found across the political spectrum, though it was less apparent in the 'anti-system' parties, the Gaullists and the Communists than in the centre and the socialist SFIO. The latter, while enjoying a substantial working-class base in the north, elsewhere consisted of little more than a coterie of *notables*, its rhetoric about class struggle and Jacobin poses no more than a veneer for a policy of manipulation and manoeuvring in the confused politics of the Fourth Republic. At both central and local levels it pursued a policy of coalition-building with whoever might be available, lacking any clear strategic vision.

At the same time the fragmentation of the state bureaucracy itself enhanced the influence of those individuals—politicians and territorial administrators—who were able to manage the relationships, pull together powers and resources and get things done. There is considerable disagreement in the literature on just how fragmented the French bureaucracy is. Tarrow (1977), in a comparative study of France and Italy, emphasises the unity of French bureaucracy based on the Napoleonic state tradition and the social and geographical homogeneity of an elitist, technocratic civil service. On the opposite side of the argument are Dupuy and Thoenig (1985) who insist that 'the administration, in the singular, does not exist.' In common with other writers of the French organisational analysis school, they present a pluralist view of the administration with a constant tendency to fragmentation. Ministries and bureaux are continually at war, each seeking to maximise its own independence and look after the interests of its own staff. So along with the prefectoral administration of the Ministry of the Interior, which at one time was supposed to supervise nearly all territorial administration, there have developed specialised services of other ministries which compete with each other and with the prefect. The status of the civil servant as the impartial administrator free from political pressures, laid down in the post-war coalition by the Jacobin Gaullist Michel Debré and the Communist Maurice Thorez, is seen as bearing little relationship to practical reality. Like Grémion (1976) and many other observers, they describe a relationship between the prefect and the local *notables* based less on regulation than on competition and collusion. Precisely because rigidly uniform administration cannot operate in a diverse set of environments such as exist in France, rules have to be bent. The bending of the rules creates a common interest between the local politicians and the state's territorial administrators; but the fiction of a uniform and unyielding administration has to be maintained so that the *notables* can take credit for the rule-bending. Additional regulations from Paris are attacked as interfering and centralist but in reality these are an asset to local politicians and administrators since the more rules there are and the more detailed they become, the more contradictory and less applicable they become, giving local actors more freedom in interpreting them.

It is impossible to reconcile these radically differing conceptions of the nature of the French state if they are regarded purely as descriptions of reality. They must also be seen as normative judgements as to what the administration should be like. Critics who assail the Jacobin model because it does not correspond with reality may thus be missing the main point. The Jacobin model is not an attempt to describe reality but a *myth* in the fullest sense of the word, that is a tale whose value is largely independent of its truth but which serves as an ideal. The differing interpretations may also tell us as much about the interpreters as about the reality which they are describing. Dyson (1980) points to the distinction in French intellectual tradition between the *esprit géometrique*, which seeks a rational understanding of the world and led to a theory of social progress based on the discovery of laws of social life analagous to those of nature; and the *esprit de finesse*, emphasising intuition as the basis of knowledge and the world as a lived experience through which man creates himself. It is not difficult to see defenders of the uniform Napoleonic state as representatives of the former and organisational sociologists of the latter.

From 1945 the state was officially impelled by the *esprit géometrique* but its efforts to impose clarity and rational purpose on the administration were continually frustrated by the territorial power network. So modernising elements at the centre began to seek ways to circumvent the local power nexus, including the prefects. The advent of the Fifth Republic in 1958 greatly accelerated this process. Civil servants re-emphasised their role as the sole guardians of the public interest or common good, distinct from fragmented political interests (Elder, 1979; Avril, 1969). On the political side, the Gaullists initially lacked local roots and saw the *notables* of the Fourth Republic both as a threat to party dominance at the centre and as an obstacle to modernising policies in the localities. With the creation of a strong executive government and the downgrading of Parliament, opportunities for influence at the centre by local elites were reduced, a factor which, combined with the absence for many years of alternation in power, was to increase support for decentralisation of power among the opposition parties. The development of party organisation, first by the Gaullists and later the new Socialist Party, reduced the importance of personalities in elections and might have been expected to undermine the *notable* system. On the other hand, the return to single-member constituencies had the opposite effect, especially after the Gaullist leaders had acquired parliamentary seats and began to put down local roots. Then a new *notable* network established itself, working within a partisan political system but continuing to bend central decisions to the exigencies of local compromises among politicians and administrators. Some foreign observers (Ashford, 1982) have seen this as an effective means of integrating territorial government, providing a policy style which is more incremental but more stable than that of Britain. By the 1970s, though, most French observers were criticising it for its inefficiency and irresponsibility. Politicians and administrators at the centre began to see that Jacobin centralisation was self-defeating, merely exposing the centre to localist pressures and risking the capture of territorial administration by local interests. Instead, they began to see decentralisation as a mean of freeing the central state from these pressures and restoring its own autonomy. The strains which this caused from the 1960s onwards combined with the effects of state regional policies and party realignment to make for a new crisis of territorial management.

Italy—The New Clientilism

In establishing a new regime, post-Fascist Italy had three major territorial issues to confront. These were separatist and irredentist movements in the islands and northern border territories; the need for a decentralised level of politics in the new, democratic and participative state; and the old problem of the south, the 'uncompleted unification'. The political forces which had to grapple with these issues were themselves in the process of formation and consolidation, pushed in many cases by contradictory pressures. The Christian Democrats were from the beginning divided between a conservative wing supported by elements of the old agrarian elite, and a reformist wing committed to progressive Catholic social doctrines, anti-capitalist in sympathy and tracing its lineage to Sturzo's *Partito Popolare*. Initially, the party was committed to regional autonomy, especially for the south where, with land reform, a class of peasant proprietors might be created to protect Catholic values and provide a bulwark against communism. The details, however, were rather vague—Christian Democrat leader de Gasperi appeared to see regions as corporatist entities to foster interclass solidarity and hamper future any socialist/communist administration in Rome, rather than as agencies for purposive government. So at the Liberation the party, while clear about the need to develop a new political class and break the politics of *trasformismo*, confined itself to generalities about regions (Zagarrio, 1981).

The Communists also wanted to break with the old politics but were torn between a doctrinal Jacobinism and the need to make contact with the masses in the south, who remained unconvinced about the need to submit to a temporary dictatorship of the northern proletariat. Despite their nightmare of a southern Vendée, a peasant reaction threatening the national revolution, their leaders were forced by pressure of events to make exceptions of Sardinia and Sicily where they convinced themselves that the masses genuinely yearned for self-government. The Socialist Party was the most Jacobin of all (Ingrao, 1973), resolutely sticking to the doctrine of the *vento del nord*, the northern wind which would liberate the ignorant masses of the south. According to a contemporary socialist, the capacity for self-government was proportional to the development of a territory, putting Lombardy in the same advanced category at Catalonia, while in the Mezzogiorno autonomy would only reinforce the *blocco agrario* (Zagarrio, 1981).

The *Partito d'Azione*, a group of radical republicans drawn largely from the professional classes, favoured regionalism as part of a general reform of the state, especially after the adherence of Guido Dorso who temporarily abandoned his vision of a purely southern party. Though there was always some doubt about the depth of the new party's commitment to southern autonomy, Dorso saw in its espousal of land reform, free trade, free market policies and administrative decentralisation as well as the purging of Fascist elements the essential prerequisites for the liberation of the south (Caronna, 1970). In 1946 the meridionalist wing of the party organised a congress at Bari, attended by all the parties of the anti-Fascist resistance, at which Dorso and his colleagues pressed the case for a new southern strategy to defeat the old ruling classes and prepare the regeneration of the Mezzogiorno. Despite general agreement on these aims, little was done and Dorso split with the *Partito d'Azione* when it refused to subsidise his meridionalist paper *L'Azione* (Caronna, 1970). Dorso's southern initiative then perished along with the *Partito d'Azione* itself and for similar reasons. The party was never more than a gathering of intellectuals without a real social base anywhere in Italy; similarly, Dorso's strategy for the south depended on the existence of the very dynamic, middle-class leadership which, according to his own analysis, the region lacked.

The Liberal Party consisted largely of the old *notabili* who had dominated politics in the pre-Fascist era. Linked in the south to the landowning classes, their aim was less to pursue a political programme than to attach themselves to whoever was likely to hold power in the new order. With some exceptions, they tended to be anti-autonomist, though prepared to accept the idea for Sicily where they might hope for influence in a regional government.

It was in Sicily that the problem of regional autonomy was first posed after the fall of Mussolini. There had been some autonomist sentiment on the island linked to opposition to Fascism in the 1930s (Ganci, 1978) but, by and large, organised opposition to Fascism had been as weak as organised support for it before the March on Rome. Instead, the various interests in Sicilian society had accommodated themselves to the new regime as they had to its predecessors. As Fascism neared its end, though, two separate and contradictory forces emerged. A reactionary separatist movement tied to landowning interests which feared the installation of a left-wing government in the north was supported by sections of the Mafia. A much weaker, left-wing separatist movement was associated with sections of the young Communists, developing a utopian vision of a free and democratic Sicily (Bonora, 1984; Mack Smith, 1968b). As early as 1941 Mussolini began to worry, issuing a futile decree to remove all native Sicilians from government offices on the island (Ganci, 1978). In July 1943 the Allies landed and all Fascists disappeared overnight. The lack of a significant resistance or partisan movement left a political vacuum into which the separatists, in the shape of the *Movimento per l'Independenza Siciliana* (MIS) under Andrea Finocchiaro Aprile, were able to move (Ganci, 1978; Zagarrio, 1981). Drawing on the old myths of *sicilitudine* and distrust of mainlanders, Aprile was able to forge a mass movement backed by reactionary and landowning elements and hoped to persuade the Allies to back independence. At this time the Allies' plans were in a state of flux, since no one knew how long the conquest of Europe would take and how long they would need their Sicilian base but it is known that they used the Mafia, including some notorious American *mafiosi*, to help establish their presence on the island (Mack Smith, 1968b; Ganci, 1978). Most of the mayors and prefects appointed by the occupying power were members or sympathisers of MIS, many with Mafia connections. Allied tolerance of Sicilian separatism, though, was short-lived. Contact was soon made with the national resistance movement on the mainland and, with the capture of Rome in September 1943, a strategy for Italy as a whole was developed, requiring the integration of the south to contain the ambitions of the Communist Party.

With the end of Allied support, the separatist bubble burst and Aprile himself moved towards federalism and then monarchy as alternative forms of support for the traditional order. Although separatism was now revealed as a tactical ploy, the ferment had powerfully affected the newly emerging political formations who hastened to incorporate concessions in their programmes. A meeting of the anti-Fascist parties in July 1943 declared the abolition of the monarchy and the establishment of a 'Sicilian republic, moving force behind the hoped-for union of Italian republics' (Ganci, 1978). The Communist Party, as well as endorsing this, put out its own statement calling for a federation of Italian republics, while castigating separatism as a reactionary plot. None of this needs to be taken too literally—these were parties seeking to establish themselves in an uncertain environment—but it does indicate that Sicilian autonomism was an issue of which the new regime would have to take account.

On the formation of a national government in 1944,

permission was given for the summoning of a Sicilian constituent assembly to draw up a scheme for self-government, in advance of the approval of the national constitution. Here all parties agreed on the need for autonomy, though for the Socialists this was limited to a grudging acceptance of an Economic Council to prepare a five-year plan. The Communists were a little more enthusiastic, fearing the separatist alternative and wanting to remove an obstruction to the agrarian reform decrees of Communist minister Gullo—which the landowners insisted had to be ratified by a regional body. The Communists also worried about cutting themselves off from the Sicilian peasantry at a time when they were developing a new approach to the land problem (Indovina, 1973; Modica, 1972); soon this was to evolve into a campaign for peasant proprietorship in the south, in defiance of the old Gramscian analysis (Tarrow, 1967). As the separatist tide had now receded and the MIS gained only 10 per cent of the vote, the outcome of the constituent assembly was a special statute of autonomy for Sicily, integrated into the national constitution in 1948.

Sardinia, where autonomist sentiment had been so powerful after the First World War, proved less troublesome this time. A right-wing separatist element with links to Sicilian separatists was few in number, while the old *Partito Sardo d'Azione* had withered under Fascism to a group of professional notables, but none of this was immediately apparent. Separatism did seem a threat for a time and the *Partito Sardo d'Azione* impressed observers with long membership lists based, as it later turned out, on letters written by its professional leaders to their clients (Azzena and Palermo, 1981)—it was virtually to die out by 1948 (Farneti, 1985). So as in Sicily, the major parties felt obliged to concede to autonomist pressures whose real potential was unknown. The Communists again conceded autonomy reluctantly, the Christian Democrats cautiously while the Socialists were at first hostile, only accepting it as a necessity of party competition.

In the frontier area Valle d'Aosta, a movement for annexation with France was headed off by the concession of regional autonomy, while in Alto Adige and Fruili–

Venezia–Guilia, autonomy was conceded through negotiation with the Allied and Austrian governments. Like the islands, these were considered special cases. The degree of autonomy varied according to demands and circumstances and, while the statutes were integrated into the national constitution, they were not seen as setting precedents for other regions. To understand the debate on the 'ordinary regions' and the failure to establish them, it is necessary first to examine the changing party and electoral dynamics in the immediate aftermath of the war.

In the 1946 elections in the south, the Liberals and representatives of the old parties of *trasformismo* suffered severe setbacks. The Christian Democrats, by contrast, made the breakthrough previously denied the *Partito Popolare*, polling 34.5 per cent in the mainland south; 33.6 per cent in Sicily and 41.1 per cent in Sardinia (Farneti, 1985; Galli and Prandi, 1970). The left-wing vote was also quite substantial. The Socialists polled 10.3 per cent, 12.3 per cent and 8.9 per cent in the three southern areas respectively, and the Communists with 11.5 per cent, 7.9 per cent and 12.5 per cent established a base on which they were soon to build with their new policy of land for the peasants (Tarrow, 1967).

Under the post-war coalition of anti-Fascist parties, a land reform programme was launched with some immediate impact in the south and the promise was held out of a serious attack on the country's divisions. The impetus was soon lost, however, as the old *notabili* of the Mezzogiorno and figures from the monarchist movement and the right-wing *Uomo Qualunque* party flocked into the Christian Democratic Party, gaining places on electoral lists in many provinces (Allum, 1972), displacing the reformist elements and pushing it sharply to the right. In 1947, with the advent of the Cold War, the coalition broke up and, with the active support of the United States and the Vatican, the Christian Democrats fought the 1948 general election on a platform of Catholic solidarity and anti-Communism. This pushed their national vote up almost to an absolute majority while the combined Communist and Socialist vote fell back. In the south, however, the Christian Democrat gains were at the expense of old parties and *notabili*, with the left-wing vote holding up. The hegemony of the Christian Democrats at the national level but without an overall majority and the exclusion of the Communists from the governmental system ended the prospects of a system of alternation in office and heralded a return to coalition politics, a new form of *trasformismo*. In the south this was mediated by the *notabili* who had found their new home in the Christian Democratic Party.

It was against this background that the new Italian constitution was formulated and put into effect. In the constituent assembly there was wide agreement on decentralisation as part of the programme to extend Italian democracy and break the habits of the past but little consensus on what this meant in practice. The Christian Democrats with their Sturzian heritage and their fear of a left-wing Jacobin regime in Rome, favoured regions throughout the country as a brake on radical change, the Socialists were essentially Jacobin, while the Communists were not so much against regions as in favour of the centralised state. Communist leader Togliatti had been prepared to make an exception for the 'special status' regions in the islands and north but criticised proposals for an extension of regionalism by the commission on local reform as amounting to a 'federal sub-state' while his colleague Gullo insisted that it was not centralisation which had caused Italy's problems in the past so much as its abuse by the ruling class (Zagarrio, 1981). At the insistence of the left, key powers over industry, commerce, mining, credit controls, public education and health were removed from the proposed 'ordinary status' regions (Good, 1976). What remained was a constitutional provision for regional government but further legislation would be required to set up regions and define their powers.

The events of 1947–8 caused a *volte face* on the part of both left and right. Installed in power in Rome on an anti-Communist platform, neither the Christian Democrats nor their patrons were willing to hand powers down to Communist-controlled regions. So the establishment of regional councils was postponed, initially to 1950 but eventually for another twenty years. For their part, the Communists, excluded from power at the centre, turned their attention to their local bases and demanded the implementation of the regional clauses of the constitution. It would be easy to dismiss this as cynical expediency as to a large extent it was, but this should not blind us to deeper forces at work. Centralist and decentralist traditions coexisted on both left and right where they confronted other ideological positions and the needs of electoral mobilisation. By the late 1940s the Christian Democrats had reinstituted the old system of clientilism and patronage in the south and this required a centralised state. The Communists, on the other hand, were abandoning the Gramscian notion that only the northern proletariat could make revolution and were throwing themselves into peasant campaigns for land reform, with considerable political reward. Regional autonomy, by breaking the power of the *notabili* and their access to state resources in Rome, might hasten the peasant revolution and bring further political benefits to the left.

This counted without the extraordinary modernisation of the Christian Democrat patronage machine, which transformed it in the 1950s from an old-fashioned system based on the individual *notabile* and his clients into a mass party machine (Graziano, 1984). The origins of this change lay, ironically, in the initiative taken by younger, leftist Christian Democrats to restore the party's reformist vocation, reduce its dependence on big business, the church and the *notabili* and create a mass political movement (Chubb, 1982). The reformist theme was taken up by Fanfani who succeeded de Gasperi as party leader in 1954. An Office for the Political and Organisational Development of the Depressed Areas was set up and control of the party in the south wrested from the old notables and put in the hands of a new breed of professional appointees subordinate to the party directorate. Instead of a democratic reform, however, this produced a larger and more powerful system of patronage differing from the old both in kind and in degree. The old loose network of notables was replaced by a party machine controlled from Rome while the mass 'membership', especially in Sicily, was largely a fiction, corresponding to the voting strength of party factions rather than active workers. Resources on an unprecedented scale were made available to the machine through the special development programmes for the Mezzogiorno and employment in the burgeoning bureaucracy of special agencies, the *sottogoverno* (Caciagli and Belloni, 1981). Patronage spread beyond the strict limits of the public sector, since the weakness of civil society in the form of voluntary and commercial organisations allowed the party a dominant position in all realms (Caciagli, 1977). There were party-controlled sporting, youth and social clubs, party-controlled unions and farmers' organisations and the need for subsidies and permits gave the party a dominant role in the business world. There was a veritable colonisation of state and society by the party machine as patronage was extended beyond favours to individual voters, to the purchase of whole groups of the population (Graziano, 1984). As a result Christian Democrat support in the south, which had fallen from the peak levels of 1948, picked up again in 1958. Since then, aided both by patronage and the greater religious attachment of the south, the party's support there has held up considerably better than elsewhere.

It can be argued that when patronage ceases to be a matter of individual favours on a personalised basis and extends to whole groups of the population, it becomes indistinguishable from the normal trading of votes for favourable policies, which characterises mature liberal democracies. What distinguishes the Italian south, however, is the environment within which this exchange takes place and its terms. In the absence of the effective political competition which might be provided by a system of alternating parties in government, the party machine holds a monopoly on the granting of favours. Nor are the organised groups with which it deals independent, as they are in the north. Rather, they are subordinate to the party machine, for which they gather votes in return for favours to their members via the party-controlled state machine (Chubb, 1982). The Christian Democrat colonisation of civil society is certainly challenged by the Communists, with their distinct counter-culture, while both Communists and, until their cooption into the spoils system, the Socialists, have provided political opposition at elections. To break the patronage system, however, a change of national government would be necessary, cutting off the supply of favours to the Christian Democratic machine. This in turn is ruled out by the impossibility—for internal and international reasons—of a Communist-led government. Any lesser challenges are dealt with by cooption according to the time-honoured rules of *trasformismo*. So the problem of the Mezzogiorno again became part of the problem of Italy itself and the one could not be resolved without the other.

Clientilism is often viewed as a transitional phenomenon, a mechanism for mediating between a pre-modern society where individualistic relationships and ascriptive norms apply, and the bureaucratic systems of the modern state (Graziano, 1984). Yet in the Mezzogiorno it has formed a remarkably resilient structure precisely by controlling the pace and form of economic and social modernisation and preventing outcomes which might undermine its own power base. As a territorial management system, it may be accounted a considerable success. Dependence of a peripheral territory on the centre, economically and politically, may itself be a centralising force, discouraging demands for peripheral autonomy. On the other hand, it may over time spawn autonomist demands where the centre–periphery mechanisms encourage the framing of demands on a regional basis and where the supply of benefits from the centre starts to dry up. In the Mezzogiorno the patronage system discourages the aggregation of demands or any form of collective expression outside the party machine. So budding autonomist movements, like other challenges, would be demobilised from the start. On the other hand, the system of mass patronage was to prove extremely expensive and constantly threatened to exhaust the resources available. At the same time the political distribution of favours was highly inefficient and failed to create economic and social structures equal to the demands of the 1960s and 1970s. So Italy was to face a territorial crisis, albeit different in kind from that of the other states and with very different outcomes.

Spain—The Extermination of the Regions

The distintegration of the Spanish state was one of the evils identified by the military insurgents in 1936 and the Francoist victory was followed by a brutal suppression of nearly all traces of regional identity. The Generalitat of Catalonia was abolished and the Basque statute of autonomy declared null and void. The remaining *fueros* were suppressed, except in Navarre and the Basque province of Alava, which had supported the rebellion or, as Franco liked to put it, 'remained loyal'. Non-Castilian languages were banned from schools and for official use throughout the regime and, in the early days, in private conversation as well (Torrealday, 1980). In Catalonia, where the local language had been encouraged under the Mancomunitat and Generalitat, fines for speaking it in public were common into the 1940s though after 1945 there was some relaxation. In the 1960s some publishing in Catalan was permitted (Vallverdú, 1980). In Galicia similar prohibitions had little effect on an underdeveloped rural society with low levels of education and literacy. At the end of the dictatorship the majority of the population, including nearly all country-dwellers, still regularly used Gallego, though for the literate the language of reading and writing was Castilian. In Andalusia the regional culture was reduced to a quaint and harmless folklore to amuse the growing tourist industry of the 1960s. The very names of regions were destroyed in the push for uniformity. Not only did the history books present the *españolista* version of truth but when for the teaching of geography in the 1960s a regional description of Spain was needed, this was based on a list of unrecognisable units provided by the Ministry of Education (Gispert and Prats, 1978).

This determination to destroy regional identities cut the regime off from large sectors of the population where it might otherwise have expected some support or collaboration, for example conservative Catholics in the Basque Country and Catalonia. Support for the regime came from the landowning classes in Andalusia and in due course from elements of Basque and Catalan big business, who were able to profit from the protectionism and subsidies which accompanied the drive for self-sufficiency and industrialisation (Solé Tura, 1985) but this was a narrow political base. The policies of Castilianisation were not without effect and for a time in the 1950s, as the old leaders died off or quarrelled in exile, it appeared that a new generation would forget their regional heritage. Overall, though, the regime's insistence on identifying Spanish national unity with itself only succeeded in delegitimising both the state and the nation in the eyes of large numbers in the traditional regions (Hernández and Mercadé, 1983). All this was to help unite the anti-Franco resistance, especially in Catalonia where movements began to prevent the loss of Catalan identity (Chapter 7) and ensure that on its fall the restoration of regional self-government would be an important element in the return to democracy.

The Resilience of Territory

This brief survey has indicated that post-war policies succeeded not so much in eliminating territorial identities and issues in the four countries as in managing them. In the three democracies this involved elaborate devices for accommodation, while in Spain there was a futile attempt at suppression. The continued existence of territorial issues was to be a factor in the emergence of new territorial movements in the 1970s as the management arrangements broke down. Before then, the salience of regionalism was further to be increased by the activities of the central states themselves, the subject of the next chapter.

6
The Politics of Regional Development

The Growth of Regional Policies

In all four countries the post-war years were marked by unprecedented economic growth and an expansion of both the responsibilities and the size of government, which was to pose a new set of territorial problems. In the three democracies Keynesian economic management at first provided an escape from the problems posed by governments' responsibility for full employment but limited capacity in a market economy to intervene in production at the sectoral or territorial level. It provided a hands-off formula for governing, in which the state would provide the conditions for growth while most production could be left to the private sector and the distribution of public services could be handled within the territorial systems described in the previous chapter.

Some more positive forms of intervention did exist in the post-war years. Under the British Labour government there was a period of 'physical control' but this had largely ended even before the return of the Conservatives in 1951. In France a more sophisticated system form of 'indicative planning' had been pioneered by Jean Monnet, but this too sought to avoid detailed control. The small *Commissariat Général au Plan* limited itself to strategic interventions, taking care not to get entangled in the territorial power networks. In Italy planning on the soviet model had been advocated on the left after the war and some left-wing Christian Democrats favoured social control over industry but the move to the right put paid to this by the end of the 1940s. In Spain until the late 1950s, a protectionist regime combined state subsidies with private enterprise to produce a force-fed industry with little regard for competitiveness but this hardly amounted to planning. On the contrary, the attempt to produce everything domestically evaded the strategic choices which are the essence of planning.

By the early 1960s, however, all four countries were converted to 'indicative planning' on the French model which itself had become more elaborate over the years. Essentially the process involves the identification of national growth potential along with the obstacles to its achievement, and an agreement and commitment between government and both sides of industry on the necessary measures. Implementation is achieved with a light hand through a planning department or semi-independent agency which seeks to pull together the various arms of central government, while consultative councils and committees provide a meeting-place for government and industry to examine the implications of the plan, agree targets and remove obstacles to its realisation. While indicative planning does have a respectable intellectual pedigree, its adoption owed something to governments' eagerness to avoid hard choices. It could be presented as a 'non-zero-sum' game in which there were no losers since cooperation among the social partners and the state could itself increase the size of the product to be distributed. At the same time it combined the market economy with the predictability and social regulation of planning. There was a strong 'technocratic' bias to the early experiments in indicative planning, a belief consistent with the 'non-zero-sum' approach that the national pursuit of growth was not a matter for partisan conflict. This idea was strongly embedded in the early French Plans, seen as the commitment of the nation, though by the Fifth and Sixth Plans they had come to be seen more as statements of the policy of the government of the day (Ullmo, 1975). In Italy national planning, demanded by the Socialists and some progressive Christian Democrats, was formally adopted when the Socialists entered the 'centre-left' coalition in 1961–2, though critics have charged that the rhetoric of planning obscured conflicting policy objectives (Pasquino and Pecchini, 1975). In Britain planning was first adopted by the Conservative government in 1961 and was elaborated by the 1964 Labour government with its Department of Economic Affairs and ill-fated National Plan. In Spain the adoption of a national plan in 1964 followed criticism of previous policies by the World Bank and a decision to integrate the country into the world economy (Cuadrado, 1981).

The post-war state was also expected to redress regional economic imbalances. In the United Kingdom the main problem was industrial obsolescence in the older industrial areas of the periphery, while in the other three countries the priority, at least until the 1970s, was the development of poorer, agricultural regions in the Mezzogiorno, southern France and the south of Spain. Regional policies required the state to make explicit territorial priorities though, like indicative planning, it was presented as a non-zero-sum game, with the political significance of choices downplayed. Underdevelopment or obsolescence in depressed regions was damaging to national efficiency while overdevelopment in boom regions risked inflationary pressures and strain on land markets and infrastructure. Intervention to correct regional imbalances could thus be justified on grounds of allocative efficiency, as the correction of a market distortion. Early policies were 'hands-off' exercises in the form of infrastructure projects and open-ended incentives to private industrialists to locate in development areas. Later, 'growth pole' theories implied a somewhat larger degree of intervention on the ground. Major investments, steered to development areas with appropriate infrastructure provision, would spark off a self-sustaining growth cycle through stimulating complementary industries, allowing the state to withdraw and leave the corrected market to take its course. By the mid-1960s, though, the need for more elaborate interventions began to be recognised, pulling the state into more detailed action on the ground and confronting local power networks.

In Britain regional policies, as an aspect of economic strategy, were strictly centralised, bypassing the elected tier of local government and, to some extent, the Scottish and Welsh Offices. They emerged as an integral part of the modernisation drive of the early 1960s, though owing something to electoral considerations on the periphery after the Scottish Conservatives' setback in 1959. In Scotland a development lobby had existed since before the war in the form of the Scottish Council (Development and Industry), bringing together industrialists and economists under the benevolent eye of the Scottish Office and from the early 1960s this began to press for stronger regional policies. In England industrial development associations were formed in the depressed regions following the run-down of traditional heavy industries from the late 1950s. While both in Scotland and in the English periphery the decline of locally-controlled industry had largely destroyed the local business voice, Scotland was able to compensate for this in some degree through the Scottish Office and its conscious efforts to construct a Scottish lobby; in England the industrial development associations were often led by local councils striving to make themselves heard in Whitehall.

Policy instruments followed the 'carrot-and-stick' approach. Regional Development Grants were available for industrialists investing in development areas, while Industrial Development Certificates restricted expansion elsewhere. At the same time large individual investments in public or state-aided industries such as steel and motor vehicles were steered to development areas. The whole policy assumed a healthy economy capable of generating growth but requiring some light-handed intervention to correct its spatial distortions. With the failure to achieve self-sustaining growth, however, the peripheral economies became increasingly dependent on state assistance which began to look like a permanent addition to the instruments of territorial management, especially in Scotland. For the state itself, the lack, even in Scotland and Wales, of an adequate field administration on the French model and the archaic structure of local government prompted a series of administrative reforms. As the coverage of regional policy extended from small 'blackspots' to more widely-drawn regions, government looked for instruments of planning and intervention, together with reliable collaborators at the regional level. At the local level, frustration with the poor programming of physical and social infrastructure to back up the industrial developments diverted into the regions prompted a search for a more professional, production-minded form of local government to replace the distributive politics of the old urban system. Such is the reluctance in Britain to discuss issues of power, however, that the political implications of all this took a long time to become apparent.

In France, too, regional policy was seen as an aspect of modernisation by technocrats at the centre and, in contrast with Italy, largely bypassed the established network of territorial representation. Their impetus came from two directions. There was pressure from emerging modernising elites in several regions usually vaguely described as *forces vives*. These included industrialists, trade unionists, farmers and academics committed to industrialisation, modernisation and planning and usually without links to the traditional political parties or the local government structure. The first and best known group was the *Comité d'Études et de Liaison de Intérêts Bretons* (CELIB) formed in Brittany in 1950 to press for the adoption of a regional plan. Similar groups followed in other regions. At the same time, a top–down modernising impetus came from civil servants, later supported by leading Gaullist politicians, seeking to tap the resources of the regions in the quest to make France a modern industrial power while relieving congestion in the Paris region. Strategically they aimed to contain the pressures from the regions themselves, while harnessing them to the policy imperative of modernisation (Hayward, 1986). It was a 'productive' strategy in contrast to the 'distributive' strategy pursued in Italy (Tarrow, 1977) where regional initiatives had been captured by the territorial network and resources allocated according to local political pressures.

In 1963 a centralised regional policy agency, DATAR, was established, completely free of the territorial *notables*. It distributed regional development grants to industry and undertook the planning and execution of major regional development 'growth pole' projects. Growth poles, in addition to their economic rationale, had the political advantage of not apparently requiring the cooperation of the local political system in their implementation. At Fos the local politicians were excluded from the project whose boundaries were drawn to avoid Marseille and Communist-dominated areas and a new town was set up under central control (Tarrow, 1978). The result, however, was to alienate local politicians and interest groups from the project, stimulating a coalition of regional defence of elected councillors, traditional territorial administrators, environmentalists and trade unionists. Other similar initiatives were undertaken by special state agencies or interministerial *missions*.

In Languedoc a massive scheme of tourist development on the coast, aimed at diversifying the local economy away from viticulture and bringing in foreign exchange, was entrusted to a *Mission interministérielle de l'aménagement touristique du littoral Languedoc–Roussillon*. Communes and *départements* were reduced to a consultative role within the *sociétés d'économie mixte* (public–private partnerships) attached to the *mission* (Allies and Dervedet, 1983). Not everyone in the region regarded these investments as manna from heaven. Some saw them as an alien intrusion unsettling the balance of the local economic and social system. More specifically there was resentment that the region's spatial development, including the motorway system, was being subordinated in the name of national policy to the needs of tourists concentrated on the coastal strip rather than serving those of the natives. Rigid state controls first controlled land prices, then when the locals refused to sell, led to compulsory purchase, depriving small landowners of their expected profit. Small traders were put at risk by the supermarkets which the development brought in its train (Bazalgues, 1972). There was resentment that the tourists tend to come from Paris and eastern France and are better off than the natives. Finally there was a feeling that tourism is a subservient trade, depriving a region of its self-respect and, indeed, a slightly puritanical suggestion that 'sea, sand and sun' tourism is a rather lazy and decadent activity to be regarded with distaste by healthy country-dwellers. The southern canal developments, intended to encourage agricultural diversification, were similarly organised from on high through the *Compagnie Nationale d'Aménagement de la Région du Bas Rhône Languedoc*. While there was some opposition to the canal (Ardagh, 1982), it was not articulated as clearly as that to the tourist developments; but if agricultural diversification were to succeed, it would have profound social and political effects, for the monoculture of the vine in Languedoc underpinned a whole way of life as well as the political system.

The local *notables* at first welcomed these developments but later became increasingly aware of the social and political costs including environmental damage, displacement of economic activity and population movement. Their inability to influence these was seriously to weaken their political status. At the same time the centre was seeking a more effective coordination of its own interventions on the ground while not surrendering control of the modernisation programme to the *notables* whose distributive preoccupations would prejudice the goal-oriented planning of the state.

In Italy regional development policies had been advocated and sporadically pursued since the 1880s and under the new democratic regime there was general support for completing the 'unfinished unification' of the peninsula. New thinking on the problems of the south came too from a generation of economists more concerned with concrete policies than the moral denunciations of previous generations of meridionalists (Barucci, 1974). In 1947 further support came from the *Associazione per lo sviluppo dell'industria nel Mezzogiorno* (SVIMEZ), though unlike regional development associations which were to spring up in other European peripheries, this was largely dominated by sympathetic outsiders, principally northern industrialists and economists. Despite all the concern there was no consensus on policies for the south. On the left were advocates of industrialisation to unify the country by 'modernising' the south. This was opposed by the employers' organisation, the *Confindustria*, who claimed that it would distort the market and damage national efficiency. Pasquale Saraceno, in a series of writings, advocated rather selective state intervention to correct market failure but even this proved too statist for the dominant political right after 1947. Others, on the left, opposed special development policies for the south as a means of marginalising a problem which should really be seen as central to national economic development (Cagliozzi, 1982).

The establishment of Christian Democratic hegemony in 1948 marked another change in governmental attitudes to the south, as the reformist element was displaced by the influx of the old notables. Land reform was a critical test issue. While a determined start was made after the war, the means of implementing reform were seriously deficient (Cao Pinna, 1979) and by the early 1950s the programme had run out of steam. Compensation money for former landowners was channelled not into productive investment but into property speculation in the cities (Caciagli, 1977). The expansion of state intervention and the advent of the Fanfani system within the Christian Democrat party changed the terms of the southern issue yet again. Development funds were now used not so much to sustain the old ruling classes but to feed the system of patronage and clientilism centred on the party machine. The effect, however, was a continued blocking of the development process since self-sustaining growth in the region would undermine the dependence on which the machine was based.

The most important innovation was the *Cassa per il Mezzogiorno*, established in 1950 with potentially wide powers to promote agricultural and industrial development. It lacked powers over land reform, though, and in the early years confined itself largely to 'pre-industrialisation', the provision of infrastructure to encourage agricultural markets and industrial development. Politically this had the advantage of not upsetting the local economic and social power structure while interventions, ostensibly governed by technical criteria, could be guided by local political pressures (Di Gaspare, 1978). Along with other special agencies set up after the war (Galasso, 1978), it fell into the *sottogoverno*, the network of patronage controlled by the Christian Democratic machine, as did the regional government in Sicily, which soon became a byword for corruption (Mack Smith, 1968b).

In 1957 the second phase of policy commenced, focused on industrial development. Regional investment incentives were increased and industries with state holdings obliged to place 60 per cent of their new investment in the Mezzogiorno until 40 per cent of the total was located there (Graziani, 1979). This did little to break the pattern of political and economic dependence or spark off self-sustaining growth and from the early 1960s a third phase was inaugurated, based on selective investment in growth poles. Growth pole theory was very much in fashion among European economists at the time but in the Italian south it was bent to the needs of the political system. Unable to prevent all industrial development, the local political bosses, in collaboration with the managers of the Cassa, ensured that it was confined to large-scale one-off projects which, instead of becoming centres of growth linked to the local social and economic fabric, remained as 'cathedrals in the desert' (Chubb, 1982). Other incentives were scattered widely according to localist political pressures and failed to have a major impact. In some areas of the south, the Mafia or Neapolitan Camorra forcibly broke up industrial developments rivalling those in which they had a stake and diverted state funds to their own objectives.

Party patronage was equally pervasive in the cities of the south which expanded rapidly in the 1950s and 1960s, not through industrialisation on the northern European model but from the influx of unemployed country-dwellers in a manner reminiscent of Third World experience. Possessing little except their vote, incomers were thrown onto the party machine which disposed of jobs in municipal and private services and access to social benefits and housing. In Naples municipal employment increased 400% between 1953 and 1968 (Allum, 1973), while in Palermo the municipal cleansing agency employed as many as that of Milan where the population was three times as great (Chubb, 1982). Urban planning was subordinated to the needs of property speculators and contractors who in return contributed to party funds and employed party nominees.

The failure to plan or coordinate state intervention in the Mezzogiorno became a recurrent theme of debate in the 1960s (Gaspare, 1985), with calls for stronger planning and programming at the centre and horizontal coordination at the regional level. Yet such purposive, goal-oriented planning would undermine the basis of party power in the south, the discretionary control of the distribution of credits and benefits and the dependence of communities and social groups upon the party machine. The reorganisations tirelessly advocated by juridically-trained professors of public administration completely missed the point. As long as the partisan power structure prevailed in the south, it would be able to absorb and turn to its advantage almost any formal change in the administrative machine.

In Spain the regional development policies of the early Franco regime were pushed through entirely from the centre. Not only was there no regional or local political input but the very term region was avoided. Instead, recourse was had to a model dating back to the beginning of the century and much used in Fascist Italy, the massive public works project, especially gigantic hydraulic engineering schemes (González, 1981). As well as fitting the regime's image of itself through their imposing scale, these could be presented as purely physical operations, devoid of all political implications, albeit only by avoiding any cost-benefit evaluation in their assessment. In 1948 the Plan Badajoz for a poor rural area in the south, had proposed comprehensive renewal but already by the time it was unveiled in 1952 the social aspects had disappeared. Land reform was progressively squeezed out of the programme as it became apparent that the regime could not afford to alienate an import part of its social base, the large landowners. Rigid central control produced further bureaucratic obstacles so that the only elements of the plan largely completed were the hydraulic and highway developments (González, 1981). Badajoz dropped from fifteenth to twenty-seventh among Spanish regions in terms of output. A similar fate befell the next plan, for Jaén and in 1963 the World Bank criticised the emphasis on capital-intensive irrigation works and called for more sensitive policies. The question of course, was whether the political basis of the regime would allow this.

By the mid-1960s rapid industrial growth, especially in Catalonia, the Basque Country and Madrid, had posed further problems of massive internal migration and inadequate social and physical infrastructure in the burgeoning cities. Territorial planning could no longer be avoided and, for similar reasons to the other three countries though in a very different political environment, Spain was pushed to the idea of regional planning and the restructuring of territorial government.

The Rise and Fall of Regional Planning

By the mid-1960s the spatial requirements of national planning, the implementation needs of regional policy, rapid demographic change and the rise of cities, had posed the need for regional planning. This in turn implied institutional reform, the reallocation of tasks, a breakdown of old central–local demarcation lines and changes in the territorial power structure. Control of the new regional level became an object of contention among central, modernising technical and political elites, seeking maximum autonomy for the pursuit of their own strategies; emerging social and economic forces in the regions; and traditional layers of territorial representation. The centre tended to seek regional bodies controlled by itself with the help of collaborative social and economic elites selected in corporatist fashion. Territorial representatives tended to favour indirectly elected bodies under their control, while a third group advocated directly elected regional councils which could develop a distinct regional perspective on development issues. The outcomes of these struggles varied from one country to another, with important effects on the conduct of territorial politics.

In Britain, Italy and France regional planning appealed to government for very similar reasons—to give spatial expression to national planning and later to coopt collaborative elites at regional level committed to a productive strategy as against the distributive orientation of local government. Early British plans were undertaken by central government and the Scottish Office, with its multifunctional basis was first in the field with a plan for central Scotland in 1962. It was later to pioneer sub-regional planning in an effort to focus central and local attention upon key development problems (Keating and Boyle, 1986). In 1963–4 a Regional Development Division was set up in the Board of Trade to produce a similar range of plans for the English regions.

In 1964 the new Labour government put the whole system on a new basis, seeking to institutionalise the regions in a corporatist mode to gain the cooperation of regional decision-makers. Regional Economic Planning Councils comprised nominees from industry, trade unions and local government, together with independent 'experts'. To coordinate its own efforts, the government set up Regional Economic Planning Boards, consisting of civil servants from the main 'economic' departments. Together, the councils and boards were to frame regional plans to give effect to the National Plan in their respective regions. As in the Italian and French cases, the composition and remit of these bodies begged a whole range of questions. Their composition was to a degree representative but government made clear that the policy objectives being served were national. In coping with this role conflict, the councils in the development regions became mere lobbies for central government support while in the 'overdeveloped' regions like the West Midlands they faced an insuperable conflict between the national policy objective of steering development away to development areas and local pressures to retain as much industry as possible against a future recession (Keating and Rhodes, 1982). Without powers, financial resources or the political legitimacy of direct election, they were unable to make their plans effective, and the central government itself seemed confused about their role. Some ministers are reported to have seen them as the basis for a future system of regional government while others saw them as no more than extensions of the centre. Whitehall departments sought to escape regional control and the Ministry of Housing and Local Government had been insistent on the inclusion of the word 'economic' in the title of the boards and councils to emphasise that its own environmental and land-use planning concerns would not be included (Lindley, 1982). In the event, government paid little attention to the councils' suggestions and, with the collapse of the National Plan in 1966-7, regional plans lost their overall framework. Members disillusioned by the experience resigned in large numbers. By the early 1970s regional planning in England had been reduced to the production of 'regional strategies', frameworks for local councils' land-use policies. Not only were these restricted in scope, largely excluding economic planning, but because of local government suspicions of the new regional machinery, new mechanisms had to be devised to produce them, typically a consortium of local councils assisted by central officials with, in a few regions some input from the REPC.

Regional economic planning had not proved a success and the incoming Conservative government of 1979 abolished the planning councils; the civil service boards had in most cases already withered away (Keating, 1985a). The experience had, however, stimulated regional thinking and the issue of regional planning has reappeared regularly on the agenda ever since. In Scotland and to a lesser extent in Wales, the experience served to reinforce territorial identity and give it a practical economic content. The idea of a 'Scottish economy' or a 'Welsh economy', while dismissed by many economists as meaningless, given the integration of the British economy, became a real factor in political debate. In 1973 the Heath Conservative government strengthened the Scottish Office's economic responsibilities and consolidated them in the Scottish Economic Planning Department. The following year Labour added the disbursement of selective industrial assistance to its tasks. The fact that the new department never actually engaged in economic planning did not detract from the importance of presenting the Scottish Office as the centre of economic debate in Scotland. Henceforth, government responsibility for the 'Scottish economy' as a distinct entity within the United Kingdom, was inescapable.

From the late 1960s British governments turned their attention to the local level, where they sought to replace the old urban machines and lethargic county administrations with modernising elites committed to development and growth. This too was presented in depoliticised terms, as official rhetoric calling for stronger local authorities concealed the difference between authorities strong enough on the ground to carry through the policies of the centre (the collaborative model) and authorities strong enough to resist the centre (political devolution). The centre in practice sought the former while resisting the latter. Local government reform was detached from the issue of English regionalism and Scottish and Welsh Home Rule, to the extent of having two separate sets of commissions, on the constitution and on local government in England and in Scotland, each of which was encouraged to interpret its terms of reference as excluding the concerns of the other. In fact the commissions on local government were set up with a serious purpose, to produce an institutional reform, while the commission on the constitution was set up to buy time but, when political circumstances forced government to take the commission on the constitution seriously, local government reform had already been enacted, prejudicing a number of possible options.

In France the first steps in regional planning were taken under the Fourth Republic with the designation in 1956 of *Régions de Programme* (Croisat and Souchon, 1979), essentially concerned with land use. The needs of the National Plan for a spatial articulation, the need to coordinate the special development initiatives and the pressures from the regional expansion committees led to further elaboration in 1960 when *circonscriptions d'action régionale* were designated under coordinating regional prefects. This was a highly centralised regionalism, designed to give the prefect stronger powers of direction but it was soon superseded as the need of the Gaullists and modernising technocrats in Paris prompted further institutionalisation. In 1964 regional prefects with reinforced powers were appointed, to be advised by CODER, corporatist advisory bodies similar to those in Italy and Britain, 25 per cent of whose members were nominated by local government, 50 per cent by business, unions and agriculture and 25 per cent by the prefect. The existing structure of local government was left intact to reassure the *notables* (Grémion, 1976) but the objective was clearly to coopt the *forces vives* into the central modernisation strategy and bypass the old territorial representatives.

Conflict within the new institutions was apparent from an early stage. Bureaucratic interests, including the *grands corps* of civil servants and central ministries like Housing and Public Works, resisted subordination to the regional machinery (Grémion and Worms, 1975; Grémion, 1976) and special initiatives for regional development passed it by (Mény, 1974). As for the *forces vives*, these rapidly became disillusioned with their lack of power and the feeling of being manipulated by the centre to lend a degree of legitimacy to its designs. In Brittany CELIB was taken over by Gaullist interests and the regionalists within it forced to accept the CODER as a substitute for the regional assembly which they wanted

(Hayward, 1969). Its toothlessness provoked the resignation of Breton revivalist Michel Phlipponneau in 1967. In Occitania, Robert Lafont, another prominent regionalist, complained about the lack of genuine regional input (Lafont, 1967). The *notables* were placated by leaving intact the existing system of local government in the communes and *départements*.

The next stage in the institutionalisation of regions came in 1969. De Gaulle had been converted to a rather vague form of regionalism while his party strategists saw an opportunity to deliver a blow at the *notables* in local government where there was still a substantial presence of the socialist SFIO, especially in the south (Mény, 1974) as well as of the old centrist parties. The assault was two-pronged. To deprive the localities of their place in the national legislature, the Senate would be reformed, and at the same time regional councils would be established, rivalling the communes and *départements* on the ground. The regional proposal, modest as it was, aroused only a little opposition but the threat to the Senate was correctly seen as an attack on the old political class and the very basis of the territorial power structure, the access of local interests to the centre. Having staked his presidency on the success of the proposals in a referendum, de Gaulle resigned when they were defeated.

His successor, Georges Pompidou, returned to the issue in 1972 with proposals which, far from using regions to challenge the *notables*, put them in charge. Indirectly elected regional councils were set up, comprising all the senators and deputies in the region together with representatives of local government. So every regional councillor was by definition an accumulator of mandates, with his power base somewhere else. The powers of the regions were tightly circumscribed and lacking their own executive, they were obliged to work through the regional prefects. In effect their activities were limited to supporting the investment programmes undertaken by other agencies in an effort to achieve some regional coherence. Their boundaries followed those of the old *circonscriptions d'action régionale*, carefully drawn so as not to correspond to historic provinces, for fear of stirring old loyalties, but not corresponding either to the needs of contemporary social and economic geography. Nantes was detached from Brittany and Normandy divided into two. Languedoc–Roussillon comprised a large part of historic Languedoc but excluded Toulouse while taking in French Catalonia (Roussillon) and part of Provence. The major interventions on the ground under the industrialisation and modernisation programmes of the centre largely bypassed this machinery altogether, entrusted as before to centralised *missions* and DATAR. As Grémion (1981) put it, Pompidou had given over the management of the consequences of change on the ground to the *notables* in return for a free hand in the industrial modernisation of France.

In the longer run, though, the reforms were to have considerable political significance. The dynamic elements in the regions, collectively described as the *forces vives*, were largely excluded both from the territorial power nexus and from influence over national modernisation policies, unless they could find their way back in through the political parties or local government; this many of them proceeded to do, bringing a new perspective into the parties of the left especially. The old Socialist Party, the SFIO, had been dealt a death blow by the 1969 referendum when, at the instigation of the *notables* who by now comprised a large percentage of its membership, it had advocated a NO vote but without offering any clear alternative (Mény, 1974). Its collapse was to give rise to the new Socialist Party with fresh ideas on regional government. Despite their composition and limited powers, some regional councils developed a life of their own, where there was strong political control and they could produce coherent plans to concentrate their limited resources. In other cases, regions proved little more than federations of *départements*, scattering their credits around in accordance with the time-honoured principles of *saupoudrage*.

So a satisfactory scheme for the region, meeting the needs of central policy, local power and coherent spatial planning, had not been achieved. Regional government had, however, been placed on the political agenda and given some institutional expression. The situation remained unstable, especially given the party realignments taking place in the late 1960s and early 1970s and the advocacy of radical measures of regional decentralisation in certain quarters. This was to inaugurate a new phase in the history of regionalism, in which it moved from a technical into an explicitly political mode.

In Italy regional planning was introduced in the early 1960s, following the centre-left government's adoption of national planning and the recognition by central officials and large industrialists of the inefficiency and wastefulness of the existing regional development measures (Ruffilli, 1970). 1965 saw the establishment of the CRPE, regional planning committees with a corporatist basis similar to the British and French schemes, bringing together representatives of both sides of industry with local councillors and 'experts' nominated by central government. After some argument from those who favoured a purely functional or technical basis, they were given the boundaries of the historic provinces but this served further to confuse their already ambiguous status. Corporatist regionalism faced the same dilemma as in Britain and France. The councils' role was technical and advisory to the Ministry of Economic Planning, their main task being to produce draft regional plans, yet their constitution was representative (albeit corporate rather than elective). The problem, however, was overtaken by their rapid politicisation by the parties and their transitional nature, given the centre-left's commitment in principle to activate the regional clauses in the constitution.

Support for proceeding to elected regions grew during the 1960s. Reformers outside the Christian Democrat ranks and even some within it saw them as a means by which the grip of the *trasformista* political tradition on the state might be broken, the patronage machine challenged, the bureaucracy reformed and a more pluralist and competitive political system established. The Confindustria, representing large industry, reversed its previous opposition (Rotelli, 1973), seeing the reform of administration as more important than the risk of left-wing control at the regional level. Some elements, indeed, saw regions as a way of taking power out of the hands of left-wing local councils seen as hostile to business development (Indovina, 1973), though the Communists now supported regions themselves, albeit with some reservations about the extent of their powers (Modica, 1972) and movements for regional autonomy had been started in the 'red belt' of central Italy (Ingrao, 1973).

Despite the consensus on the desirability of regions, there were fundamental disagreements on just what they should do and the hopes of a new modernising power axis based on them were dashed. As early as 1972 observers were able to equate their limited planning role with the restricted French experiment rather than a move to regional autonomy (Zariski, 1972).

Political manoeuvring at the centre delayed regional elections until 1970 and none of the parties showed itself ready to concede wide autonomous powers (Good, 1976). So powers were transferred piecemeal in two phases and drawn narrowly to correspond to the responsibility for administering existing legislation and programmes rather than for determining policy over broad functional areas (Merloni, 1982) while financial powers were tightly constrained. Once elected, regional councils were rapidly colonised by the existing power structure based on the parties, and, especially in Christian Democrat-controlled regions in the south, became little more than an extra relay in the patronage system. As the incorporation of the Socialist Party in the governing coalition in practice degenerated into old style *trasformismo*, the Socialists were allowed a share of patronage at central local and regional levels. Electoral lists were made in Rome where regional coalitions were also decided and, instead of becoming autonomous centres of power, regions became, at best, channels of access to the centre. All this demonstrated what previous Italian history had shown, that to reform territorial administration, it was necessary to reform the political system itself and in particular to replace the politics of *trasformismo* with those of responsible party government.

After its adoption of economic planning and economic liberalisation in the early 1960s, Spain faced the same need for a regional level of planning and policy integration. It also needed the collaboration of dynamic economic actors on the ground, freed from the town and provincial councils dominated by the Francoist *Movimiento*. Whereas in the three democracies this aroused suspicion and opposition on the part of existing central and territorial elites, in Spain the suggestion was calculated to produce paranoia. As Richardson (1975, p. 197) remarked, the 'incompatibility between the requirements of regional planning and the present political structure is unlikely to find an easy, or early, solution'. So the whole issue of regional planning had to be approached with great circumspection.

Regional collaborative elites were unlikely to be found in most Spanish regions or, if they could, they would serve only to weaken the system. Economists might complain that 'the potential challenge to the bureaucratic elite in the regime from the middle classes in Catalonia has been severely restricted by their chasing the delusion of regional autonomy' (Richardson, 1975, p. 13). The fact was, however, that the dynamic elements of the Catalan middle classes were organising themselves around Catalan themes and organisations such as Jordi Pujol's Banca Catalana, with a view to making their region an economic as well as a cultural reality (Baiges et al., 1985) and that drawing them into collaborative development policies would require concessions on regional autonomy. In Andalusia the promotion of dynamic elements of the middle classes would undermine the regional basis of the regime in the landowning classes—one could make similar arguments elsewhere.

So the early national plans had little spatial content. Lopez Rodó, head of the *Comisaria del Plan* and the technocrats surrounding him were not only inhibited in looking to regions but sought to remove policy as far as possible from the influence of civil governors and local councils dominated by the *Movimiento*. The first plan did certain talk of the 'need to correct the economic inequalities existing among the various regions of the country' (Cuadrado, 1981) but took the matter no further. In the second plan, it was recognised that 'the Spanish provinces, individually considered, are too narrowly drawn to serve as objects of economic planning' (Cuadrado, 1981) but in practice decentralisation of the plan was confined to municipal and provincial councils (Richardson, 1975). By the early 1970s there was more movement towards the regional idea but a 1973 proposal from the new Planning Ministry for regional consultative planning committees with a corresponding administrative team from central departments—on the French and British model—was stillborn. An early proposal in 1971 from economics professor Alfonso García Barbancho for a planning hierarchy of state, region, province and *comarca* had also received short shrift (García, 1979). Ideas were floated for 'regions' based on purely functional/technical criteria, which would not correspond to old loyalties but by this time the regime was nearing its end and the oil crisis disrupted the progress of planning with the position of the region unresolved.

Regions had thus become an object of political struggle in all four countries, contested among central elites, the old territorial representatives and emerging regionalist forces. Attempts to contain regionalism through corporatist devices subordinate to the centre had failed but in the process had sharpened regional consciousness, raising the issue of elected regional government. In France and Italy the old territorial representatives were largely able to take over the regional level themselves but even this had dynamic effects in promoting the regional idea. Everywhere the experience of regional policies and regional planning had destabilised old patterns of territorial representation and government, created new expectations and brought into question the existing functional divisions of government and central control of economic matters.

7
The New Territorial Politics

The Crisis of Territorial Representation

With the economic crisis of the early 1970s and the collapse of the Keynesian consensus, diversionary regional policies ceased to be a non-zero-sum game, becoming a costly add-on to policies for national efficiency, justified on 'social and political' rather than strictly economic grounds. With national efficiency and regional development no longer two aspects of the same growth strategy but competitive with each other, territorial questions became more highly politicised. At the same time European and international integration were both increasing territorial disparities in economic development and reducing the ability of the state to address these. While the European Community did not herald the demise of the 'nation-state', it did serve to accentuate rather than diminish the importance of territory within member states (Keating, 1986a). Free trade had differential effects on regions and sectors, penalising peripheral areas furthest removed from the markets of the Golden Triangle. Community policies in agriculture and industry similarly had a major territorial impact, given the spatial concentration of agricultural sectors and industries subject to control and intervention, notably coal and steel. The ability of national governments and territorial representatives to mitigate these effects was limited by the free movement of goods and capital and Community restrictions on aid. The European Regional Development Fund, a response to this, was used by national treasuries simply as an extra source of revenue and attempts to establish direct links between regional interests and the Community were obstructed.

In the United Kingdom the role of the 'motor' regions as sources of investment to be diverted north and west was undermined by crises within these regions and a wider national deindustrialisation. In Scotland the discovery of offshore oil offered the promise of an alternative route and undermined the position of the old territorial mediators as the only source of help. In France similar processes were at work. Regional development policies had increased dependence so that by 1972 more than half the employees, producing nearly three-quarters of the value-added in Languedoc–Roussillon, worked for firms owned outside the region (Trempé, 1980), many of them state-owned or aided. Viticulture under the patronage of the *notables* had not been modernised to the degree it had elsewhere (Bartoli, 1981, 1984) but after the establishment of the EEC wine regime in 1970, the *notables* were unable to deliver protection from Italian competition and domestic subsidies.

In Italy the corruption and political skewing of regional development programmes resulted in gross inefficiency and a lack of self-sustaining growth. The north–south gap actually widened apart from a brief period in the early 1970s (Giannola, 1982) while dependence of the south on the central state increased. Integration with the advanced economies of northern Europe merely increased the Mezzogiorno's peripherality and emphasised Italy's economic dualism. In Spain signs of obsolescence were appearing in Basque and sections of Catalan industry, while the new policies of integration in the European and world economy pursued from the 1960s heralded a reordering of the economic geography of the country.

The social, economic and environmental costs of the regional and urban development policies of the 1960s also began to appear in the balance; and there occurred a crisis of the local government institutions whose distributive role had formed an important element of the post-war welfare settlement. In southern Italy, and in the cities of Britain and Spain, large profits had been made by property speculation. In all four countries urban development had displaced large numbers of people without necessarily offering them a greatly improved lifestyle. Now in the 1970s, the end of the large-scale redevelopment and the economic crisis reduced the largesse available for distribution by urban political machines while proposals for reform threatened their very bases. The ideology of participation, so much in fashion after 1968, involved further attack on the traditional forms of local government and representation.

In Britain a series of corruption scandals in major cities damaged the reputation of local government while swings against Labour governments in 1967–8, repeated a decade later, swept away many of the old urban politicians. The destruction of the city machines was completed by the end of major redevelopment schemes, drying-up patronage and by the increased professionalisation of local administration. Redevelopment policies in a city like Glasgow had removed large numbers of working-class people to peripheral housing schemes lacking in amenities or jobs but also largely free of the disciplined Labour Party machines which had operated in the older parts of the city (Keating, 1988b). Britain's local government reform of 1973–5 redrew the map of power and cut away much of the political base of the old guard.

In France the 1969 Gaullist assault on the *notables* had largely been repulsed but major development initiatives simply passed them by. Despite a wide consensus that the structure was an anachronism, attempts by successive governments to consolidate and modernise local administration met with limited results. In Italy reform of territorial government between 1969 and 1976 left intact the communes and provinces while introducing a regional level but there was some tendency, as in France, for central administrators to bypass the system of territorial representation, especially on the big issues such as major investment decisions (Dente, 1985). At the same time the advance of the Communist Party in local government brought in a new type of urban politics. Excluded from the *trasformista* coalitions at the centre, Communist representatives could not function as territorial intermediaries. Instead Communist municipalities set new standards of efficient, honest government, which in themselves posed a challenge to the old system. Clientilism in the cities was further undermined by the economic crisis and the slowdown in the construction industry, traditionally a major source of patronage (Caciagli, 1977). In Francoist Spain local government was always weak but its influence was even further reduced by the centralised planning and development policies pursued by Madrid technocrats removed from the *Movimiento*, the sole political organisation which dominated the municipalities and provinces.

The resulting breakdown in the pattern of territorial politics could lead to a variety of outcomes. Just which occurred in each case was conditioned by developments in national politics and by factors peculiar to individual territories. In Britain and France the territorial crisis coincided with breakdown or realignment of national party systems, providing an opening for new political movements. British electoral behaviour became increasingly volatile and detached from class ties, presenting opportunities in Scotland and Wales for territorial parties. In France the demise of the old Socialist Party, the SFIO, after the 1969 referendum was confirmed by the subsequent presidential election campaign in which its candidate scored a derisory 5 per cent. On the right the Gaullist Party itself had problems after losing the presidency in 1974. It was in this period of political flux that territorial political movements began to make some impact. In Italy, by contrast, the party system held largely intact. The Christian Democrats remained the basis of all coalitions in Rome and the nearest the regime came to radical change was the 'historic compromise' experience of 1976–9, in which the Communists became part of the governing coalition, albeit without seats in the Cabinet. Whether this was to provide the basis for a new regime of party alternation or prove the ultimate in *trasformismo* by including the Communists in the spoils system was never clear during the brief life of the experiment. In Spain the mid and late 1970s saw a regime change in which the pattern of territorial politics, along with much else, was open to radical remodelling.

The 1960s and 1970s also saw a cultural revival on the European periphery comparable to that of the late nineteenth century. The origins of this are complex but a common theme is rejection by sections of the educated youth of mass commercial culture and, in particular, the 'cultural imperialism' of the United States. There are strong links to the rediscovery of community as a basis for political organisation against the impersonal centralised government machine, with regional languages and culture seen both as valuable in themselves and as a bulwark against the leviathan state. The tradition of folk-song with its popular roots, lent itself to the protest movement of the new generation and in Brittany, Catalonia, Ireland, Scotland and Wales was revived and politicised.

Participation was very much in vogue in the late 1960s, with calls for more direct forms of democracy both at the workplace and in the state. This was a challenge not merely to the conservative right but also to the social democratic left, since protest movements were aimed as much at the bureaucratic socialism of the welfare state as at the traditional establishment, particularly after the student-led events of 1968. The 'new' socialism was a throwback to the anti-statist and anarchistic tradition of early socialism, especially that of European peripheries, and with its distrust of authority and search for more human levels of social organisation, the 'new left' could make common cause with movements for regional recognition, themselves moving leftwards. As we shall see, however, the resulting amalgam of ideas and policies was often more united in identifying its enemies than in presenting practical visions of the future.

The Return of Territorial Politics

Some territories, as we have seen, had retained or reforged a sense of identity carried by three factors of cultural distinctiveness, economic differentiation and political/institutional identity. In some cases social and economic change, breaking down barriers within territories and producing common economic interests, had strengthened or even created the sense of territorial distinctiveness in a manner reminiscent of late nineteenth-century experience. It was here that territorial political movements grew in the course of the late 1960s and 1970s. The political dimension, as ever, was critical, since the new movements had to accommodate these cultural, economic and political or institutional concerns within coherent ideologies and policies appealing to a sufficiently large constituency. This did not prove easy, at least beyond the early phase of mobilisation.

Postulating a common territorial economic interest involved denying the primacy of interterritorial class interest. Yet in the course of mobilisation, territorial movements have been forced to address class issues—just as class or sectional parties have been forced to accommodate territorial issues. One response to the problem has been to seek an interclass alliance against the centre. Avoiding anything which might divide the territory, this type of response often ends up endorsing the socio-economic *status quo*, an attitude which easily gives way to right-wing populism. The other type of response is to equate class and territory through variants of the 'internal colonialism' argument. While never having been entirely convincing intellectually, this does provide a series of slogans for mobilisation. In the longer run, though, it has suffered from an inability to specify just who within the territory concerned is to be numbered among the exploited and just who are the exploiters.

Reconciling economic with political demands raises further problems. Economic grievances may feed on a sense of neglect or failed expectations but demanding help from the centre is inherently centralist, requiring the maintenance or even strengthening of the centre's redistributive capacity. Demands for territorial autonomy imply a weakening of that capacity. Despite this contradiction, political mobilisation may require both types of appeal and in the short run, a confluence of both types of grievance, of neglect by the centre and of excessive centralisation, may be possible. In the longer run, the political programme of a territorial movement will have to specify just how they propose to restructure territorial power relations in order to achieve autonomy without sacrificing the benefits of access to the centre. Of course, if separatism can be presented as economically attractive, as in the case of Scotland in the 1970s, then a territorial movement can sidestep this whole problem. Even then, however, the realisation that separatism will involve a redistribution of power *within* the territory as well as between it and the former centre, serves to stimulate opposition.

Reconciling cultural demands with political and economic ones raises more difficulties again. In most cases peripheral languages and cultures are the property of a minority and emphasising them may be an obstacle to broad-based territorial mobilisation. Yet de-emphasising culture and language may lose the most-committed partisans. Maintaining political commitment is itself difficult. Public opinion on regional self-government is notoriously fickle but polls rarely reveal it to be in itself a major priority. This is hardly surprising. Regional government is not a substantive policy goal but an instrument by which goals might be achieved. Territorial identity itself, while often strong, is only sporadically politicised and even then it is not necessarily aimed at securing territorial autonomy but may be focused on economic or cultural aims. Even when there is enthusiasm for constitutional change, it is difficult to sustain. So territorial movements need economic and cultural issues to bolster their support over the long term.

The party competitive context is important here. A territorial party whose sole policy was a rejection of the existing constitutional arrangements and a desire to change them would be unable to participate in governing coalitions under existing constitutional arrangements and thereby deliver some rewards to its supporters. It would therefore be vulnerable to competing parties able to satisfy at least some types of territorial demand. Class or ideologically-based parties, for their part, may be able to take on board some territorial demands to erode the support of territorial parties. This type of competition and accommodation is the essence of territorial management and by and large it has been successful in the countries in question.

There are several types of response available to parties at the centre faced with territorial challenges, ranging from 'output' concessions, that is substantive policy changes, leaving the structures of power intact, through changes in central decision-making procedures, to the concession of regional autonomy (Rudolph and Thompson, 1985). One of the most common 'output' techniques is to try and reduce all territorial issues to economic ones which are thus negotiable by redistributing resources. Despite their frequent commitments to equity, state-wide parties have rarely refused on principle to do this, though it is an expensive strategy with the risk of a backlash from less-favoured territories. Another device is to concede forms of social or cultural autonomy, which do not raise constitutional issues. So regional languages may be encouraged in education, administration and broadcasting, not only satisfying the substantive demand for their use but providing jobs and quasi-autonomous institutions for the intellectuals at the forefront of the language movements.

A range of institutional and constitutional concessions is possible. Peripheral interests may be given greater access to central decision-makers. Administrative decentralisation may allow a more sensitive and differentiated central response to peripheral problems, without a loss of power or control by the centre. Institutions of local government might be reformed and strengthened as rivals to the regional level. Finally autonomous regional government might be conceded. So governments, central bureaucratic elites and political parties retain a considerable capacity to manage territorial dissidence through accommodating certain types of demand while resisting others, dividing and demobilising the movements of the periphery. To illustrate these themes, the next two chapters will look at the process of territorial mobilisation in individual territories and the reactions of the central state elites in each case.

The United Kingdom

Scottish Nationalism Revived
In Scotland, Home Rule long commanded majority support (Miller, 1981) but the sentiment lacked a political outlet and few electors felt strongly enough to break the bonds of party loyalty. So the Scottish National Party (SNP) drifted along as a minority group of few enthusiasts and little political vision, its policy on social and economic issues formally based on old Social Credit ideas (Hanham, 1969). By 1958 Labour

felt secure enough officially to drop the traditional Home Rule policy which after the early 1920s had become a dead letter. In the late 1940s the interparty Covenant Movement had aroused some enthusiasm but its bluff was called by the Labour government which, despite some pressure within its own ranks, refused to make any compromise. Spurned by the main parties and unable to mobilise electoral support against them, Scottish nationalism relapsed into a side issue. The twenty-year period from the late 1940s to the late 1960s, however, proved merely to be a lull in the Home Rule movement.

Scottish political behaviour had during this period of quiescence diverged markedly from that of England (Welfhofer, 1986), initially to the benefit of Labour. In 1964 the SNP started to pull itself off the electoral floor and in 1966 polled over 5 per cent of the Scottish vote. Its first real breakthrough, though, came in 1967 with a spectacular by-election win in the Labour stronghold of Hamilton. In local elections in 1968 the nationalists took twelve seats on Glasgow city council, many in the new peripheral housing estates where the Labour machine had not taken root and discontent with redevelopment and displacement was strong. In 1970 the SNP polled 11 per cent of the Scottish vote but their greatest moment, was in 1974 when Edward Heath, preoccupied with the miners' dispute and the world energy crisis, called a snap election which was to have profound effects in the UK periphery. The SNP, fresh from a by-election victory against a dilapidated Labour machine in Glasgow Govan, polled 23 per cent and gained seven seats; in the second election of that year, in October, they raised this to over 30 per cent of the vote and eleven seats. Campaigning on the slogans 'It's Scotland's Oil' and 'Rich Scots or Poor Britons', the nationalists seemed unstoppable. Yet by 1979 their star had declined and in the election of that year they lost all but two of their seats. Reduced to 17 per cent of the vote, they had failed even to use their position in the hung Parliaments of 1974–9 to secure an elected Scottish assembly.

Early commentators were inclined to dismiss the SNP performance as a 'protest vote' against the two-party system, but this fails to explain why rejection should have taken a territorial form in Scotland but not in England or most of Wales. The 'protest-vote' explanation also betrays a curious assumption that the two-party split represents 'normal' voting behaviour. Similar problems arise with the theory that it was all to do with the discovery of oil off the Scottish coast and the appeal of the SNP to self-interest. This must assume a strong existing sense of Scottish identity such that Glaswegians or the inhabitants of Argyll, far removed from the oilfields, could still see the oil as theirs. Miller (1981; Miller *et al.*, 1977) is on firmer ground in showing SNP voters in the 1970s as being detached from traditional party loyalties by distrust, indifference or generation but also as having definite orientations towards specifically Scottish issues, including that of self-government. It appears that oil, along with the general disillusion with the major parties, removed a constraint on people's expressing support for Home Rule at the ballot box. This represents a failure of the territorial management practised in Scotland since the war, based as this was on the encouragement of Scottish identity, its perception in economic as well as historical/cultural terms and its channelling into support for the major parties, especially Labour which promised access to the centre as a substitute for Home Rule. No longer able to deliver, the major parties were outflanked by a party which, with the help of North Sea oil, could promise both Home Rule and wealth. This explanation does not depend on a theory of relative deprivation and, indeed, in the early 1970s Scottish conditions were improving relative to those of England, in contrast to the 1950s when nationalism had been weak. SNP voting can thus be seen as a rational response to rising expectations and the changing geography of wealth in the form of a call for the restructuring of the territorial power system. It may also be an example of the 'revolution of rising expectations', in which discontent occurs not at times of greatest deprivation but when the means for improvement are at hand.

The rational explanation is sometimes contested on the ground that a substantial number of SNP voters did not actually favour the party policy of independence. A Downsian analysis of rational voting (Downs, 1957), however, requires merely that the SNP should be nearer the modal point in the distribution of public opinion along the separatist–unionist spectrum than the two major parties still tied to the centralisation/access model of governance. This was, nevertheless, a weakness in the SNP basis of support, allowing the major parties to recover votes by moving a little nearer the modal point themselves. A related weakness was that devolution was in itself never a major priority for most Scots. SNP support also drew on a more diffuse sense of Scottishness which could, as in the past, be channelled in other directions to material goals, or depoliticised altogether.

This argument depends on the existence of a sense of Scottish identity which was strengthened or politicised in the 1960s and 1970s. In addition to the institutional and economic identity fostered since the war, Brand (1978) points to the critical importance of a range of factors such as the church, Scottish army regiments, football—in which Scotland, to the bewilderment of overseas observers, fields its own national team—and the folk-song revival. The Scottish media too have become somewhat more distinctive in style and even content, especially since the advent of commercial television, while the lessening of sectarian tensions and of Highland–Lowland suspicions has united the country to a greater extent than before. This sense of identity does not, of course, dictate support for a political nationalist party. It could be expressed in other ways and the heyday of the SNP in the 1970s was merely one incident in the history of Scottish nationalism.

The presence of an organised party was critical in bringing nationalism to the top of the agenda in the 1970s but as a vehicle for achieving constitutional change it suffered from several weaknesses. One was a failure to agree on a measure of Home Rule short of complete separation, an unrealistic goal calculated to lose it supporters as soon as the other parties moved towards devolution. The party did reluctantly support the Labour government's devolution legislation but insisted that this was a stepping-stone to independence and when the legislation failed, was convulsed in argument about whether they should again lend their support to a half-way measure. There was even confusion about terminology, with the word 'separatism' avoided in favour of 'independence' and later 'self-government', each term less threatening than its predecessor but obscuring the issue of whether there would be a new nation-state on the model of the old one with the boundaries redrawn, or whether the party was seeking a new political formula for the UK or Europe. An insistence on full sovereignty was accompanied by frequent assurances that they would not place customs posts at the border, while party representatives boasted about how a Scottish currency would float high on the foreign exchanges without seeming to worry about the effect of this on manufacturing industry.

At the same time the SNP failed to establish a clear position on major socio-economic issues within Scotland. Its official position appeared to be that with oil all could become rich Scots and priorities would be unnecessary. This catch-all approach was a source of strength in the early days of the nationalist revival, allowing differing appeals in differing constituencies, but by the end of the 1970s, the party was embroiled in a left–right battle over policy and strategy. On the left the 79 Group insisted that the SNP must break Labour's hold on the working class in the central belt with a socialist platform and a moderation of the separatist line—though it is doubtful how far socialism explains Labour's grip on this constituency. On the other side the traditionalists went for an interclass strategy, emphasising the common interest of all Scots in independence. Another option, largely ignored, was for the SNP to become a party of Scottish interest on the lines of the nineteenth-century Irish Party, promoting Scottish material interests within the UK and recognising that constitutional reform is a matter of sporadic interest to the public. This would have required a commitment to work within the institutions of British government and was unacceptable to the fundamentalists who were already unhappy about dealing with Labour on devolution. The weaknesses in the SNP made it possible for the unionist parties, primarily Labour, to recuperate their position in Scotland, taking over elements of the SNP appeal while suppressing others, though as a result of their own confusion and errors, it looked at the time like a very close-run thing.

The Nationalisms of Wales

Organised nationalism in Wales was quite different from that of Scotland, with prominence given to the cultural and linguistic element. In 1962 the Welsh Language Society was founded, dedicated to militant but non-violent direct action. The Society was dominated by students and young professionals, the basis of the youth political movements elsewhere in Europe in the 1960s (Butt Philip, 1975), but with the proportion of Welsh speakers stabilising around 20 per cent of the population, linguistic nationalism, and especially militant action like sit-ins at courts and broadcasting offices, risked alienating the majority of Welsh people. A Welsh schools movement had started after the war, led by middle-class revivalists with support from ministers of religion concerned about the threat to their traditional Welsh congregations. By the 1960s this was active in the English-speaking areas where the lack of Welsh schools was most keenly felt by language enthusiasts but in South Wales the new generation of self-conscious Welsh speakers remained a small professional elite. Other linguistic initiatives included the formation of a Welsh teachers association in 1940 and a Welsh breakaway from the Women's Institutes in 1967 (Butt Philip, 1975).

A nationalist party, Plaid Cymru, had existed since 1925 but until the late 1950s, more as a cultural and political pressure group than a serious political party (Osmond, 1977). The event which thrust it into prominence and gave it its campaigning edge was the proposal to flood the Tryweryn valley in Mid-Wales to provide water for Liverpool. This apparent plundering of a Welsh resource by an English city both mobilised local opinion and produced a coalition of territorial defence throughout Wales. After the bill to permit the reservoir had been passed by English MPs with the support of none of the Welsh members, Plaid Cymru scored 5.2 per cent in the general election of 1959.

Its breakthrough came in 1966 when shortly after Labour's spectacular general election victory, Gwynfor Evans won a by-election at Carmarthen, shaking the Welsh Labour establishment. At the 1970 General Election, though losing Carmarthen, Plaid Cymru increased its share of the vote to

11.5 per cent. This was to be its high point. By 1974 it had slipped to 10.7 per cent, though picking up two seats in February and recovering Carmarthen in addition in October. There were also some notable advances in local government at the expense of the Labour machine in the southern valleys. Here was a pattern of nationalist advance more complex and varied than that in Scotland, reflecting the complexities of Welsh society which both stimulated and limited the potential for territorial politics.

Labour after the Second World War, had managed to take over the old radical, non-conformist traditions of 'Welsh Wales', the Welsh-speaking areas of the north and centre, which had provided the basis of the old Liberal ascendancy. These were added to the mining and heavy-industrial areas of the south where its 'natural' class supporters were to be found, so that with around 60 per cent of the vote in the years 1945–66, it could claim with some justice to be the national party of Wales. It was in 'Welsh Wales' that Plaid Cymru, taking on the old radical mantle, extended its influence, especially after the Labour government of the late 1960s had so disappointed expectations. In English-speaking Wales, Plaid Cymru made some advances in local government, capitalising on the discomforture of the old Labour machine in the wake of a series of corruption scandals. Like the SNP in Glasgow, they offered a non-Conservative alternative but again like the SNP, they never learnt to operate the local machine so as to build a solid basis of support and their successes were short-lived. In a third part of Wales, populated increasingly by English immigrants, the Conservatives began to advance from the late 1970s, squeezing the Labour vote from another direction (Balsom, 1985).

In these circumstances, it was difficult for Plaid Cymru to speak for Wales as a whole. Nor was it able to find an economic issue which could offer a vision of a more self-reliant Wales and rewards for all. 'Welsh Water' provided an emotive issue but it lacked the significance of 'Scotland's Oil'. Plaid Cymru suffered too from a lack of a strategic policy, though some ideological themes recur strongly in its campaigns. These express a strongly anti-statist vision, seeking not a separate Wales but a looser state system for the British

Isles and Europe as a whole. Within a self-governing Wales, there would be ample local and community self-government and participation (Osmond, 1977). This type of thinking can trace its roots to Welsh traditions of community self-reliance as well as to anarchism and the European new left—but it is essentially utopian and of limited appeal in the industrial world of modern South Wales.

At the same time, though, a new sense of Welsh identity was emerging, focused not on the language or the old nonconformist agenda, but on economic issues and the institutions of Welsh society and government. These included the Welsh Office, founded in 1964 and gradually extending its scope to become the focus for a Welsh political debate, and the economic planning machinery of 1964. A Farmers' Union of Wales was founded in 1955 and in 1974, after a long period of debate, a Wales Trades Union Congress was set up. Within the Labour Party the old Welsh radicalism represented by the half-dozen MPs who supported the Parliament for Wales Campaign in the 1950s, was supplemented in the 1960s by new figures eager to build on the Welsh Office as a practical improvement in the machinery of government. In 1966, before the Carmarthen by-election, proposals for an elected Welsh Council as a top tier of local government were approved by Welsh Labour's annual conference. While even this mild measure was opposed by centralists in the parliamentary party, it did represent a recognition of the Welsh question within the Labour Party itself. Yet another dimension of Welsh nationality was tapped by the Investiture of the Prince of Wales in 1969. The ceremony, intended to demonstrate both the British state's recognition of Welsh identity and its attachment to the Crown, was opposed by Plaid Cymru and most nationalist opinion as an abuse of Welsh identity for the purposes of imperial propaganda and manipulation. Yet the monarchy remained popular in Wales as in Scotland and opposition to the Investiture did the nationalist cause little good except among already devoted partisans.

Plaid Cymru and the language issue thus represented but parts of a growing sense of Welsh identity. The question was whether their vision of nationalism could be merged with the sense of common interest developing in English-speaking Wales to create a new sense of Welshness for the latter half of the twentieth century. Polls in the late 1960s seemed to give some encouragement to this, showing majority support for devolution to an elected Welsh assembly (Butt Philip, 1975) but there was also evidence of the divisive potential of language.

Accommodating the New Nationalisms

Scottish and Welsh nationalism posed an electoral problem for the major British parties, the danger of losing seats to the SNP and Plaid Cymru, and a constitutional one, the danger of the breakup of the British state. As long as territorial demands were confined to Scotland and Wales, however, the problem could be presented as marginal to mainstream British politics, to be resolved by special devices which would leave the essentials of the central state intact.

Labour's first reaction was to reduce the whole matter to an economic grievance to be handled by more public expenditure adjustments and regional development policies. At the same time the linguistic challenge in Wales was accommodated at little cost through measures like the Welsh Language Act of 1967, which in principle conceded the equality of Welsh and English in administration. In due course, Welsh-medium education was expanded, bilingual road signs were introduced and Welsh-language broadcasting was given an allocation of air time considerably more generous than that of Europe's other minority languages. Indeed, it was occasionally suggested that Westminster government was in the best interests of the Welsh language since a Welsh government responsive to the English-speaking majority might have found concessions more difficult. Welsh-language administration, education and broadcasting did, however, bring into being a Welsh-speaking elite and cause friction over access to various types of employment among the two language groups. This was a factor in the growing hostility to Welsh-speaking and by association to nationalism generally among English speakers.

Constitutional concessions were made more reluctantly. In 1969 the Labour government set up a Royal Commission on the Constitution in an attempt to bury the issue in discussion. Surprisingly in view of their history, the Conservatives made more positive moves, albeit with a curiously contrived scheme for an elected assembly to take the committee stages of Scottish bills which would complete the rest of their parliamentary passage at Westminster. In government after 1970, the Conservatives had more pressing concerns and in 1973 their Scottish conference formally rejected the scheme.

Nineteen seventy-four brought the issue back with a vengeance. Within a few months the SNP won the Govan by-election, the Royal Commission issued its long-delayed report and the February 1974 General Election produced a hung Parliament including seven Scottish and two Welsh nationalists with a minority Labour government. The Royal Commission ploy had backfired, for now Labour was under intense pressure to act and could no longer prevaricate, since while the Commission was divided, it had produced a scheme for Scottish and Welsh assemblies. With a second general election inevitable within months, private pollsters told Prime Minister Harold Wilson that he could lose up to thirteen Scottish seats to the SNP. Labour now had three strategic choices. Some left-wingers urged it to suppress the territorial issue and stress purely class or ideological/socialist policies. This advice was too late since Labour's whole strategy since the 1930s had involved accommodating territorial politics and presenting itself as the party most committed to Scotland and Wales. The second possibility was to divert the issue back into the economic channel, rolling out the pork-barrel and stretching the scope of administrative devolution. This was done. The whole of Scotland and Wales were declared development areas, Scottish and Welsh development agencies were promised and the economic powers of the Secretaries of State were extended. On the economic issue, however, Labour was always going to be upstaged by the SNP's oil campaign, and it soon became apparent that the third option, a concession on self-government, might be necessary.

Labour had been rediscovering its old devolution traditions since the late 1960s, slowly in Scotland, more rapidly in Wales, influenced by the growing sense of territorial identity, the new fashion for decentralisation and the as yet unclear implications of EEC entry. Now the British leadership decided that a rapid move was essential whatever their Scottish and Welsh followers thought. The Scottish Labour conference was reconvened to vote in favour of a legislative assembly and pledges were inserted into the October 1974 Election manifesto. Following Labour's narrow victory, legislation was drafted, providing for elected assemblies, the Scottish one with legislative powers, the Welsh one with executive powers only. This cut through the old dilemma of access to the centre versus territorial autonomy by providing for both. Scotland and Wales would get elected assemblies while keeping the Secretaries of State, their offices and the full complement of Scottish and Welsh MPs. Social and environmental policies currently administered through the Scottish and Welsh Offices would move into more strongly autonomous spheres of elected assemblies, leaving economic and industrial policies centralised and continued privileged access for Scotland and Wales through their Secretaries of State. This was less a radical break than a reformulation of the 'dual polity' which had formed the basis for the existing regime. English MPs, and unionists in general, were assured that nothing was being done to abridge parliamentary sovereignty or the political and economic unity of the United Kingdom.

As a strategy for defeating nationalism and preserving the union, the proposals suffered from several weaknesses. Despite the critical importance of economic and financial issues, Labour's revised dual polity could not concede the assemblies any economic or fiscal powers. Instead, a block grant would be negotiated with the Treasury. Anti-devolution Scots were quick to point out that conducting Scotland's expenditure negotiations under the eyes of English MPs, would put at risk its traditional advantages; English MPs made the opposite complaint that an assembly would enhance Scotland's already excessive bargaining power. The role of the Secretaries of State posed further problems, particularly their tutelary role, with the right to propose orders overruling assembly actions. They would also retain those matters, mainly economic in nature, not considered suitable for devolution and continue to lobby for Scotland and Wales in government, a matter of concern to English MPs.

This was a characteristically British solution, a package put together to meet immediate needs with little regard for basic principles or consistency. With devolution conceded only in Scotland and Wales, Scottish MPs would continue to vote on English affairs but neither they nor English MPs would have a vote on Scottish affairs. In itself this might have been no great matter, since England, Scotland, Wales and Northern Ireland had long been governed rather differently and the sovereignty of Parliament was unimpaired. Yet the failure to make a positive case for devolution or to present it as a means for improving the government of Britain as a whole fostered the impression that Labour was pandering to separatist pressures and the argument was advanced, as though it were a demonstrable fact, that devolution would inevitably lead to the breakup of Britain (Dalyell, 1977). In Wales where devolution had gained some support in the Labour Party and in the English-speaking south, the perception that it was really a concession to the nationalist movement of the Welsh heartland cost a massive loss of support.

Anxieties among the government's English supporters were met by some pork-barrel and a consultative paper on English regional government, but to little avail. Regional sentiment in England had certainly developed since the 1960s but it was nowhere as strong as in Scotland, and anti-devolution English MPs, unskilled in the politics of territorial accommodation, were unable to decide whether they merely wanted to stop Scottish and Welsh devolution, obtain a measure of devolution for their own regions or bargain their support in return for material concessions. Meanwhile the Conservative Party, having retreated from its brief flirtation with devolution under Edward Heath, imposed a three-line whip against the legislation.

Devolution was to haunt the Labour government for nearly five years and provide the instrument of its downfall. From the beginning it was subordinated to the imperative of the survival of the government, dependent on the support of nationalist MPs. Sceptical English backbenchers were corralled into line but guerrilla tactics by opponents succeeded in forcing concessions and damaging amendments (Keating and Lindley, 1981). Referendums, seen as a way of sinking the Welsh proposals, were accepted at an early stage, but assuming that they would lose the Scottish referendum, anti-devolution MPs insisted the proposals must have the support of 40 per cent of the eligible voters. Given British abstention rates of around 30 per cent at general elections, 35 per cent at the EEC referendum of 1975 and 60–70 per cent at local elections, this was a formidable obstacle. Yet the government made no attempt to reverse the amendment at a later stage in the legislative process.

In the referendum campaigns a YES vote was urged by the official Labour Party, the nationalists and a few Scottish Conservatives. While Labour was urging a YES vote as the means of keeping the UK united and staving off the dangers of separatism, the SNP was urging a YES vote for precisely the opposite reason. NO was urged by the Conservatives and a substantial block of Labour dissidents, including passionate unionists on the right of the party and some left-wingers who saw territorial issues as a dangerous distraction from the politics of class. The Conservatives opposed devolution while promising, through Lord Home, author of the devolution proposals of the 1960s, and their spokesman Francis Pym, that a rejection of the Scotland Act would lead to a new and better devolution bill from a Conservative administration. Thoroughly confused, voters in Scotland and Wales shifted to the NO side or to abstention to produce a massive NO majority in Wales and a small YES majority (well short of the 40 per cent threshold) in Scotland.

For Wales this was the end of the matter. Substantial support for devolution had been registered only in the Welsh-speaking areas of the north and centre, with overwhelming rejection in the English-speaking south where it had been seen as an attempt to impose the values of the Welsh culture on the principality as a whole. In Scotland the position was more complex. There had been a majority for devolution and the government needed the SNP to survive in Parliament, yet they hesitated, knowing that there was no genuine majority for devolution in Parliament and unconvinced that they could persuade their English supporters to push through the Act. The hesitation was fatal and the government fell.

Winning the subsequent election with a working majority, the Conservatives repealed the Scotland Act and declared devolution a dead issue. The SNP, their support falling, were reduced to two MPs and ceased to play a major role in Scottish politics.

The Doomsday Scenario

The argument presented here is that the elaborate system for territorial management in Scotland and Wales had broken down in the mid-1970s because of the failure of the parties to satisfy the expectations which they had created. Labour's attempt to build a new territorial system incorporating many elements of the old had also failed under the weight of the party's internal confusion and the assaults of its opponents. The 1979 General Election did not, however, mark a return to the *status quo ante* 1974. Labour, by adopting devolution, however reluctantly, had stemmed the nationalist tide. At the same time it had reinforced its own position as a Scottish party of territorial defence. Enthusiasm for constitutional issues is difficult to sustain over a long period, and as attention moved back to economic concerns in the 1980s recession and the credibility of the oil issue wore out, it was Labour and not the SNP which was able to pose as the defender of Scottish material interests. In the 1980s, social and economic changes further served to differentiate Scotland from much of England where the values of individualistic, market-oriented conservatism have had more appeal. As a result, while Conservative support has fallen steadily to 24 per cent of the vote and ten seats in 1987, Labour has advanced, taking fifty of the seventy-two seats. Wales, by contrast, appears to be becoming more like England, with a steady Conservative advance and a retreat of Labour from its hegemonic position of the 1950s and 1960s. Even here, though, a setback occurred in 1987, reducing the government to just eight Welsh seats. These developments ensured that territory would continue to be an important feature of British politics, despite the poor performance of the nationalist parties (who gained three seats each in 1987).

Problems were posed both for the Conservative government and for the Labour opposition, primarily in Scotland but also to some extent in Wales. For the Scottish Conservatives, the essential problem in 1979 was that of political legitimacy in a situation in which they had lost both the referendum and the general election but had to run the distinctive institutional apparatus of the Scottish Office. Under Secretary of State George Younger, territorial management entered a new phase. His strategy was to avoid policy initiatives of his own but to apply the centre's policy to Scotland with the appropriate institutional modifications while acting as a lobby for Scotland in Whitehall, a reversion to the traditional role but with some important new elements. Government now insisted, against some sceptical comment (Keating, 1985), that a formula determining Scotland's expenditure levels over a wide range of functions gave the Secretary of State absolute discretion to shift spending from one programme to another. This made him both the administrative and political manager of Scotland since, prohibited from coming back to the Treasury for more, he had to find money for new demands by cutting back elsewhere. At the same time he had to lobby for Scotland, knowing that the government had little political stake there and that Scottish nationalism was no longer an effective scare tactic. There were some successes. The Scottish Office forged a cross party lobby to save the Ravenscraig steel works, the Scottish Development Agency, Labour's creation of 1975, was spared the Treasury axe and Conservatives supported the fight to keep Scotland's last independent clearing-bank in Scottish hands. Within Scotland, Younger's manner was conciliatory, and while forcing cuts in the expenditure of Labour local councils he did not follow his English colleagues in removing the local power bases of the Labour Party through structural reform.

The basic problem for the Secretary of State as territorial manager, though, is that he is expected to calm Scottish discontents without the power and resources to do so. At the same time Conservative policy, while refusing political devolution, was maintaining Scottish identity and focusing debate around Scottish administrative institutions. By late 1985 Younger was locked into battle with local councils over their spending levels which the Treasury counts against his own totals; with Scottish teachers, traditionally more militant than English but with whom he could not make an independent settlement; and with middle-class ratepayers over a property revaluation. He had been unable to prevent the closure of the Gartcosh steel mill and Ravenscraig was still in danger. The Conservative Party, at 14 per cent, lay fourth in the opinion polls. At this point Younger was replaced by Malcolm Rifkind, an Edinburgh advocate with an altogether more aggressive style, determined not merely to manage the Scottish Office but to rebuild Conservative fortunes in Scotland through bold policy initiatives. The constraints on him, however, were the same and the one major initiative which he was able to get through Cabinet and Treasury, a poll-tax to replace domestic rates, proved an electoral disaster. In June 1987 the Conservatives scored their lowest-ever share of the Scottish vote.

In Wales the stakes were not as high since the referendum defeat had removed the constitutional issue from the agenda, while the Conservative advance seemed to herald a political assimilation with England. The language issue did resurface in the controversy over the fourth television channel and whether it should be the sole and exclusive medium of Welsh broadcasting (Madgwick and Rawkins, 1982). Welsh language campaigners might have been expected to favour the dispersal of Welsh programmes across all four channels, to expose the maximum number of viewers to chance encounters with Welsh. This consideration, however, was overridden by the desire for a strong institutional base for the Welsh language such as could be provided by a television channel—which would also be a source of jobs for the talking professions. Such a solution was also widely acceptable to English speakers, who could thus avoid chance encounters with Welsh. It took a threatened hunger-strike by veteran nationalist Gwynfor Evans to make the Conservative government concede the issue but concede it they did. Another modest concession to Welsh identity was the parliamentary Select Committee on Welsh Affairs which, for all its ineffectiveness, kept alive the idea of a distinct Welsh political arena (Jones and Wilford, 1986).

1987 brought the 'Doomsday scenario' in which the Conservatives were returned with a safe majority in the UK as a whole but were badly defeated in Scotland. They also suffered some setbacks in Wales. This, it was widely expected, would produce a crisis of legitimacy as well as severe practical difficulties in working the system of administrative devolution which requires a government to have, not a majority of Scottish seats but enough presentable MPs to form the Scottish administration. In the event a Scottish Office team was, with some difficulty, assembled though losses in Wales meant that an English Secretary of State had to be drafted in there. More serious in the long run was the question of legitimacy and authority in Scotland and to a lesser extent in Wales. The constitutional position is quite clear. Government as long as it disposes of an overall parliamentary majority, can govern whatever the territorial distribution of its support. Yet the conventions underpinning the system of territorial management do involve government of the periphery through local elites with some basis in local society. For its part, the opposition, where it is dominant in the periphery, accepts rule by the Westminster majority because under the system of alternation, its turn will come. In the 1980s one party is in long-term, if not permanent, control at the centre, while another party enjoys hegemony in the periphery. Under these circumstances the incentives to play by the old rules of the game are sharply reduced.

So far the rules have held because Labour has continued to play the role of loyal opposition, channelling Scottish and Welsh support into its Westminster strategy but there are serious questions as to how long this can last. After 1979 Labour was able to convince itself of the merits of its own policy on Scottish devolution, rather than letting it lapse as it had in the 1920s. Support was particularly marked on the Scottish left, reflecting a changed ideological perspective common to many European socialist parties. The party as a whole, however, had to reconcile Scottish devolution with its support for economic centralisation, and with the need to win back support in the south and midlands of England in order to form a government. There were several attempts to link Scottish devolution to a strategy for decentralising power throughout Britain, notably the proposal by parliamentary spokesman John Prescott (Prescott, 1983) but they were all defeated by the weight of entrenched party, trade union and local government interests (Jones and Keating, 1985). In 1983 and 1987 the party manifesto promised a Scottish assembly but left the reform of territorial government in England and Wales to the vaguest generalities.

After 1979 some devolutionists argued that the Conservatives, having lost the election and the referendum, lacked a democratic mandate in Scotland and that direct action to resist government policy would be justified. In the run-up to the 1987 election, this was the basis for the 'Doomsday scenario'. In practice, the argument was impossible to sustain as long as Labour was attached to the doctrine of parliamentary sovereignty and aspired to govern England with Scottish and Welsh votes. Labour's official position attempted to hold the line, insisting that an assembly would come from a Labour majority government at Westminster. It would be based on a strengthened version of the Scotland Act and be elected on a first-past-the-post electoral system. Scottish interests in Whitehall and Westminster would continue to be looked after by a Secretary of State and the full complement of seventy-two MPs. This position was regarded with considerable scepticism outside Labour's ranks for three reasons. Firstly many people doubted Labour's ability to win the necessary UK majority. Secondly many doubted the ability of a Labour government to put through an assembly bill, given the difficulties encountered from its own backbenchers last time. Thirdly there was an inconsistency in Labour's claims to favour devolution as a democratising measure while insisting on the first-past-the-post electoral system which would ensure a permanent Labour majority on as little as a third of the vote. What this amounted to was that Labour was now committed to Scottish devolution but even more committed to the traditional parliamentary regime and the two-party adversary system of government which underpins it. So it regarded interparty organisations like the Campaign for a Scottish Assembly with suspicion and rejected the Campaign's proposal that a Scottish constitutional settlement could be produced within Scotland by a convention and then negotiated with Westminster, as an assault both on parliamentary sovereignty and on party government. Up to 1987 Labour's strategy in Scotland and to a lesser extent in Wales, was paying electoral dividends, but the party has now built up expectations to a level which, without a return to government, it cannot meet, while even if it did return to office it would find these extremely difficult to reconcile with its other pledges and priorities. A resulting collapse in Labour support would leave a political vacuum in Scotland, which could be filled again by autonomist or separatist forces.

In the 1970s the territorial crisis in Britain concerned the intrusion of minority nationalist parties into the old two-party system. It was a marginal issue to be dealt with by pork-barrel policies and a mild form of devolution. In the 1980s the situation, while less dramatic, may prove more serious. While the assembly policy failed, Scottish political identity was enormously strengthened in the 1970s, and despite the decline of the SNP, remains an important political force expressed through the Labour Party. For its part the Conservative party is governing Scotland with an unprecedentedly low share of popular support. So the territorial issue is coming to correspond with the major fault line in British politics (Jones and Keating, 1987).

Northern Ireland—The Problem with No Solution?
The Northern Ireland problem is extremely complex and there may be some doubt as to whether it fits into the present scheme of analysis, since it exhibits neither separatism nor autonomism but rather a conflict between irredentism, the desire on the part of one group to join with a neighbouring state, and unionism, the desire to remain part of the existing state on the best terms which might be obtained. It does, however, merit inclusion in this section for what it tells about the territorial management policies of the United Kingdom.

London's neglect of Northern Ireland ended abruptly in 1967–8 when a civil rights movement posed a series of demands on behalf of Catholics, not for separation from the UK but for the rights which UK citizenship might be expected to entail. This was a demand to which no British government could be deaf, especially as the early civil rights movement gained considerable sympathy on the mainland. Encouraged by the political openings created by the reformist

O'Neill government at Stormont, the civil rights movement grew rapidly, only to encounter a Protestant backlash. By 1969 this threatened the lives and security of Catholics and the British Army was sent in to protect the Catholic community. The IRA, after the failure of its border campaign of the early 1960s, had faded, with sections of it moving to the left and pursuing political activity with a non-sectarian purpose, but after 1969 it reappeared in the form of the Provisional IRA, posing as the defender of the Catholic community. Soon the IRA was attacking British troops while the latter, untrained for a police role and unclear just who the enemy was, began to behave like an army of occupation. Unwilling to take over direct responsibility, the British government left Stormont in place, so that the army appeared as the defender of the Unionist regime, further alienating Catholic opinion. The introduction of internment without trial in 1971 and the killing of civilians by troops in 'Bloody Sunday' in 1972 produced a greater gulf between Britain and the Catholic minority, allowing the historic animosities to emerge and the historically unusual posture of 1969—British troops defending Catholics—to be forgotten.

Meanwhile the civil rights movement had galvanised the constitutional nationalist movement into action and in 1970 the Social Democratic and Labour Party (SDLP) was formed. Though its ultimate aspiration was for Irish unity, the SDLP was prepared to work within the UK system to improve the lot of the Catholic community, a major break in the long abstentionist tradition. On the other side of the sectarian divide, the Ulster Unionist Party progressively disintegrated under pressure for reform from the British government and resistance from Protestant extremists. The latter, whether in the form of Ian Paisley's Democratic Unionists or the paramilitary Ulster Defence Association, was to make it impossible for Unionist leaders to deliver on any agreements with Britain, leaving the state without reliable collaborators within the Protestant community. In 1972, unable to form an administration acceptable both to the British and to Protestant opinion, Stormont was dissolved and direct rule from Whitehall imposed. On top of the political, constitutional and security crisis of the 1970s was then imposed the economic recession, hitting Northern Ireland's old industries particularly hard and creating large-scale unemployment among urban youth, an ideal recruiting-ground for the paramilitaries on both sides.

Many proposals have been canvassed as a political solution to the Northern Ireland problem. The two limiting cases, integration with Britain and unity with the Republic, illustrate the issues at stake. Full integration is the logical consequence of the oft-stated unionist belief in their essential Britishness. The problem is that strictly speaking, Northern Ireland is not British but part of the United Kingdom and that the Britishness of which the unionists speak is a phantom identity. In 1987, asked about his identity, Ulster Unionist MP Harold McCusker replied: 'The symbols of my national life are Buckingham Palace, Big Ben, Westminster, Windsor Castle' (*Guardian*, 13 February 1987). These, of course, are symbols of an *English* identity which would never occur to a Scot or a Welshman and McCusker's evocation of them merely confirms the absence of a sense of UK nationality. Politically the values of Ulster Protestants seem far removed from those on the mainland with its traditions of tolerance and non-sectarianism, and attempts to introduce the Northern Ireland issue into Scottish politics in the 1987 by running unionist candidates came to naught. There is even a problem as to just what integration would mean in institutional terms. Some integrationists call for Northern Ireland to be administered like Yorkshire, that is, as a part of England; but it is not in fact part of England. Most take the model of Scotland; but there administration is in the hands of a Secretary of State who is a member of the ruling party but sits for a Scottish constituency, while the opposition, even when in the majority locally, accept the position. Neither the Conservative nor the Labour party has local representatives available to do this. Labour refuses to organise there, essentially because of its support for Irish unity but also because of a feeling that its candidates would get no support. Conservative links with the Ulster Unionists were broken in 1972 over Unionist opposition to the suspension of Stormont.

Irish unity is supported in principle by most of the Catholic community and by successive governments of the Republic of Ireland. A large portion of the British Labour Party has long sympathised with the aspiration and in the 1980s it has become official party policy. Some figures on the left of the party have even forged links with Sinn Fein, the political wing of the IRA, and ignoring the essential social conservatism of the Irish republican movement, have wishfully seen it in the light of Third World national liberation movements. In practical terms, however, Irish unity has not been on the agenda because of the entrenched opposition of the Protestants who, few can doubt, would resort to armed resistance against it, and because the Republic does not really want to absorb a million hostile Protestants along with the chronic economic problems of the north. In the early 1980s the electorate of the Republic made clear its lack of concern for an Irish unity which would encompass those of both religions and none by voting down a referendum proposal to allow divorce.

Advocates of both integration and unity illustrate a key aspect of the situation, the ability to assume away the aspirations, indeed the very existence, of the other side. In conversation, republicans will either ignore the Protestants altogether or ask, in a rather bemused way, why they should fear a united Ireland, given the toleration extended to Protestants in the south. For their part, unionists in the past may have supported the Stormont system as a guarantee of Protestant supremacy, the right not to be truly British. With Stormont long gone, though, many express a wonderment at the attitude of Catholics closely paralleling that which supporters of Irish unity express at Protestants. In the mid–1980s the Ulster Political Research Group, an offshoot of the paramilitary Ulster Defence Association, produced proposals for a non-sectarian constitution and power-sharing with guarantees for civil rights, all on condition that the border was accepted as permanent and the Catholics abandoned their aspiration to Irish unity. It is clear that their essential demand was not related to specific public policies which might or might not be adopted under one regime or another for on economic issues working-class Protestant spokesmen have a great deal in common with their Catholic counterparts. On social issues, too, Ulster Protestantism and Catholicism often have more in common with each other than with the secular, permissive values prevalent on the mainland. The essence of the Protestant position is simply the right to be 'British', just like the Scots and the Welsh, and the denial of the equivalent posture on the Catholic side. In view of these entrenched attitudes, it may indeed be correct to say that the problem of Northern Ireland has no solution.

Given the intractability of the problem and the difficulty of reducing it to economic terms—as was done for so long in Scotland and Wales—British parties have sought as far as possible to contain Northern Ireland, to prevent it becoming an issue within British politics. In their efforts to externalise the problem, they have been prepared to introduce a range of expedients which have been ruled out on the mainland and which are accepted, by a bipartisan consensus, as setting no precedents there. One approach tried in 1974, following the Sunningdale agreement and pressed on various other occasions, has been the consociational one of bringing the representatives of both sides together in a power-sharing government to which powers could be devolved, so allowing a gradual withdrawal of direct British involvement. This approach, however, assumes that leaders can bind their followers to power-sharing agreements. In practice, while the SDLP was able to use power-sharing to increase its standing within the Catholic community, each Protestant leader who has tried to share power with Catholics has been overthrown by more intransigent elements. The failure of Sunningdale was followed by a constitutional convention, a device rejected for Scotland and Wales on the ground that it would prejudice the unity of the kingdom and the sovereignty of Parliament. In the event its deliberations were fruitless, since the British government refused to accept its proposals for an effective return to Protestant ascendancy. This was not the end of devolutionary experiments, though, for the 1979 Conservative government, while repealing the Scotland Act which had gained majority support in a referendum, pressed ahead with devolution for Northern Ireland where, in the absence of any popular consultation and against most of the evidence, they insisted that there was a demand for it. The resulting assembly faltered on the same problem as its predecessors, the unwillingness of the Protestants to contemplate real power-sharing and the inability of the SDLP to settle for anything less.

In the absence of an agreed constitutional model, direct rule has continued through a Secretary of State appointed in London and representing a British constituency. This is not quite a 'colonial' regime, since Northern Ireland does send representatives to the House of Commons but it bears some similarity to the nineteenth-century Irish constitution in that the Irish representatives, not being part of either British party, can never form part of the government. By the same token, Northern Ireland electors, having neither Conservative nor Labour candidates, are effectively denied a say in the choice of government. Direct rule involves governing without local collaborators and, if necessary, without consent, though in practice it is widely regarded as the least-unacceptable option. Direct rule has been accompanied by repeated searches for a political solution to the problem but also by a preoccupation with the security situation and the war being conducted by the IRA.

At times this has come near to a belief that the problem is purely a security one and violence simply a criminal matter to be resolved by tough law-and-order policies. The problem here is the complex and subtle relationship of political violence to Catholic opinion. Most Catholics will deplore the tactics of the IRA, are repulsed by individual acts of terrorism against civilians and give their electoral support to the constitutional and democratic SDLP. Yet they do not regard IRA violence as purely a criminal matter and are prepared to concede the IRA a degree of legitimacy stemming from historical memories of the 1920s and their own fear of the old Protestant B-Specials of Stormont days and the Protestant paramilitaries of the present. Above all, they recognise that the IRA, though misguided, are on 'their side'. The IRA are able to play on this complex of beliefs and traditions of resistance to the state by presenting themselves as victims of state policy. Catholic opinion can then swing almost overnight from revulsion at an IRA atrocity to condemnation of the British, the traditional enemy. Failure to understand this has led to some of the worst blunders of British policy, such as internment in 1971 and the reactions to the hunger-strikes of 1981. In the latter, a group of IRA prisoners went on hunger-strike in order to win 'political' status as represented by a right to wear their own clothes and not do prison work. The Thatcher government's refusal to 'give in' to the moral blackmail of the hunger-strikers was seen by conservative circles in Britain as a mark of steadfastness in the fight against terrorism. Elsewhere it was seen as a gift to the IRA of precisely what they wanted—not the concession of their relatively trivial demands, but its refusal so that the hunger-strikers would die and join the pantheon of Catholic martyrs. The resulting deaths served to radicalise a large section of Catholic opinion and give an impression that the British government was more concerned with its reputation for not changing direction than the fate of Northern Ireland. Republican extremism and British conservatism proved, as in the past, to be objective allies in polarising the situation by conjuring up an issue of deep principle, which by more skilful political manoeuvring could have been avoided.

Direct rule has also been accompanied by a return to the 'exceptionalism' so strongly criticised in the 1880s by the Unionist Dicey. Laws applying only in Northern Ireland have gone beyond what might reasonably be expected in a federal state, let alone one whose governments have continually insisted on its unity. In 1976 the Labour Government's Prevention of Terrorism Act even allowed the expulsion of British citizens from the mainland to Northern Ireland, an obvious attempt at containment of the province but an extraordinary measure in a unitary state.

Yet another type of solution canvassed is to tackle the problem of dual identity through some sort of condominium of Northern Ireland by the Republic of Ireland and Britain. The most recent step in this direction is the 1985 Anglo-Irish agreement. Though not providing for joint sovereignty, this involved the Irish government assuming the role of safeguarding Catholic interests, a position largely acceptable to the SDLP but not to the IRA which opposes both states. It is unacceptable, too, to most of the Protestant community who feel that no one speaks for them and resent the interference of a 'foreign state' in Northern Ireland affairs. Indeed the Anglo-Irish agreement, by recognising both the reality of the border and the legitimacy of the Republic's intervention in the North, has offended intransigent elements on both sides of the sectarian divide. It is significant in representing the first occasion on which a British government has faced up to Protestant opposition without yielding and this, together with the collapse of the unionist campaign in Scotland in 1986–7, may force Protestant leaders to face the reality that they are neither Irish nor British and to acquire an identity of their own.

There have been moves in this direction in the past. In the late 1970s the idea of an independent Northern Ireland was floated. In practice, this would be extremely unlikely to kill the aspiration to Irish unity and would very likely result in a Protestant-dominated autocracy. If this were to be avoided, there would need to be firm arrangements for power-sharing and civil rights, with international guarantees which could only be enforceable by Britain and the Irish Republic. This would be more like a condominium than real independence.

If the problem of Northern Ireland really is about identity and an exclusive notion of nationality, then it is amenable neither to economic remedies nor to constitution-making within the parameters so far observed. Any reform satisfying one side will alienate the other. On the other hand, this should not be seen as a problem which was inevitable. Protestants and Catholics live in peace in England and Wales and in Scotland institutions and policies have developed to defuse rather than exacerbate the sectarian issue. Northern Ireland thus remains a failure of British policy, a failure rooted in the short-term response to the crisis of 1920–2 but also in more recent mistakes. Economic recession has further exacerbated the problem and allowed the IRA–Sinn Fein to exploit urban discontent, especially among the young. Any advances in opening up job opportunities for Catholics have been overwhelmed by the loss of jobs stemming from the recession and the economic policies of the early 1980s. The political events of the 1970s too have polarised opinion on sectarian lines, which are likely to leave an imprint for generations. Instead of moving to a solution, territorial management has left the problem in a worse state than it found it.

The Success of Territorial Management
British territorial management in the 1970s and 1980s has 'succeeded' to the degree that no part of the state has broken away and the principle of parliamentary sovereignty has been preserved more or less intact. On the other hand, attempts to achieve constitutional change or a new territorial order have foundered because of their subordination to short-term expediency. Not one important constitutional change has been successfully implemented in the post-war period. Even membership of the European Community, which might be cited as an exception, has been accepted only reluctantly and its supranational implications denied so as to reduce it to the status of an international organisation. Serious constitutional issues in Ireland and Scotland remain unresolved but the major parties are still heavily committed to the traditional parliamentary regime of centralised but alternating governments. Given the tensions within the polity, this is likely to produce a reassertion of territorial interests in the years to come.

France—The New Regionalism

In France, cultural revivals and new economic issues also coincided with party realignment to produce a crisis of territorial representation. A series of territorial movements in Brittany, Occitania and elsewhere enjoyed brief periods of success but were prone to fission and to the absorption of many of their demands by the parties of the left

The Breton Revival
In the immediate post-war years Breton nationalism, discredited by the collaboration of some activists, reached a low point, and with the continued exodus of the rural population and the expansion of modern media the death of the language was widely predicted. By the mid-1960s all this appeared to be in reverse and Breton identity to be growing ever stronger, tied to modernising themes rather than the defence of the old order. Change occurred first in the economic sphere,

followed by cultural and political action. In 1950 modernising elites in business, trade unions, farmers and local government (the famous *forces vives*) came together in the *Comité d'études et de liaison des intérêts bretons* (CELIB) to press the government to adopt and finance a plan for Brittany. Though the Communist-dominated trade union, the CGT, initially opposed the CELIB as 'class collaboration', it too joined in 1961, giving the movement a wide basis of social support which was to prove both a strength and a weakness. The sense of territorial solidarity drew on Breton traditions of social cohesion and was considerably helped by modernisation which reduced divisions between clerical and secular forces. A coalition of territorial defence was forged over a series of issues including the battle to keep open the *Forges d'Hennebont* and the *bataille du rail* to force the railways to withdraw a new tariff which would have disadvantaged Breton traders. A regional plan was obtained, though its financial backing was meagre, and in 1962 CELIB was able to extract from the majority of Brittany's parliamentary candidates a pledge to put the interests of Brittany above those of party (Hayward, 1969). Such a pledge was easy to give, as it had been in 1936, but difficult to enforce against party loyalty and the inducements of office. The election returned a right-wing majority in Brittany and René Pleven, president of CELIB, accepted government office under de Gaulle. In 1964 the regime's centralist regionalism produced a Breton CODER into which the Breton movement was invited to channel its energies.

Despairing of the interparty approach, Michel Phlipponneau, Rennes professor and leading Breton activist, concluded that the only hope for the movement was to throw in its lot with the left-wing opposition and in 1965 supported Gaston Defferre's abortive bid for the presidency. Unable to persuade the movement as a whole to follow him and excluded from the CODER in 1964, Phlipponneau resigned from the CELIB in 1967, complaining of a *trahison des notables*. While the CELIB continued its strategy of non-partisan pressure on the state, the CGT pulled out in 1972 and other sections of the left deserted it for a distinctive left Bretonism which had developed in the wake of the anti-state protests of the events of May 1968. Territorial solidarity was cemented by a series of industrial struggles such as that at the *Joint Français* where wage parity with Parisian workers was demanded, but this was a left-wing solidarity very different from the interclass approach of the CELIB. Other protests in the early 1970s focused on the problems of milk producers, plans for military bases and nuclear power.

A linguistic and literary revival started in the 1960s, encouraged by the church but largely confined, as in Wales, to the young professional middle class and students. Of wider appeal to youth was the electric folk-rock of Alan Stivell who blended Breton musical traditions with the popular music and protest songs of the 1960s and 1970s in a pan-Celtic theme. In some measure the relative weakness of the linguistic revival helped the cause of Breton solidarity since too heavy an emphasis on language could have proved as divisive as in Wales.

The Breton political movement which emerged from all this proved fissiparous and unstable, torn between the interparty, interclass approach and alignment with the left, with sections occasionally veering to the right. In 1956 a *Mouvement pour l'organisation de la Bretagne* (MOB) emerged, calling in its manifesto for decentralisation of the French state, a special statute for Brittany with an elected assembly and economic reforms. Some of its members were elected to municipal councils in the 1950s but in 1963 it split on the issue of Algerian independence to give birth to the socialist and internationalist *Union démocratique breton* (UDB). This adopted the 'internal colonial' analysis, claiming that the Breton proletariat was doubly exploited as workers and as Bretons and calling for a European federation of regions. Forming tactical alliances with other left-wing parties, it succeeded in putting several of its members onto local councils in union-of-the-left lists (Guillorel, 1981). The UDB was not to be entirely successful in marrying socialist and regionalist ideologies and even less so in building a mass base. In 1968 it expelled members sympathetic to the violent *Front de libération de Bretagne* (FLB) and in 1970, after moving to a strict Leninist line, aligned itself with the Communist party. Despite the divisions in the movement, the 1960s had seen a firm association of the Breton cause with the political left, in sharp contrast to the movements of the late nineteenth and early twentieth centuries. Morvan Lebesque (1970) recalls how his left-wing Parisian friends used to tell him that Breton nationalism was reactionary and wonder how he could interest himself both in Vietnam and Brittany. In the wake of 1968, with decentralised socialism back in fashion, this no longer looked so strange.

The MOB, left with the right-wing rump of the Breton movement, transformed itself in 1972 into the interclass *Srollad ar Vro* whose motto was 'neither red nor white but only Breton', but after vacillating between extreme right and extreme left (Phlipponneau, 1981) it disappeared into obscurity. In the late 1960s and early 1970s a fringe of violent groups emerged, attacking the symbols of 'French occupation' but confining their aggression to property rather than persons. While these attacks were few in number, a wave of arrests in 1969 netted some rather respectable citizens who were never brought to trial but released under an amnesty by the new Pompidou government. In 1972, after another wave of arrests, leaders of the law-abiding Breton groups took the attitude of deploring the methods of the accused but understanding their aims but in 1974 the most prominent of the extremist groups, the *Armée révolutionnaire breton*, was banned.

The activities of these fringe groups perhaps distracted attention from the consolidation of the mainstream of the Breton movement within the democratic socialist fold, enabling them to contribute to the contemporary realignment of the left. Political clubs such as the *Bonnets rouges* and *Bretagne et démocratie* and conferences on regionalism and socialism at Saint Brieuc and elsewhere paved the way for the entry of Breton activists into the new *Parti Socialiste* and its adoption in turn of a regionalist platform.

Occitania and the Failure of Regionalism

In Occitania cultural and economic issues gave rise to political movements as unstable as those of Brittany. The cultural revival stems from 1949 when the *Institut d'études occitanes* was founded, while a new generation of writers started to produce Occitan poetry and prose and sought agreement on a written standard for the language. The political implications of this soon became apparent. Supporters of local variants of the language, for example Provençal, the language of Mistral, were suspicious of the movement for linguistic unity as an artificial exercise or even 'Occitan imperialism'. Others saw the language as it had survived as a peasant one, tied to concepts and ways of thinking which were conservative, rural and unfitted for the emerging urban society and called for the creation of a modernised Occitan as an instrument of social progress. The tension between traditionalists and modernists, between left and right, was thus present from the start.

On the economic front, a coalition of territorial defence forged in 1961 against the closure of a mine at Décazeville, generated considerable regional solidarity and Robert Lafont and others founded the *Comité occitan d'études et d'action* as a more politicised movement situated firmly on the left and drawing ideological inspiration from Lafont's concept of internal colonialism. A series of crises followed in the viticultural industry with overproduction and the establishment of the European Community wine regime in 1970. As earlier in the century, the viticultural crisis could be presented as a regional issue, not merely a class or sectional one since large and small growers, the towns of the wine-producing areas and the wine cooperatives were all affected. With the resentment at state-imposed regional policies and the inability of the *notables* to control the situation, a crisis of representation developed, brought to a head in the referendum of 1969 when the locally-dominant SFIO was able to offer no alternative to de Gaulle's proposals and its subsequent presidential campaign, headed by the southern city *notable* Gaston Defferre, collapsed. May 1968 had sparked off a new political and cultural movement, mixing peasants, intellectuals, *gauchistes*, anarchists, Trotskyists and others in an anti-capitalist, anti-state movement. The committees of action of May 1968 soon came together with the left-wing elements of COEA to form *Lutte occitane* which by 1971 had displaced the COEA altogether (Touraine *et al.*, 1981).

The campaign against the extension of the Larzac military

base in the Cévennes mountains which was the main focus of *Lutte occitane*'s activity in 1971–2 showed up the strengths and weaknesses of the movement. Larzac provided it with a clear target which could unite peasantry threatened with displacement, pacifists and ecologists, and the Occitan regionalists. On the other hand, the industrial unions hoped for jobs from the base, and while Larzac committees sprang up in many places few were in the viticultural areas of the coastal plain, the other main area of regionalist fervour. The most successful ones appears to have been in the larger towns of Toulouse, Montpellier and, indeed, Paris, where they could group a wide coalition of the 'alternative left' (Lucha Occitana, 1975). The Communists and the local Socialist Party supported the campaign but looked for a solution in the context of the French state. *Lutte occitane* declined after the Larzac campaign though continuing to give support to the viticultural and language movements. It never had more than about 1,200 members, and while engaging in dialogue with a variety of social and economic forces remained essentially a group of writers and intellectuals. By the late 1970s it had put most of its faith in an alliance with the parties of the French left, albeit with considerable misgivings about the commitment of the signatories of the Common Programme to genuine regionalism (Pais Occitan, 1978; Alcouffe, 1980).

In 1974 the death of President Pompidou opened up the political game and Robert Lafont was put forward as the candidate of the minorities and regions of France. When his nomination was rejected by the constitutional court, a new tack was adopted and the slogan of the abortive campaign, *Volem Viure al Pais* (VVAP) became the name of a new organisation dedicated to decentralisation and socialism. Under Lafont's influence, VVAP initially attempted to forge a new regionalist coalition in alliance with the parties of the French left, following a precedent set as long ago as 1964 when COEA had affiliated to François Mitterrand's *Convention des Institutions Républicaines*. Never far below the surface, though, was a tension between the fundamentalists and those merely pushing for decentralisation within the French state.

Occitan regionalist agitation reached its peak in the mid-

1970s under the impetus of the viticultural protests, the Larzac campaign and the cultural revival. Cooperation with the French left, however, proved a double-edged weapon. While providing a realistic prospect of achieving results, it did tend to demobilise the movement as an independent force. So the breakup of the union of the left in 1977 and the subsequent defeat at the 1978 legislative elections came as a severe blow, producing two contradictory tendencies, to unity and to disintegration. A series of attempts was made to unite the former activists of *Lutte occitane* and *Volem Vuire al Pais*, culminating in a meeting in 1979 to approve a manifesto and constitution for a new body to be called *Movement Socialista Occitan—Volem Viure al Pais*. The meeting failed to bridge the gap and Lafont and other left-wingers left VVAP, aligning themselves again with the French left in the period up to the 1981 presidential elections. VVAP, for its part, moved increasingly in the direction of fundamentalist nationalism, with attacks on the French left as well as the right. The old *Lutte occitane* activists continued to publish their journal for a while but then dropped out of active involvement. VVAP's strategy of political independence yielded meagre results.

Like so many other territorial movements, the Occitan movements had difficulty in integrating the various elements of regional protest and formulating an ideology and programme. There is evidence of a 'revolt against modernity' in the viticultural protest, with its ambivalent attitudes to the state as protector and enemy. There is regional chauvinism seen in the right-wing *Parti Nationaliste Occitan*, in the opposition to Spanish entry into the EEC or the suggestion by VVAP that jobs should be reserved for natives. There is a libertarian socialism suffused with community ideas and dreaming of a Europe of the regions. There is an anti-militarist and pacifist element (Lucha Occitana, 1975). Drawing these elements together, then, we can see a contrast between a tendency to a fundamentalist, inward-looking, conservative and defensive regionalism on the one hand and a left-wing, outward-looking, cosmopolitan vision which places Occitania in the context of a Europe in which nation-states are reduced in importance. The same tensions are evident in the cultural field with, on the one hand, the *Félibrige* tradition, romantic and passeist and, implicitly at least, conservative, and on the other, the movement for a modern, living Occitan culture. Social and demographic changes in the cities, however, have made them infertile ground for the latter since the language has long died out there, and in contrast to Brittany there has been little by way of mass Occitan youth culture or rock music. The movement, even on its progressive wing, has failed to produce a serious economic or social programme to take it beyond the stage of social protest, and in contrast to the early Breton experience there has been little involvement by modernising economic elites. Consequently the state-wide parties were able to recoup the position. The Communists and the CGT trade union sided with the viticultural protest and gave voice to Occitan themes (Barelli *et al.*, 1980) though their concept of regional autonomy was limited (Giard and Scheibling, 1981) and their main appeal an offer of regional protectionism within a protected French market. The Socialists found matters more difficult in view of their modernising ideas and support for European integration but did take on board the decentralist and participative aspects of the movement, as did the CFDT union and were to incorporate a vision of locally planned regional development into their programme. Once the viticultural crisis was transcended, this put them in a strong position to claim the leadership of the new Languedoc.

The End of the Jacobin State?

The Jacobin tradition in French politics was challenged in the 1960s when a number of proposals were floated for a consolidated and elected regional level of government in the interests of democratic decentralisation and efficiency. Pierre Mendès-France proposed ten large regions while at the end of the decade Jean-Jacques Servan-Schreiber made regional reform the centrepiece of the platform of his Radical Party (Gourevitch, 1980). In 1965 Gaston Defferre had made a gesture to regional reform in the programme of his abortive presidential bid.

It was, however, the demise of the old SFIO and the emergence of a new *Parti Socialiste* under François Mitterrand in 1971 which gave regionalism a place in the programme of a major political party and tied it to the democratic left. Along with Mitterrand's CIR group, there joined a variety of left-wing clubs along with various independents. In contrast to the SFIO, dominated by middle-aged civil servants and middle-class professionals (Johnson, 1981), with fully half its membership in 1965 being local councillors (Frears, 1977), the new party received an influx of younger members, many of them secondary and university teachers. Despite the continued 'workerist' posturing inherited from the SFIO, manual workers were to be scarce in the ranks and in practice the party was to pitch its appeal well beyond the industrial working class (Portelli, 1980), taking on board new issues and the concerns of newly emerging groups. Early adherents included regionalists such as Michael Phlipponneau as well as libertarian socialists from the generation of 1968. In 1974 Michael Rocard and his *Parti Socialiste Unifié*, which in 1968 had advanced an 'internal colonialist' analysis of France's problems, came in while the CFDT trade union, though not formally affiliated, infected the new party with its ideas on participation. The pluralist perspective which this gave the *Parti Socialiste* represented a major break with the recent French left, albeit echoing the anarcho-syndicalism of the early movement.

At its 1971 Avignon congress, the PS adopted a regionalist resolution which became part of the programme (Mény, 1974). Refined and strengthened in the course of the 1970s, this received its fullest expression in the 1981 document *La France au Pluriel* (Parti Socialiste, 1981). This recognised the need for centralisation under the Third Republic to protect the revolution and extend democracy, human rights and public services, but condemned the increasing centralisation of the twentieth century, which it blamed on the natural tendencies of capitalism. Regional cultures and languages had been swamped and suppressed in the same way as French was being swamped by the English language and American culture. Centralised regional policies had unbalanced local economies, local businesses had gained little from the tourist developments on the Mediterranean, local cultures had been devalued to tourist spectacles and holiday homes had pushed up land prices. The party espoused the slogan *Volem Vuire al Pais* but this meant that people should have work in industries and not merely in services. In side-swipes at Communists as well as the right, the document saw three possible models of regional development policy:

1. Providing incentives to private industry as in the past. This had been shown not to work.
2. Nationalisation and management of the regions from the centre as in the Soviet Union. This would not work either and would inevitably lead to policies favouring the centre as against the regions.
3. Increasing the power and resources of the regions themselves. This was the solution favoured by the party. Decentralisation underpinned by a strategy of indigenous economic development, the key level for which would be the region, would attack not only state power but also the structure of capitalism itself, given its tight collusion with the central state. So socialism and decentralisation, far from being incompatible, were part of the same struggle.

This is not quite the full internal colonialist argument but it is close enough to strike a chord with many of the Breton and Occitan activists. It also ingeniously allows the socialists to broaden their appeal socially as well as territorially for the villains of the peace are the big Parisian enterprises and the multinationals, with small local business seen as a natural element in the progressive coalition.

Specifically, the socialists proposed the direct election of the regional councils whose boundaries would be redrawn to reflect regional loyalties more accurately. There would be a reform of finance, and regional investment banks, while the national economic plan would be revived and regionalised. Regional languages would be encouraged in schools, and in the programme for the 1981 election, a special statute for Corsica and a *département* for the Basque country were promised. It was a programme of cultural, economic and political measures to satisfy the demands of most regional activists, few of whom were seriously pushing for separatism or even federalism.

There were, however, some problems within the *Parti Socialiste* in coming to terms with the new decentralist perspective. Though opposed in principle only by the remaining Jacobin element largely concentrated in the left-wing CERES group, it meant different things to different people. There were regionalists, themselves divided into modernisers who saw the region in technical terms as a planning unit and sympathisers with Occitan and Breton cultural and autonomist aspirations. These competed for influence with the *notables*, rooted in the *départements*, many of them from the old SFIO, and with both old-style bosses and younger, modernising elements in the big cities, who looked for an extension of municipal power. Unable to reconcile these pressures, the party agreed to leave each level of sub-national government intact but with strengthened powers. This could only work to the disadvantage of the regions which would be unable to increase their influence at the expense of the outmoded *départements* as advocated by modernisers and regionalists.

In government after 1981, the socialists moved rapidly to carry out their pledges, with the first legislation within weeks of the election. Over the course of the next four years, a series of texts was put through, lightening central control and transferring functions and personnel to regional and local councils (Keating and Hainsworth, 1986). In the course of this, regions emerged as an elected tier of government but with their powers and status highly restricted by the way in which the reform was carried out. Entrenched political interests created since the 1972 regional reform frustrated the redrawing of regional boundaries so that Nantes continued to be separated from Brittany and Languedoc–Roussillon persisted as an untidy federation of *départements*. Under pressure from the Spanish government, the proposal for a Basque *département* was abandoned. Fear of the political damage of mid-term reverses together with the influence of socialist *notables* led to the postponement of direct regional elections until literally the last moment of the government's life, the legislative elections of 1986. By this time the greatly strengthened *départements* had occupied much of the political space earlier coveted by the regionalists. Powers devolved to the regions proved to be modest and their financial resources constrained. There was, it is true, a reform of the national plan with the involvement of regional councils, but the plan was not the centrepiece of the government's economic strategy and the negotiation of planning contracts with the regions was centralising in effect, tying the regions into national policy objectives. The nationalisation programme contradicted the thrust of decentralisation as there was no decentralisation of the nationalised industries or the banks.

Some concessions were made to regional cultures, building on the 1951 *Loi Deixonne*, with more provision for the teaching of regional languages in schools and a major report was commissioned on cultural pluralism. Though the Giordan report recommended a *droit à la différence* and even that there should be *réparation historique* for past French treatment of cultural minorities (Loughlin, 1986), relatively little had been achieved before the elections of 1986. The Ministry of Culture remained a stronghold of centralisation, seeing its role as the diffusion of French culture to the provinces rather than the promotion of regional cultures.

Despite these qualifications the 1980s have seen moves towards the accommodation of regional and cultural minorities in France, which would have been inconceivable in the past and this, together with the institutionalisation of regions, can be expected to maintain regional identity and a regional politics for the future. By the mid-1980s, fearful of the right, especially the extreme right National Front which had made inroads into Languedoc, most regional activists maintained a wary support for the *Parti Socialiste* despite considerable disillusion about the extent to which the latter had accommodated their demands.

Spain—The Re-emergence of the Regions

Under the Franco regime from 1939 nearly all visible signs of regional identity in Spain were destroyed, yet regionalism survived in the form of a cultural and linguistic identity in Catalonia, the Basque Country and Galicia, in the calls for regional economic development and in the political dimension.

Regional activists of necessity formed part of the anti-Franco coalition, and as the new party system emerged in the mid-1970s regionalism was one dimension along which it divided.

A survey conducted in 1975–6 (Jiménez Blanco, 1977) indicates a strong popular sense of regional identity but weakly politicised. In a factor analysis of the survey, Jiménez Blanco (1977) classifies regional consciousness along four dimensions. The economic dimension measures the sense of regional economic grievance and the belief that this is caused by structural factors in the economic and political system rather than the character of the people or the land. Most pronounced in their regionalism in this respect were Galicia, Andalusia, Murcia, Madrid and Extremadura. The linguistic dimension refers to support for the promotion of regional languages. Most regionalist in this respect were Catalonia, Galicia and the Basque Country. The administrative and political dimensions are rather similar, both referring to the question of regional autonomy. Most regionalist on these dimensions are the Barcelona part of Catalonia, the Basque Country, Galicia, Asturias and the Canaries.

So the four regions we examined earlier emerge as having some sense of identity, though not equally along all dimensions. Andalusia, notably, showed a strong sense of economic grievance but supporters of centralisation exceeded autonomists by almost two to one, reflecting the tendency of a poor region to look to the centre for help. Surveys have also detected a link between high levels of economic development, urbanisation, education, youth and support for autonomy (López-Aranguren, 1983; Gunter et al., 1986). The existence of various types and degrees of regional sentiment does not in itself mean that these will be an element in political alignments for there was considerable public confusion about the constitutional implications of regionalism (CIS, 1985). The intervening variable is the political parties and the extent to which they exploit, express of ignore this dimension in building their bases of support. So we see a complex pattern of party activity, with Spanish parties seeking to incorporate the regionalist dimension while regionalist parties, often interclass in principle, had to confront divisive social and economic questions within their own territories. In the course of this, regionalism was to become a major issue which the state-wide parties would have to accommodate in the constitutional and political arrangements of a democratic Spain.

Catalonia—Making the country
Though Catalan was still, in the 1970s, spoken by over three-quarters of the population (López-Aranguren, 1983) and used regularly by some 60 per cent (Vallverdú, 1980) the ban on its use in education and most of the media meant that literacy levels were low, with around 40 per cent being able to write Catalan (López-Aranguren, 1983). It was concern about the threat to Catalan as a viable language of scholarship and literature rather than a mere spoken *patois* which prompted the movement for linguistic revival in the 1950s and 1960s once the paranoia of the regime had relaxed a little. *Omnium Cultural* and other groups were formed to promote Catalan culture and some pupils were able to study the language in voluntary classes outside school hours (Strubell, 1984). In the 1960s, work started on the *Gran Enciclopedia Catalana*, Catalan sporting and social clubs were founded and Catalan music revived.

By the late 1960s the cultural revival had linked with the youth culture and the spirit of protest in the universities to produce the *Nova Cançó*, a modern type of folk-song familiar in Brittany, the United Kingdom and North America, expressing current social and political themes. Nineteen sixty-eight, with the student revolts in the western democracies and the Soviet invasion of Czechoslovakia, encouraged the emergence of the new left, more libertarian and decentralist than the previous generation of socialists. In the search for a more humane variety of socialism, the idea of community and region featured strongly. Religion provided another element in the Catalan revival. The abbey of Montserrat, traditional centre of Catalanism, became a centre of opposition to Francoism, and with the liberalisation of the church after the second Vatican Council progressive Catholics began to attack the links between the church and the regime and to address themselves to current social and economic problems. While most of the hierarchy supported the regime until its end, the break between Francoism and a section of Catholicism was made easier in Catalonia by the regime's anti-Catalanism; among the demands of the reformers was the appointment of more native Catalan bishops.

Despite the regime's political prejudices, the economy of Catalonia made great strides forward during the years of expansion (Trias, 1972), retaining first place among Spanish regions but there was resentment about subsidising the rest of Spain and thus sustaining a regime with little base in Catalonia. The large industrialists, it is true, were integrated into the regime, benefiting from the policies of protection and subsidy, but among the professional middle classes there was considerable contempt for the Madrid machine and little inclination to credit it with Catalonia's advance.

Until the 1960s there was no political outlet for Catalanism. The last remnants of armed resistance had been broken in 1947, and in 1954 Josep Tarradellas, elected president of the exiled Generalitat, opted to dispense with the pretence of a government in exile and instead to embody in himself a purely symbolic Catalan legitimacy (Gispert and Prats, 1978). Within Catalonia the revival of organised activity dates from the early 1960s and cannot be separated from the figure of Jordi Pujol. Son of an upper-middle-class Barcelona family, a devout Catholic and conservative, Pujol was obsessed with the idea of creating a modern Catalonia. Certainly his beliefs are suffused with the myths of a historic Catalonia, the great 'nation-state' of the Middle Ages, and with a religious dimension but his political ideas concerned the here and now, the necessity to *fer pais*, that is, to make a modern Catalonia (Pujol, 1976). In the absence of political structures, making the country would involve work in culture and economics, with politics coming later, and to this Pujol was to devote his energies. In 1959, worried about the lack of native control over vital sectors of the economy, he founded the Banca Catalana (Baiges *et al.*, 1985) which was to become the centre of a vast financial and political movement. His reputation established by a gaol sentence for organising the singing of a Catalan song at a concert attended by Francoist notables, Pujol used the resources of the bank as well as his own to help not only Catalan businesses but a range of cultural and political activities (Baiges *et al.*, 1985). Though preference was given to those sharing his own Catholic and conservative views, some help did go to socialists and even striking workers, where they seemed to be helping the Catalan cause.

On the left there was a constant ambiguity about Catalanism. From the late 1940s the Catalan Communists, the PSUC, following the lead of the Spanish Communists, downplayed the issue and presented the workers' struggle as a Spanish-wide one. In 1952 Joan Comorera, leader of the PSUC, was expelled from the Communist Party, despite his impeccable Stalinist credentials, for Catalan nationalist deviation (Oltra *et al.*, 1981). The Socialist PSOE, concerned with its position among the non-Catalan immigrant workers, also downplayed the issue. By the late 1960s, though, the success of the new Catalan movements and the ideological rethinking prompted by the emergence of Third World national liberation movements had caused the left to change their line again. In 1965 PSUC resumed its support for Catalan autonomy while PSOE gave more circumspect support.

As the regime approached its end in the early 1970s, the democratic forces in Catalonia made common cause in demanding autonomy as part of a new political settlement (Solé Tura, 1985). In 1969 a broad front, the *Coordinadora de Forces Politiques*, was formed and in 1971 an *Assemblea de Catalunya* demanded liberty, amnesty and a statute of autonomy. With the legalisation of political parties in 1975, Catalonia divided on nationalist, class and ideological lines. Pujol founded his own party, *Convergència Democratica de Catalunya*, ostensibly propounding a moderate centre-left position but in practice representing the democratic right; the historic *Esquerra Republicana de Catalunya* re-emerged on the centre-left, while the *Partit Socialista de Catalunya* (PSC) was the local affiliate of the Spanish socialist party PSOE and the PSUC maintained the same relationship with the Spanish Communists. All were pushing for autonomy, creating a serious problem for the government of Adolfo Suarez whose own UCD party lacked a solid base in Catalonia.

Basque Conflicts
In the Basque country, cultural repression under Franco together with large-scale immigration from other parts of Spain had combined to reduce the proportion of the population speaking the language to a third by 1981, with perhaps a quarter, concentrated heavily in the rural areas, using it as their regular means of communication (Llera, 1986). It was above all the language of the home, where over 80 per cent of all Basque speakers used it regularly, though only some 17 per cent used it at work (López-Aranguren, 1983). The 1960s, however, saw a cultural revival. A network of voluntary schools, the *ikastolas* grew up and by the 1970s were enrolling some 50,000 pupils (Torrealday, 1980). Other ventures focused on adult literacy and publishing, while a Basque Summer University was organised annually from 1973. Given the attitudes of the regime and the historic experiences of the Basques, such cultural activity was in itself political, bringing new recruits into the democratic resistance and the cause of Basque autonomy.

The impact of economic change was complex, producing some contradictory trends (Roiz, 1984). As in Catalonia, there was a rapid industrial expansion in the 1950s and 1960s, accompanied by an increase of the urban population from 47 per cent in 1960 to 78 per cent in 1980 and large-scale immigration. Given the difficulties in learning the language, this created a greater division among natives and immigrants than in Catalonia, with attitudes towards the newcomers often ranging from indifference to a contempt bordering on racism. By the 1970s, though, there were ominous signs of obsolescence in Basque heavy industry. The global recession struck particularly hard and unemployment levels soared, particularly among youth.

Like its Catalan equivalent, the Basque movement was divided and ineffective after the Civil War, especially following the failure of a series of strikes in the late 1940s and early 1950s. The Basque Nationalist Party (PNV) continued its line of conservative nationalism and opposition to Franco but in 1959 a militant offshoot, ETA, emerged, committed to a modern nationalism adapted to the new age, but still tied to the old interclass assumptions. In 1968 it began an armed guerrilla campaign, sparking off a cycle of attacks and repression which marked the final years of the Franco regime. The 1970 Burgos trials and executions of ETA members gained world attention while the assassination of Prime Minister Carrero Blanco showed that ETA was capable of threatening the Spanish state itself. In 1974 ETA split into two and in 1976 the *politico-militar* wing renounced violence. The remaining elements carried on their campaign and, like the IRA, moved into the cities, drawing in unemployed youth and adapting their ideology to a left-wing 'national liberation' line based on Third World models.

With the legalisation of political parties, Basque politics, like those of Catalonia, divided on nationalist, class and ideological grounds, with an additional division between militant and moderate nationalism, based both upon ends—separatism versus autonomy—and means—violence versus electoral activity. The PNV (Basque Nationalist Party) was to emerge as the strongest force, drawing in the conservative and Catholic Basque vote, while from the late 1970s Herri Batasuna, the political wing of ETA, appealed to the Basque disaffected youth, particularly the urban unemployed (*Cambio* 16, 20 February 1984). On the left the Spanish socialists, PSOE, contended with the PNV as the largest party, drawing heavily on the working-class immigrants but also gaining some support among the Basque working class. In addition the parties of the Spanish centre-right competed with some limited success.

The Politicisation of Andalusia
In Andalusia the regional question largely revolved around economic issues, with no linguistic dimension and only later a briefly forceful but unstable political expression. Andalusia emerged from Francoism as an underdeveloped region, with an agricultural sector larger than that of Spain as a whole, a developing industry highly dependent on outside capital, and a service sector based on tourism providing largely seasonal employment. Unemployment and emigration were constant facts of life, with nearly two million people leaving between 1951 and 1981 (Sevilla Guzmán, 1986). Rapid industrialisation which had reduced the agricultural population from 60 per

cent in 1950 to 20 per cent in 1981, caused further social dislocation, while on the land there was a combination of overlarge *latifundia* and undersized *minifundia* together with an army of landless labourers. Politically the dominant landowning classes had supported the Franco regime which in turn looked after their interests, abandoning the dreams of land reform and colonisation propounded by radical sections of the *Falange*. So the economic problems of the region were widely seen as related to the political structure of the regime.

At the first democratic elections of 1977, the socialist party, PSOE, led, closely followed by the centrist UCD of Prime Minister Suarez. PSOE was strongest in the towns, while among the landless peasants the Communists polled well and the poorest, most marginal sectors were amenable to populist appeals from the extreme right, though eventually gravitating towards PSOE (Porras Nadales, 1984; 1985). The middle classes tended to support the UCD. Towards the end of Francoism, a number of movements pressing an internal colonialist line (Alburquerque, 1977) emerged and in 1973 the *Alianza Socialista de Andalucía* was formed, later transforming itself into the *Partido Socialista de Andalucía* (PSA). While the PSA initially pushed a left-wing regionalism, the need for territorial solidarity, along with the attractions of a populist line in competition with the Communists, pushed it towards an interclass strategy and eventually to the political right. On the centre-right, including sections of the UCD, support for autonomy came from middle-class professionals and intellectuals seeking a break with the old structures of landowner dominance in order to pursue policies of modernisation and industrial development. Many socialists in PSOE were carried along with the new sense of Andalusian identity forged in the 1970s but others stuck to the Jacobin line and worried about the exploitation of Andalusianism by the Communists and the PSA. The problem for PSOE was particularly acute, since Andalusia was one of its main power bases in Spain, an essential pillar if it were to hope for power in Madrid, and was the home of party leader Felipe Gonzalez and other prominent socialists.

These autonomist elements drew on traditions of Andalusian

identity and the sense of regional economic grievance but the project for regional autonomy had to be constructed without a clear historical guide. It was the example of Catalonia and the Basque Country which crystallised Andalusian autonomist sentiment, a feeling that regions already privileged economically were gaining further advantages. In December 1977 a million and a half people took to the streets calling for Andalusian autonomy and the parties in Madrid were forced to respond.

Galicia—The Absence of Politics
Galicia at the end of the Franco regime retained a strong sense of linguistic identity, with some 94 per cent of the population able to speak Gallego and nearly 80 per cent using it in the home, though usage at work, especially in the cities, was much lower (López-Aranguren, 1983). A sense of common economic identity has already been noted, but given the persistence of the apolitical tradition of the region, these did not easily gain political expression. Galicia, indeed, is a case of a lack of 'modernisation' coinciding with a lack of territorial political assertion, a finding consistent with the general argument being presented here. Social and economic change had been more limited than elsewhere in Spain, with nearly half the population still employed in the primary sector in 1970 (Vilariño and Sequeiros, 1986). Local peasant societies still regarded themselves as self-sufficient, and under Franco, the persistence of a form of *caciquismo* satisfied most desires for political expression. In the 1950s there was some revival of cultural activity by Gallego enthusiasts within Spain while the exiles from the Civil War tried unsuccessfully to pursue a political campaign. By the 1960s cultural activities by the Gallegos of the 'interior' had led into politics and a number of left-wing movements emerged, taking up the themes of internal colonialism and national liberation (Maiz, 1986). These attracted little support, while among the middle classes interest in Gallego themes did not extend beyond cultural matters. A Christian Democratic *Partido Popular Gallego* appeared in 1976 but disappeared almost immediately.

The absence of a centre-right option for Gallego nationalism reflected the weakness of the middle class and its absorption in the machinery of the state, where many Gallegos had found employment in administration and the military. In the transition to democracy, the client networks of the Franco regime were to a large degree taken over by the *Alianza Popular* of Manuel Fraga Iribarne, himself a native of Galicia (Gunter *et al.*, 1986). While remaining essentially centralist, the *Alianza Popular* toned down its *españolista* rhetoric within Galicia and accepted the increased use of the regional language. The middle classes and, where they voted at all, the small peasantry, thus gravitated towards it while left-wing voters and industrial workers tended to vote for PSOE. A range of small Gallego parties came and went, mostly situated on the left and none able to develop a secure electoral base. Eventually in 1982 a *Coalición Galega* was formed, on a centrist and moderate nationalist platform. Taking over some of the support of the defunct UCD, this was able to poll 13 per cent at the autonomous elections of 1985, with the left nationalists taking another 10 per cent. This, however, was too late to influence the move towards regional autonomy or the shape of the autonomy statute.

Territorial Management and the Transition
The party system emerging from the old regime was caught between ideological and class imperatives on the one hand and the need to accommodate regionalism on the other. The UCD of Prime Minister Adolfo Suarez was divided and uncertain on the issue of regional autonomy. While most of its leaders accepted the need to do something for Catalonia and the Basque Country, many were unwilling to go further. The socialist PSOE's nominal commitment to a federal republic coexisted with a belief in the essential unity of the Spanish people and a significant Jacobin element. In practice it saw the political necessity for conceding autonomy to Catalonia and the Basque Country, and in due course was to support Andalusian autonomy as well. *Alianza Popular* and the right generally were opposed to autonomy as a threat to the unity of Spain. The extreme right were against any concession to regionalism and this was to be a factor in the coup attempt of 1981. The Communists supported autonomy following their change of line in the 1960s but splits both at

national level and in the regions did not help to clarify their policy line.

The position was complicated by the overlaying of class and ideological issues with territorial ones and the links between parties in Madrid and in the regions. Catalonia and the Basque Country developed their own party systems, with only *Alianza Popular* operating on the same basis throughout Spain (Botella, 1984; Brabo and Ortiz, 1984). The Catalan socialist party, PSC, had merged with PSOE in 1977, enabling the socialists to appeal on Catalanist themes while retaining the support of immigrants (Gunter et al., 1986). PSUC, affiliated to the Spanish Community Party, played a similar role. The UCD had a local affiliate but it was squeezed by Pujol's centre-right CiU party. In the Basque Country the Spanish parties competed under their own names, but the dominant Basque Nationalist Party (PNV) squeezed out the Spanish centre-right.

While in the other countries regional autonomy was handled by a stable central regime, in Spain the autonomy process coincided with the formulation of a new constitution and the alignment of the new party system, and so involved a large element of negotiation between central political forces and the new territorial representatives. At one point central forces appeared to be losing control, though by the early 1980s they had begun to reassert the authority of the central state. The result was a constitution which, like that of the Second Republic, was neither unitary nor federal and whose future evolution is still a matter of uncertainty.

Negotiating Autonomy

The Catalan problem was manageable since separatist feeling was negligible and, unlike Scotland and Wales, there was no organised opposition to autonomy outside the discredited extreme right. On the other hand, there was indifference shading into suspicion of Catalanism among the non-Catalan immigrant population, a factor of which the Madrid parties had to take account. In the case of PSOE, this was experienced as an internal tension between its Catalan and Madrid-based wings. The 1977 general elections brought victory for the left in Catalonia, with the Socialists and Communists between them polling 47 per cent and the old leftist ERC scoring another 4.5 per cent. Pujol's new Catalanist CiU gained 16.8 per cent of the vote, exactly equalling the governing UCD. The result guaranteed that autonomy would become a major issue, and shortly after the election a million and a half people took to the streets in Barcelona to demand it. Recognising his weak position in Catalonia, Prime Minister Suarez sought to outflank the new Catalan representatives by recalling Tarradellas, exiled president of the old Generalitat, to head a new provisional Generalitat (García, 1980; Lores, 1985). To preserve a semblance of equity, the decree also provided for the formation of provisional assemblies by deputies elected in other regions. In 1978 a royal decree removed the proscriptions against the Catalan language and made its teaching compulsory in schools. Despite Suarez's manoeuvring, though, the initiative was taken by the newly elected Catalan deputies who set about framing a new statute of autonomy.

In the Basque Country the problem was more severe, given the campaign of violence by ETA, and in an effort at reconciliation, the opposition parties made a priority of securing an amnesty which was duly brought in in 1977. In the elections of that year, the Basque National Party (PNV) led with 27.9 per cent of the vote, followed by PSOE at 25.4 per cent, with the governing UCD gaining a mere 12.5 per cent. The evidence available also points to a strong polarisation between native Basques, the strongest supporters of the PNV, and immigrant workers, the basis of PSOE's vote. The primacy of the autonomy question was immediately apparent in the UCD's decision to support the PSOE candidate for the presidency of the pre-autonomous assembly (Corcuera, 1986), rather than allying with the PNV to which it was closer on social and economic matters. Negotiations on the form of an autonomy statute started immediately, though the process was to prove more difficult than in Catalonia.

One of the most remarkable features of the Spanish case is the way in which the movement for regional autonomy during the transition became so strongly associated with democratic reform that it spread from the old historic regions to engulf the whole country. Pre-autonomy assemblies were formed in Andalusia and other regions so rapidly as to alarm the government and to some extent the opposition. It was to control this process which threatened eventually to leave the central state as little more than a residual entity, that the new constitution of 1978 incorporated three routes to autonomy (Esteban, 1982). While establishing a formal equality among regions, the object was to confine full autonomy to the three historic regions with a capacity to threaten the stability of the state. In those regions where autonomy had been voted by referendum under the Second Republic, a statute drawn up by the pre-autonomous assembly and agreed by the Parliament in Madrid could be adopted by referendum by a simple majority of those voting in each province of the region. For other regions aspiring to full autonomy, there was a two-stage procedure, clause 151. Autonomy proposals had to be initiated by vote of three-quarters of the town councils and an absolute majority of the electors in each province of the region in a referendum. The statute then had to be negotiated and voted by an absolute majority of all the deputies and senators of the region and agreed with the constitutional committee of the Madrid Parliament. The text then had to be submitted to a further referendum where it required a simple majority of those voting in each province. Finally it had to be approved by an absolute majority of the members of both Houses of Parliament. The 50 per cent threshold for the initiating referendum had been imposed by pressure from centralist forces during the passage of the constitution to prevent any region joining Catalonia, Galicia and the Basque Country (Clavero, 1981). Other regions would have to make do with a lesser degree of autonomy under clause 143 of the constitution. Thus Spain joined the UK, France and Italy in permitting extended autonomy for selected regions but limiting it so that the central state itself could escape federalisation.

The autonomy process for Catalonia went fairly smoothly, with the statute supported by all but the extreme right. Despite a 40 per cent abstention rate, largely accounted for by the immigrant population, 88 per cent of those voting supported the statute (ESE, 1979). The first elections for the new Catalan assembly again saw a 40 per cent abstention rate and a corresponding 6 per cent drop in the immigrant-based socialist vote, allowing the CiU to lead the ballot with 27.7 per cent. Subsequent elections were to show the socialists emerging as the dominant party in national elections in Catalonia, while the CiU led in the regional elections (ESE, 1980).

In the Basque Country the lack of a constitutional consensus caused more serious difficulties. Support for separatism registered around 9–10 per cent in opinion polls and was the ultimate aspiration of most of the Basque National Party (PNV). Though the PNV were prepared in the meantime to settle for more modest measures, they were under pressure from more intransigent elements associated with ETA, which in 1978 came together in the party *Herri Batasuna*, with a left-wing, revolutionary and separatist programme. The PNV's philosophical commitment to the idea of a Basque nation distinct from, and not part of, the Spanish nation, made it impossible for them in principle to accept autonomy as a gift of the Spanish state. They based their case instead on the natural rights of the Basques and the historic *fueros* which owed nothing to Spanish law. It was because of the 1978 constitution's reference to these historic rights and a suggestion, albeit extremely confused, that they stemmed from it (Clavero, 1981), that the PNV recommended abstention in the constitutional referendum. As a result the turnout was just 45.5 per cent and though a large majority of these voted YES, they comprised only 31 per cent of the Basque electorate (Corcuera, 1986). Thereafter the complaint that the Basques had not endorsed the constitution became a rallying cry for the most intransigent Basque nationalists. For their part the socialists of PSOE, though supporting Basque autonomy, regarded the *fueros* as a relic of class privilege within the Basque Country and preferred to base the statute on the general right to autonomy of the various *nacionalidades* and regions of Spain.

Another serious problem was posed by Navarre, claimed by Basque nationalists but which had opted out of the autonomy programme of the Second Republic and supported Franco in the Civil War—in return for which they had been allowed to keep some foral privileges. In 1977 Navarre had returned a majority of UCD deputies who refused to participate in the pre-autonomous assembly, while polls showed a majority of Navarrese against incorporation in the Basque Country (Clavero, 1983). Eventually it was agreed that the matter be decided by referendum, and PSOE, which had initially favoured incorporation, moved to defend the rights of an autonomous Navarre. Basque nationalists, however, continued to claim the province as well as the French Basque Country.

ETA's continuing campaign of violence provided an incentive to the constitutional parties to produce a political solution of the Basque problem and a statute of autonomy was negotiated in 1979. It provided for a Basque assembly and government for the first time in history, apart from the brief experience of the Second Republic, and while the historic *fueros* were not explicitly accepted as the basis of the statute, much of their substance was incorporated in a new *concierto económico*, allowing the Basque government to collect all taxes and hand over a negotiated share to Madrid. At the referendum of 1979, the PNV, which had played a large part in negotiating the statute, joined with PSOE and the UCD in urging a YES vote, with *Herri Batasuna* (whose electoral support was around 10 per cent) urging abstention. The abstention rate was again high at 41 per cent, comprising non-Basque immigrants and die-hard separatists. As very few people voted NO, the statute managed a bare overall majority of 53 per cent of the electorate as well as a majority in each of the three provinces, a critical step in protecting its legitimacy against the sort of attacks directed against the Spanish constitution. Elections to the Basque parliament have shown some similarities to those in Catalonia, with the nationalists winning the largest share of the vote and PSOE suffering badly from the abstention of its immigrant supporters, while in national elections PSOE recovers.

In contrast to Catalonia, however, there remained an intransigent nationalist group around ETA and *Herri Batasuna*, endorsing a continued campaign of violence and able to count on some 10–15 per cent of the vote. This posed a security problem for the Spanish state while destabilising

Basque nationalist politics to the point at which the PNV itself split into warring factions. By the mid-1980s the situation was as complex and seemingly hopeless as that of Northern Ireland. ETA, while not remotely reflecting majority Basque opinion, was well entrenched in the cities, drawing on the support of unemployed and despairing youth and able to count on a political culture which, like that of Northern Irish Catholics, did not actively support violence but which, given their historical experiences, refused to regard it as purely criminal. The Spanish government of PSOE was taking the line that there could be no political negotiations with ETA since they did not represent Basque opinion and would not renounce violence for democratic politics. The constitutional Basque nationalists were caught in the middle, supporting negotiations to resolve the problem of violence but aware that any political negotiation with ETA representatives would undermine their own representativeness.

The third historic region, Galicia, posed fewer problems. Autonomy could be provided on the same terms as in Catalonia and the Basque Country, and though there was no regionalist party powerful enough to insist on it there was no real opposition. A statute of autonomy was negotiated, and despite high levels of abstention approved at a referendum.

In Andalusia experiences at end of the Franco era and the movement towards autonomy in Catalonia and the Basque Country, served to politicise the sense of regional identity and produce a strong demand for a statute of autonomy. The resulting movement, though not as deeply rooted or sustained as those in Catalonia and the Basque Country, was capable of generating bursts of considerable enthusiasm. At the beginning of the transition, Andalusianism was represented not by separate parties but as a tendency within PSOE and the Communist Party, both of which adopted Andalusian suffixes as the PTA and PCA (Porras, 1980). This left-wing Andalusianism was based on opposition to the imposition of change on the region from outside and resentment of the privileges of the wealthy regions of the north, and tended to find expression in high-flown rhetoric about the future of a self-governing Andalusia rather than in precise policy formulations. Within the UCD too, there were decentralist currents representing the middle-class regionalism committed to modernisation and change. As a result the pre-autonomous body set up in 1978 leaned to a wide measure of autonomy and work was started immediately. In the 1979 legislative elections a new Andalusian Socialist Party, the PSA, gained 10 per cent of the vote, pressurising the state-wide parties to move faster on the issue. The president of the pre-autonomous body was replaced by a more regionalist fellow-socialist and a pact was concluded among all the parties to press for autonomy by the challenging route of clause 151, giving the possibility of equality with the Catalans and Basques. Ninety-five per cent of the town councils supported the initiative and moves towards the necessary referendum were taken.

At this point the UCD government in Madrid began to worry about the uncontrolled spread of full autonomy and turned against the Andalusian initiative. The Andalusian UCD, together with the right-wing *Alianza Popular*, refused to ratify the autonomy pact, and while a compromise was reached on a date for the initiative referendum the campaign was limited to two weeks and the question posed in a rather confused manner. Thereafter the UCD did all in its power to secure the failure of the referendum, calling on its supporters to abstain, preventing television from covering it and state-owned papers from taking advertisements about it. Autonomy was presented as a left-wing ploy and Manuel Clavero, an Andalusian moderate who had resigned from the government over the issue, painted as a dupe of the left (Porras, 1980). As the campaign became openly partisan, PSOE and the Communists pressed hard for a YES vote, while insisting on the unity of Spain and reminding voters that autonomy in itself would not solve their economic and social problems. The Andalusian Socialist Party also campaigned for a YES vote but was by now discredited by a deal which it had struck in the Madrid Parliament with the UCD to keep the government float. It was also in the process of sliding from the radical left to the populist right, emphasising its Andalusianism more than its socialism.

The result was defeat for the government and victory for the autonomist left, with the 50 per cent threshold passed in every province except Almeria and the NO votes amounting to just a handful. It was estimated that 60 per cent of the UCD's own supporters had ignored the abstention call and supported the referendum (Porras, 1980). Nevertheless the vote had technically been lost since one province had failed to register the requisite level of support. Spanish television announced simply that the Andalusian referendum initiative had failed and the government stated that Andalusia would have to proceed to limited autonomy through clause 143. PSOE's reaction was to press a censure motion in Parliament, promising clause 151 powers to Andalusia. This sealed the fate of the Andalusian Socialist Party which, like the Catalan nationalists, was bound by their pact to support the UCD government. When the censure failed, an attempt to change the law to allow Andalusia to proceed by clause 151 was rejected by just one vote (Clavero, 1983).

Despite the controversy over Andalusia, the state-wide parties were moving towards agreement on the autonomy question. PSOE, though pressed by its own supporters and the electoral situation to support full autonomy in Andalusia, turned against further application of clause 151, and even before the Andalusian referendum had opened talks on a pact with the UCD (Clavero, 1983). Now the parties agreed Andalusia could proceed with clause 151 but all other regions would have to settle for clause 143. On the other hand, clause 143 itself would be expanded and clarified to ensure that it provided for a full elected assembly, bringing some of the advantages of clause 151.

The attempted coup of February 1981 provided a further spur to action. Autonomous governments under clause 143 provisions were set up for the remaining regions of Spain and government and opposition agreed to set up two expert commissions, on economic and on political affairs, to examine the autonomy process and recommend ways in which the various autonomy statutes could be harmonised. In 1981–2, this gave rise to two laws, LOAPA and LOFCA, on powers and finance, and a pact between the UCD government and the PSOE opposition to support them in Parliament. LOAPA sought to bring some coherence to the various autonomy statutes and to protect the powers both of the state and of local governments within the autonomous regions. As both

Prime Minister Calvo Sotelo and PSOE leader Felipe Gonzalez made clear, this reflected the principles of the unity of the Spanish state and nation and the subordinate position of regional governments and rejected the idea that Spain was the mere sum of its parts. Gonzalez added that there could be no discrimination between regions (Congreso de los Diputados. 1 Legislatura. Diario de Sesiones, 21 de junio, 1982).

To Catalan and Basque deputies, this type of reasoning was anathema. They saw their statutes of autonomy as stemming not from common rights of Spaniards but from the intrinsic rights of their own communities. Nor could they accept that all regions should have the same powers. As the constitution itself was far from clear on the matter, a definitive interpretation had to await the outcome of an appeal to the constitutional court by the Basque and Catalan nationalists who argued the three historic regions were different from the rest of Spain and, accordingly, the principle of autonomy should be applied differently there. The Catalan government added that LOAPA was an attempt to change the constitution through unconstitutional means.

In its verdict the Tribunal struck down several of LOAPA's provisions and declared that it could not be promulgated as a harmonising law. While the constitution did indeed guarantee equal rights of citizenship to all Spaniards and the civil equality of all social groups, this did not mean that all autonomous communities had to be equal in their powers or in the procedure by which they acceded to these powers. All that was required was their common subordination to the constitution and the constitutional tribunal and that their different statutes should not enshrine social or economic privileges. In this way the divergent needs of national unity and regional autonomy could be safeguarded (Tribunal Constitucional, 1985).

This all left the status of the autonomous regions unclear. Certainly the idea that they were subordinate in the manner of French or Italian regions did not prevail; but on the other hand, Spain was not yet a federal structure with clearly defined limitations on the powers of central government. Territorial management continues to be a preoccupation for the parties at the centre, and with Catalonia pressing for wider powers it is likely to be some years before the situation stabilises.

Italy—The Exception to Prove the Rule

Italy in the late 1960s and 1970s experienced great political turbulence, from the 'hot autumn' of 1969, through rumours of coup plots, to right and left-wing terrorism. There were continued irredentist pressures in the northern border regions. Yet in the Mezzogiorno there was not the upsurge of peripheral regionalism found in the other three countries. This needs to be explained, given that many of the correlates of regionalism/peripheral nationalism identified in the literature were present. Despite all the measures for regional development, the economic gap between north and south grew over most of the post-war period. There were social strife and recurrent urban crises in the overexpanded cities of the south. An ideology of regionalism was available in the historic proposition of southern autonomy and the need to break the power of successive ruling blocs at the level of the Italian state. The component parts of Italy had a history of independent existence as recently as a hundred years ago. Admittedly there was no great linguistic differentiation between northern and southern Italy by the mid-twentieth century as the southern dialects had never developed the status of separate languages, but this is not a necessary condition of political mobilisation and can be a divisive force. The reason why nothing happened in the Mezzogiorno in fact lies in the political system, helping to substantiate the argument that regionalism and peripheral nationalism are to be explained largely in the realm of politics itself from the way in which political actors respond to and exploit social and economic conditions within peripheries, and do not arise spontaneously from the influence of social and economic change. In so far as social and economic conditions do provide the base on which autonomist movements can work, it is modernisation and the development of a participative culture which is the key. In the case of the Mezzogiorno, the system of territorial management used local social and economic conditions both to maintain its position and, as a corollary, to prevent modernisation. Paradoxically the very failure of policy in the south was a key to political 'success' in heading off the development of autonomist movements.

From the early 1960s, attempts to reform the system for managing the south focused on the need for greater policy coherence. They failed because the problem lay not in the south but in the structure of the state itself and the party system which underpinned it. Had governments in Rome succeeded in framing coherent policies for the south, this might have stimulated and focused debate on the southern question and brought back into play the issue of regional autonomy. Instead, the problem continued to be handled in a disaggregated manner. A series of attempts to reform the *Cassa per il Mezzogiorno* was made, starting with a law of 1965 to strengthen the control of the Minister for the Mezzogiorno, within the context of the national plan. A 1971 law sought further to strengthen central control and reduce the autonomy of the *Cassa*, and thus its connections with local clientilist networks. While these moves towards central control failed, the role of the *Cassa* itself was progressively downgraded, as central departments dealt directly with large firms, the *Cassa*'s affiliate bodies came to exercise more independent power, regional councils came to exercise more functions and sectoral interventions by central government began to override regional policies (Torchia, 1984). By the mid-1980s, the *Cassa per il Mezzogiorno* had officially ceased to exist, though there were still people on its payroll spending substantial sums of money! An increase in regional policy spending together with the impact of regional government did produce some advances. By 1975 public spending in the south was greater than the national average, having been lower in 1963 (Cao-Pinna, 1979). The early 1970s also saw a brief growth spurt, but based on external and state capital, this did not produce a self-sustaining cycle and was killed off in 1974–5 by the aftermath of the oil crisis—growth since then has been attributed to the traditional factors of low pay and exploitation rather than modernisation (Giannola, 1982). So the central state itself had failed to generate and carry through the policies which would be needed for a transformation of southern society and economy (Cagliozzi, 1982) into the modern, participative political system which might sustain an autonomist movement.

The establishment of regional government in the 1970s was part of the response to the crisis of governability on the part of the centre-left governments of the 1960s, an attempt to hand over responsibilities to local collaborators and channel discontents away from the centre (Good, 1976), as well as improving the quality of administration. In practice the regional reforms made little difference to the practice of clientilism focused on the central state through territorial intermediaries. Instead, they were captured from the beginning by the party machines and tended, at least in the south, to become just one more link in the chain. Special agencies continued alongside the regions (SPS, 1984) and the councils themselves were subordinated to the needs of the party machines (see Chapter 8). This failure to institutionalise regionalism tended to reduce the salience of regional politics and diminished the likelihood that discontent would find a regional framework and means of expression. It also served to discredit the idea of regionalism as a solution to the problems of the south or, indeed, Italy as a whole.

The attitudes and practices of the major parties, the Christian Democrats and the Communists, were also critical. While the party system came under great strain in the 1970s, there was not the realignment which allowed regional and peripheral nationalist forces to emerge in the UK, France and Spain. Though the Christian Democrats had accepted regional reform as the price of the centre-left coalition and because of pressure from industrialists and their own reformist wing, they soon reduced the southern regions, controlled by themselves, to the old clientilist logic (Barbera, 1985). It is this clientilism which has been widely credited with sustaining the Christian Democrat position in the south where, after reverses in the 1960s, they have held their vote up better than in the north. While directed principally at the Communists, the strategy also diffused other forms of potential opposition, and by reducing politics to patronage relations focused on itself, discouraged the aggregation of demands essential to political mobilisation on the part of opposition movements. In the early 1970s they played their other major card which had proved a trump in 1948, the Catholic appeal, backing the 1974 referendum to repeal the 1970 divorce law. In Italy as a whole, the ploy backfired, with divorce being approved by 3–2, but six out of seven regions in the mainland south voted against divorce and in Sicily the pro-divorce majority was just 1 per cent (ICS, 1975). So despite the crises of the period the Christian Democrat power base in the south held.

For its part the Communist Party was primarily concerned with maintaining the stability of Italian democracy and paving the way for peaceful alternation in government. This involved supporting existing institutions, combating political violence of the right and left, controlling spontaneous outbursts of social protest and channelling them into support for itself, while seeking a rapprochement with the Christian Democrats. The historic compromise of 1976–9, which had its origins in the early 1970s, was the culmination of this strategy, involving the Communists in support for a Christian Democrat government as a preliminary to full participation in the governing coalition. All the while the Communists were consolidating their position in local government, presenting a model of clean and efficient administration while the transfers of powers to the regional councils in the 1970s worked to their considerable advantage in the 'red belt' of central Italy. In the south too they were able to mark some steady advance and in 1976 captured the city council of Naples. In these circumstances they were unlikely to place themselves at the head of a movement for southern home rule, especially after the divorce referendum had shown up the continued clerical influence there and the neo-Fascist MSI had demonstrated considerable strength as well as the ability to profit from social disruption.

The ability of existing elites to channel social discontent to their own purposes was vividly illustrated by the events at Reggio Calabria in 1970. The riots which shook this southern city may have had their origins in discontent at underdevelopment and the corruption of the administration (De Felice, 1983) but their course was determined by local political considerations. The immediate grievance was the choice of Catanzaro over Reggio as capital of the new region of Calabria, resulting in a loss of patronage opportunities but the riots appear to have been encouraged and financed by local right wing Christian Democrat, business and agrarian interests opposed to reforming elements who were gaining the ascendancy (Cooper, 1970). Anti-reform elements were able to use the mob to undermine the reformists as well as advancing the claim for the regional capital with its patronage potential, and to turn discontent away from political channels. In due course, both at Reggio and at Aquila and Pescara (Abruzzi) where there were similar disturbances, the neo-Fascist right moved in to exploit the situation, encouraging rioting while calling for tough law and order policies. The central government's response, once the rioting at Reggio had subsided, was a piece of traditional pork-barrel. Instead of a plan for the development of the region's resources, they promised Italy's largest steel-works, a project with little relation to the local economic structure but which, while continuing the region's dependence, would be a source of jobs.

So the Mezzogiorno's urban and regional crisis was used by the territorial power brokers further to consolidate their own position. Failing an alternation of power in Rome or a crisis severe enough to bankrupt the system of patronage, this pattern is likely to continue.

8
The State and the Regions

Configurations of Territorial Politics

The previous chapters have shown, through a series of necessarily fragmentary case studies, that territorial politics and regionalism, far from disappearing under the influence of modernisation, recur regularly as social, economic and political changes generate new interests. While it is difficult to build a statistically significant thesis on a limited range of cases, sustained regional mobilisation aimed at autonomy appears more common not in underdeveloped regions as a protest against modernity but in the more advanced peripheries, where a sense of identity has been maintained and especially where there has been some institutional development. The critical point, though, is the use made of the issue of regional autonomy by organised political formations in debate and mobilisation. Autonomism has manifested itself both in the form of separate regionalist or peripheral nationalist parties and as a force within the state-wide parties, and the regionalist/peripheral nationalist parties themselves have assumed a variety of positions in relation to social and economic questions.

Separatist nationalism is represented in an extra-constitutional and violent form by ETA–*Herri Batasuna*, the IRA–*Sinn Fein*, and Corsican separatists (not examined here). For these the issue is not how to reconcile differing territorial identities or the aspirations to self-government of populations, but rather how to realise the existing 'nation' whose identity is not recognised by existing constitutional forms. For this purpose the wishes of the population of the nation are in the last resort irrelevant, since the nation is more than the sum of its constituent members and its realisation not to be denied by mere transitory majorities. For the central state this type of demand is strictly non-negotiable since nothing less than capitulation and the dismantling of the existing state would satisfy it. Further, to negotiate or make concessions to violence undermines the legitimacy not only of the state and the constitution but also of non-violent peripheral nationalist movements attempting to work through building majority support within existing institutions. On the other hand, to see political violence merely as a problem of criminality to be dealt with by security measures, may be self-defeating since the support for violence is often based on political grievance. So states have sought to make deals with constitutional nationalist movements in order to undercut violent action. The picture is further complicated by a marked move to the extreme left on the part of most of the violent separatist movements. To some degree this is mere rhetoric for external consumption, allowing them to become part of the world 'national liberation' community and draw support, arms and funds from sympathetic sources. It also, however, reflects conditions on the ground in Northern Ireland and the Basque Country, where the IRA and ETA have been able to tap the discontent and despair of unemployed youth in decaying cities where heavy industry has died, with the promise of a social as well as a national revolution. So the regional crisis of the 1960s and 1970s has been overlaid with the urban crisis of the 1980s to create an even more intractable problem, for even if the constitutional question should be resolved, the urban problem would remain.

Separatist nationalism in its constitutional, democratic form is represented by the Scottish National Party, the fractured Basque National Party and the SDLP (which aspires to separate the province to unite with the Republic of Ireland), though many of their supporters would in practice settle for a good deal less. Constitutional nationalist parties tend to be interclass, since they aspire to majority support in the electorate, though they do in practice lean towards the left (SDLP) or right (PNV). State responses to this type of nationalism have alternated between insistence on the unity of the state-nation and concessions of autonomy, ranging from a mild administrative devolution to elected legislative assemblies, in an effort to isolate the intransigent separatists. Such concessions do not, of course, succeed in taking the territorial issue out of politics in order to allow 'normal' politics to resume, since each concession helps to reinforce the sense of territorial identity. Despite the protests of intransigent Jacobins, however, this type of nationalism is amenable to negotiation and compromise, albeit at the cost of considerable confusion on the part of central politicians about what national unity means in practice and what limits it imposes on the devolution of power to subordinate units.

A number of parties of the periphery describe themselves as nationalist but without serious pretensions to separatism. This is the case with the Catalan CiU and the Welsh Plaid Cymru, as well as some of the Breton and Occitan movements. Outside the three historic regions of Spain, the terms nationalism and nationality are used rather loosely in the autonomy statutes of Andalusia and Valencia and, in debate, in other regions as well. These movements, which many would not classify as nationalist at all because they are not separatist, seek a restructuring of the state so as to recognise their own specific identity and would insist on their right to negotiate for autonomy with the centre rather than having it presented to them by sovereign power. In their opposition to the centralised state, they will often stress their own Europeanist and internationalist orientation, aiming ultimately for a Europe of the regions, though in practice the limited political development of the European Community makes this a distant dream (Keating, 1986a). The Catalan CiU tends to the right politically while pursuing an interclass strategy and stressing the primacy of Catalan interests as a unifying factor. Others are on the libertarian left, seeking a wider transformation of state structures with an emphasis on community and opposition to the inherently centralising bias of capitalism as well as to centralised government. Their attempts to build support on this dual opposition, with both class and territorial appeals have had little success. Either they have appealed only to small minorities within the region or else have had to redefine working class into an all-embracing concept excluding only large-scale externally-owned capitalism. In some cases this has led back to an interclass strategy which, in its concern not to alienate any regional interests, can slide towards right-wing populism. We have noted in the case studies the fragility of libertarian regionalist movements and their difficulties in building support, given the utopianism of their ideology and the competition of the mainstream left-wing parties with their access to the central state and its resources. Given the limited nature of their immediate demands and the utopianism of their ultimate aspirations, this type of regionalism/nationalism is amenable to negotiation and compromise, though again not without conflict.

There are also movements for regional/national autonomy crossing party lines, such as the Campaign for a Scottish Assembly, founded in the aftermath of the 1979 referendum but drawing on a long Scottish tradition, various of the movements for Spanish regional autonomy and some of the Breton movements. These are neutral on social and economic questions and, not challenging the established parties electorally, can mobilise wide support. Yet their support tends to be weakly rooted, their members have prior commitments and loyalties and there is a constant problem in maintaining enthusiasm for a movement based purely on constitutional issues. Where the major parties refuse to make concessions, interparty movements have no real sanctions short of contesting elections, that is, becoming political parties themselves, losing members in the process and usually condemning themselves to the political margins.

A means of avoiding such a marginalisation is for regionalist and peripheral nationalists whose goals fall short of separatism to work within the state-wide parties. In the 1980s this usually means working with the parties of the left. Though left-wing regionalism/peripheral nationalism has had a long history as a minority strand, there has been a remarkable shift in recent years, due to a combination of external and internal factors. Externally the decline in the social base of left-wing parties together with competition from the new movements has forced them to broaden their electoral appeal which has included a more explicit territorial dimension.

Prolonged periods of opposition at the national level have also led left-wing parties to consolidate their urban and regional bases. Internally European socialism has become more pluralist to the extent that the French Socialist Party could publish a document called *La France au Pluriel* while the British labour Party has been agonisingly reappraising its view of the state and the distribution of power (Jones and Keating, 1985). In Spain, Felipe Gonzalez was able, after a struggle, to persuade PSOE to abandon its traditional Marxist view of the world in order to compete effectively in a post-Francoist Spain emerging as a complex and plural society. The Italian Communists have gone beyond destalinisation to abandon the doctrine of the dictatorship of the proletariat and the principle of democratic centralism and have, with some success, sought a wider and more diverse social base. The process is less evident in the French Communist Party which has girated between Eurocommunism and Stalinism while its support has steadily shrunk.

Regionalism has been taken furthest in the social-democratic parties, the French Socialist Party, the British Labour Party and the Spanish PSOE, helped by generational change. This has channelled into the parties of the left much of the regionalist/peripheral nationalist impulse and even personnel in Andalusia, Scotland, Brittany and Languedoc. In Italy much of the potential for a regionalist movement in the *Mezzogiorno* has been taken up by the Communist Party which has espoused both territorial economic demands and the cause of regional autonomy. This is evident to a lesser extent in the French Communist Party where the commitment to regionalism often takes the form of populist campaigns of territorial defence, combined with a continued insistence on nationalisation and centralised control as the basis of economic policy and the persistence of democratic centralism within the party.

The parties of the democratic left are in a good position to benefit from regionalist sentiment since they are able to offer a combination of limited territorial autonomy, regional defence within the institutions of the existing state and a guarantee against separatism. Regionalist/peripheral nationalist parties are able to offer only the former, limiting their appeal to a public which is nowhere overwhelmingly separatist. On the other hand, regional autonomy has been adopted by left-wing parties only at the cost of a potential clash with other elements of their policy prospectus. They are all, in principle, committed to centralised control of the economy, and even where they have begun to back away from this they have not worked out the relationship between decentralised government and centralised capitalism. They are all committed to national welfare standards. Finally the need to win power at the centre may require them to downplay their commitment to regional particularism. In opposition this sort of policy dissonance is just about manageable, but should the French Socialists or British Labour Party return to power they would have to face up to the problem. This requires a new model for the territorial dispersal of power, adapted to the needs of the late twentieth century and able to reconcile central and non-separatist regional aspirations.

What this shows is that just as territorial politics is a perfectly normal mode of political activity, so territorial demands, like social and economic demands, are usually negotiable within the framework of liberal democracy. The process of negotiation has produced conflicts and the contemporary west European state has not yet found the perfect formula for accommodating regional autonomy within previously unitary regimes—but as much could be said about the difficulty of accommodating other social and economic interests. The difficulties can be seen from a brief examination of proposals for experience of regional government in the four states.

Regional Government

While movements of the periphery have sought regional autonomy, the central state itself has used regionalism to reduce administrative overload and coordinate its territorial interventions. The tension between autonomist and centralised regionalism has already been noted as have the attempts since 1970 to build a regional level of government satisfying both sets of goals. In the absence of a developed theory of regional government in Europe, concepts must be taken eclectically from the study of federalism, local government and intergovernmental relations (Keating, 1988a). These suggest that the critical issues are the need for central autonomy, for regional autonomy and for mechanisms of intergovernmental accommodation and cooperation.

In the quest for central autonomy, none of the states has accepted the federal principle with its restraints on both levels. Nor have they accepted any element of regional sovereignty allowing territories to negotiate their own arrangements with the centre, though the circumstances of Spain in the 1970s, with the central regime being built along with the regions, entailed some element of this, and Catalan and Basque nationalists insist on this reading of the Spanish constitution. LOAPA represented the attempt by central forces to clarify the position in their favour and resist federalisation. In the United Kingdom it is the insistence on retaining the unitary parliamentary regime which has made it easier for governments and Parliament to concede secession than Home Rule for the periphery. In France the insistence on state sovereignty prevented a referendum on Corsican independence even when the centre knew that it would win it, since this would concede the principle. The need for central autonomy has also led governments to retain extensive override powers in all cases (Cammelli, 1980), though these are the subject of constitutional challenge in Spain. It is the insistence on central autonomy which has led all these 'unitary' states to allow special status regions, upsetting their constitutional symmetry since, while the pressure from these territories has proved to hard to resist, extending the provisions to the whole state would have meant federalisation.

Regional autonomy is partly a matter of power and resources, partly a matter of political circumstances. Powers are most generously, though confusingly, drawn in Spain, least so in France where the 1972 regions had no power of their own and the new regions since 1986 have limited competence. In Italy, as under the Scotland and Wales Acts, powers were narrowly drawn to devolve individual pieces of legislation rather than broad functions and this has led to close dependence on the centre (Merloni, 1982) and fragmentation of regional policies (Pastori, 1982). Financial powers, too, are greatest in Spain, especially in the Basque Country and Navarre, with their *conciertos económicos*. In Italy regions depend for 90 per cent of their finance on central grants (Buglione and France, 1984) and the Scottish and Welsh assemblies would have had no taxing power at all. In France the major reform of local finance promised for years has not materialised.

Generally speaking, it has proved easier in the modern state to devolve powers in social and environmental policy fields than in economic. Yet much of the pressure for regionalism has come from regional aspirations to control the process of economic change and the inability of traditional territorial representatives to do this. Central reservation of economic and industrial policy has led in turn to recentralisation in other fields, given the interdependence of policy fields. Central control of finance has had the same effect. More generally the difficulties of drawing clear lines between functional areas has led to complex patterns of collaboration and joint working. In contemporary federalism, where this trend has been observed, the effect is an interdependence of the two levels, each of which has powers and resources needed by the other. With regional devolution, however, the centre has the capacity unilaterally to change the distribution of powers or to override the lower level. This too is subject to some dispute in Spain but it is clearly the case in France, Italy and the abortive Scotland and Wales proposals. So interdependence leads to regional dependence (Salerno, 1983; Aniasi, 1982), unless the latter can become a 'locus of political power' (Bogdanor, 1986) able to constrain it.

One mechanism for structuring central–regional relations in economic matters and managing their effects in other fields has been planning. While planning exercises of the 1960s assumed consensus on goals and means, the 1981 proposals of the French Socialists, like the Prescott (1983) proposals in the British Labour party, envisaged planning as a political dialogue and negotiation between regions and the centre. In the French proposals put into effect for the Ninth Plan, there was a regional input into the national plan while regions were free to adopt their own priorities as long as they did not conflict with the national ones. In practice the revival of planning was overtaken by the economic crisis and the major industrial restructurings bypassed it. In the absence of substantial financial devolution, regional plans were mostly designed to lever the maximum financial support from the centre and presented little coherent vision (SPELEO, 1985).

The ability of regional governments both to retain their own field of autonomy and to carry weight in intergovernmental bargaining is critically dependent on the political circumstances and power structures. Unlike most federal systems which have brought together disparate territories, regional devolution involves taking powers away from an existing centre (Frenkel, 1986) and this has met with resistance. Bureaucratic influences can be a powerful recentralising force. In Italy regional bureaucracies have fallen into the old clientilist/centralist pattern, while in France the civil service, though divided by *corps*, remains territorially unified. In the Scotland and Wales Acts, no provision was made for separate civil services. Central governments have also maintained their own field administrations in the Spanish civil governors, Italian prefects and French *commissaires de la république* while the British proposals would have retained the Secretaries of State for Scotland and Wales. Existing levels of local government are another force against radical change. In no case has it proved possible to suppress a tier of local government to make way for the regions, and except in Navarre and Sicily (King, 1987) and the abortive Scottish proposals, all retain their direct links with the centre and its field officials.

Political parties and career patterns are an important factor in structuring central–regional relationships. In France and Italy, national parties dominate regional councils which have been largely reduced to relays in the unitary political systems (SPS, 1984; Bassanini, 1985). Regional elections follow national trends. Proposals to limit the French accumulation of offices are intended to give the various tiers a life of their own but these are timid and to be phased in over several years. In Catalonia and the Basque Country, separate party systems operate, allowing for an autonomous political life, but at the cost of reducing regional weight in national politics.

Where a regional party system is completely separate and regional politicians do not participate in national governments, the incentives to cooperate in making the system work are sharply reduced. What is required to meet the goals of central autonomy, regional autonomy and central–local cooperation is an identifiable level of politics focused on the territory, participation of territorial politicians in national political life, together with a willingness to engage in territorial and bargaining and compromise. Putnam *et al.* (1985) have found that Italian regional government works best and can most easily break the old political habits where there is an established democratic participative culture, social and economic relationships based on exchange rather than tradition and patronage, secular values and social stability—in other words, a 'modernised' political culture. Regional participation in national politics can also be encouraged through second legislative chambers with a regional basis (Hebbert, 1987), but though the idea is often floated and is implicit in the constitution of Spain and Italy it has not been implemented since it would be a threat to central autonomy. All four countries at present have weak second chambers and central elites are unwilling to share their power.

So regional government has not yet shown the capacity to transform the unitary state. Yet the issue is not going to go away. As the power of national governments to manage the territorial economy is reduced by the internationalisation of trade and business, the pressure for regionally-based responses to change increases. This book has concentrated on politics and government, but social and economic interests have also focused attention on the regional level (Miguelez, 1984; Indovina, 1973). Should the movement to European integration resume, the power of national governments would further diminish. Of course, regional governments or an independent Scotland would have even less leverage over the world economy than the existing states but the significance of territory will only increase and the need to find some formula to accommodate it in the modern state remains. That is a subject for another book.

Bibliography

Acosta Sanchez, J. (1978), *Andalucía. Reconstrucción de un identidad y la lucha contra el centralismo* (Barcelona: Anagrama).

Agnew, J. (1987), *Place and Politics. The Geographical Mediation of State and Society* (Boston: Allen and Unwin).

Alburquerque, F. (1977), 'La cuestión nacional y el subdesarrollo en Andalucía', *Negaciones*, 3.

Alcaras Ramos, M. (1985), 'Cuestión nacional y al subdesarrollo en Andalucía', *Negaciones*, 3.

Alcouffe, A. (1980), in *Pais Occitan*, 39 estiu-auton (Lutte Occitane).

Allies, P. and Dervedet, M. (1983), *L'aménagement touristique du littoral Languedoc–Roussillon: d'une logique étatique à une gestion décentralisée* (Montpellier: CERTE).

Allum, P. (1971), 'The south and national politics, 1945–50', in Woolf, S.J. (ed.), *The rebirth of Italy, 1943–50* (London: Longman).

—— (1973), *Politics and society in post-war Naples* (Cambridge University Press).

Anderson, N. and Anderson, P. (1967), *Political Institutions and Social Change in Continental Europe in the Nineteenth Century* (Berkeley: University of California Press).

Andriani, S. (1979), 'I nuovi termini della questione meridionale', in Accornero, A. and Andriani, S. (eds), *Gli Anni '70 nel Mezzogiorno* (Bari: de Donato).

Aniasi, A. (1982), *Rapporto 1982 sullo stato delle autonomie del Ministro per gli Affari regionali, Aldo Aniasi* (Rome: Istituto Poligrafico e Zecca dello Stato).

Arcangeli, F. (1982), *Italia: Centri e Periferie* (Milan: Franco Angelo).

Ardagh, J. (1982), *France in the 1980s* (Harmondsworth: Penguin).

Armengaud, A. and Lafont, R. (1979), *Histoire d'Occitanie* (Paris: Hachette).
Ashford, D. (1982), *British Dogmatism and French Pragmatism. Central–Local Policymaking in the Welfare State* (London: Allen and Unwin).
Aumente Baena, J. (1980), 'Por Que la "nacionalidad" andaluza', in *Hacia una Andalucía Libre* (Seville: Edisur).
Avril, P. (1969), *Politics in France* (Harmondsworth: Penguin).
Azzena, A. and Palermo, L. (1981), 'Coscienza autonomista e sviluppo della "Specialità". Verso un nuovo rapporto stato–regione sarda', in Mori, G. (ed.), *Autonomismo meridionale: ideologia, politica e istituzioni* (Bologna: Il Mulino).
Baiges, F., Gonzalez, E. and Reixach, J. (1985), *Banca Catalana. Más que un banco, más que una crisis* (Barcelona: Plaza y Janes).
Balsom, D. (1985), 'The Three-Wales model' in Osmond, J. (ed.), *The National Question Again. Welsh National Identity in the 1980s* (Llandysul: Gomer).
Barbera, A. (1985), '1970–85; como superare le insufficienze del decentramento', *Democrazia e Diritto*, XXV.1.
Barelli, Y., Boudy, J–F., Carence, J–F. (1980), *L'espérance occitane* (Paris: Entente).
Barker, R. (1978), *Political Ideas in Modern Britain* (London: Methuen).
Barrio, J.R. del and Sevilla Guzman, E. (1983), 'Nacionalismo y corporatismo: aproximación al caso andalúz', *Revista Internacional de Sociologia*, XLI.45.
Bartoli, P. (1981), 'Politique viticole: note de discussion', *Nouvelles Campagnes*, 16.
—— (1984), 'Résultats départementaux des primes d'arrachage et de reconversion viticole, 1976–82', *Séries Études et Recherches*, No. 79, École Nationale Supérieure Agronomique, Montpellier.
Barucci, P. (1974), *Il Meridionalismo Dopo La Ricostruzione, 1948–57* (Milan: Guiffre).
Bassanini, F. (1985) 'La repubblica delle autonomie: rilancio o declino', *Democrazia e Diritto*, XXV.1.
Bayona, A. (1987), 'The autonomous government of Catalonia', *Environment and Planning C. Government and Policy*, 5.
Bazalgues, G. (1972), 'L'aménagement du littoral méditérranéan' in *La Régionalisation. Espoirs ou illusions?* (Wanquetin: Mouvement d'Action Rurale).
Beer, W.R. (1977), 'Social class of ethnic activists in contemporary France', in Esman, M.J. (ed.), *Ethnic Conflict in the Western World* (Ithaca: Cornell University Press).

—— (1980), *The Unexpected Rebellion. Ethnic Activism in Contemporary France* (New York University Press).
Berger, S. (1977), 'Bretons and Jacobins: Reflections on French regional ethnicity', in Esman, M.J. (ed.), *Ethnic Conflict in the Western World* (Ithaca: Cornell University Press).
Bernard, P. (1983) *L'état et la décentralisation. Du préfet au commissaire de la république* (Paris: Documentation Française).
Birnbaum, P. (1982), *La logique de l'État* (Paris: Fayard).
Blas Guerrero, A. de (1978), 'El problema nacional–regional español en los programas del PSOE y PCE', *Revista de Estudios Políticos*, 4.
Bogdanor, V. (1986), 'Federalism and devolution: Some juridical and political problems', in Morgan, R. (ed.), *Regionalism in European Politics* (London: Policy Studies Institute).
Bonora, P. (1984), *Regionalità. Il concetto di regione nell'Italia del secondo dopoguerra (1943–1970)* (Milan: Franco Angeli).
Botella, J. (1984), 'Elementos del sistema de partidos de la Cataluña actual', *Papers*, 21.
Brabo, P., and Ortiz, C. (1984), 'Las Elecciones autonómicas en Catalunya', *Leviatan*, 16.
Brand, J. (1978), *The National Movement in Scotland* (London: Routledge and Kegan Paul).
Braudel, F. (1986), *L'Identité de la France* (Paris: Arthaud).
Breuilly, J. (1985), *Nationalism and the State*, 2nd edn (Manchester: Manchester University Press; Chicago: Chicago University Press).
Buglione, E. and France, G. (1984), 'Skewed fiscal federalism in Italy: Implications for public expenditure control', in Premchand, A. and Burkhead, J. (eds), *Comparative International Budgeting and Finance* (New Brunswick: Transaction Books).
Bulpitt, J. (1983), *Territory and Power in the United Kingdom. An Interpretation* (Manchester: Manchester University Press).
Butt Philip, A. (1975), *The Welsh Question. Nationalism in Welsh Politics, 1945–70* (Cardiff: University of Wales Press).
Caciagli, M. (1977), *Democrazia Cristiana e Potere nel Mezzogiorno. Il sistema democristiano a Catania* (Rimini: Guaraldi).
Caciagli, M. and Belloni, F.P. (1981), 'The "New" clientilism in southern Italy: The Christian Democratic Party in Catania', in Eisenstadt, S.N. and Lemarchand, R. (eds), *Political Clientilism, Patronage and Development* (London: Sage).
Cagliozzi, R. (1982), 'A regional or a national industrial policy', *Review of Economic Conditions in Italy*, 1.
Cameron, D.P. (1974), 'A theory of political mobilisation', *Journal of Politics*, 36.1.

Cammelli, M. (1980), 'Cent'anni di regionalismo e dieci di regioni', *Il Mulino*, 268.
Canals, R.M., Valles, J.M. and Viros, R. (1984), 'Las elecciones al parlamento de Catalunya de 29 abril de 1984', *Revista de Estudios Políticos*, 40.
Cao-Pinna, V. (1979), *Le Regioni del Mezzogiorni* (Bologna: Il Mulino).
Caronna, M. (1970), *Guido Dorso e il Partito Meridionale Rivoluzionario* (Milan: Cisalpino-Goliardica).
Carr, R. (1975), *Spain, 1808–1939*, 3rd edition (Oxford: Clarendon).
Carr, R. and Fusi, J.P. (1981), *Spain: Dictatorship to Democracy*, 2nd edition (London: Allen and Unwin).
Chevallier, J., Rangeon, F. and Sellier, M. (1982), *Le Pouvoir Régional* (Paris: Presses Universitaires de France).
Cholvy, G. (1980), *Histoire du Languedoc de 1900 à nos jours* (Toulouse: Privat).
Chubb, J. (1981a), 'The social bases of an urban political machine: The Christian Democratic Party in Palermo', in Eisenstadt, S.N. and Lemarchand, R. (eds), *Political Clientilism, Patronage and Development* (London: Sage).
Chubb, J. (1981b), 'Naples under the Left: The limits of local change', in Eisenstadt, S.N. and Lemarchand, R. (eds), *Political Clientilism, Patronage and Development* (London: Sage).
Chubb, J. (1982), *Patronage, Power and Poverty in Southern Italy. A Tale of Two Cities* (Cambridge: Cambridge University Press).
CIS (1985), *Actitudes y Opiniones de los españoles ante la Constitución y las Instituciones Democráticas* (Madrid: Centro de Investigaciones Sociológicas).
Clavero, B. (1981), 'Los Fueros en la España contemporánea: de la reacción anti-liberal al federalismo vergonzante', *Revista de Estudios Políticos*, 20.
Clavero Arevalo, M. (1983), *España, desde el centralismo a las autonomías* (Barcelona: Planeta).
Cooper, P. (1970), 'The wreckage of Reggio's riots', *New Society*, 16, 12 November.
Connor, W. (1977), 'Ethnonationalism in the First World: The present in historical perspective', in Esman, M.J. (ed.), *Ethnic Conflict in the Western World* (Ithaca: Cornell University Press).
Corcuera, J. (1986), 'La configuración del nacionalismo vasco', in Hernández, F. and Mercadé, F., *Estructuras Sociales y Cuestión Nacional en España* (Barcelona: Ariel).
Croisat, M. and Souchon, M.-F. (1979), 'Regionalisation in France' in Lagroye, J. and Wright, V. (eds), *Local Government in Britain*

and France (London: Allen and Unwin).
Cronin, S. (1980), *Irish Nationalism. A History of its Roots and Ideology* (Dublin: Academy Press).
Crozier, M. and Friedberg, E. (1977), *L'acteur et le système* (Paris; Seuil).
Cruise O'Brien, C. (1972), *States of Ireland* (London: Hutchinson).
Cuadrado Roura, J.R. (1981), 'La política regional en los planes de desarollo', in Acosta España, R. (ed.), *La España de las Autonomías*, Tomo 1 (Madrid: Espasa-Calpe).
Curto, V. Lo (1978), *La questione meridionale* (Florence: D'Anna).
Dalyell, T. (1977), *Devolution: The End of Britain?* (London: Jonathan Cape).
Dangerfield, G. (1979), *The Damnable Question. A Study in Anglo-Irish Relations* (London: Quartet).
Davis, J.A. (1979), 'Introduction' in Davis, J.A. (ed.), *Gramsci and Italy's Passive Revolution* (London: Croom Helm).
Dente, B. (1985), *Governare la frammentazione* (Bologna: Il Mulino).
Deutsch, K. (1966), *Nationalism and Social Communication. An Inquiry into the Foundations of Nationality*. 2nd edition (Cambridge, Mass.: MIT Press).
Dicey, A.V. (1886), *England's Claim Against Irish Home Rule*, 1973 edition (Richmond: Richmond Publishing Company).
Dorso, G. (1978), 'La rivoluzione meridionale', extracts in V. Lo Curto (ed.), *La questione meridionale* (Florence: G. D'Anna), 2nd edition.
Downs, A. (1957), *An Economic Theory of Democracy* (New York: Harper and Row).
Dulong, R. (1975), *La Question Bretonne* (Paris: Presses de la fondation nationale des sciences politiques).
Dupuy, F. and Thoenig, J–C. (1985), *L'administration en miettes* (Paris: Fayard).
Dyson, K. (1980), *The State Tradition in Western Europe* (Oxford: Martin Robertson).
Elder, N. (1979), 'The Functions of the Modern State' in Hayward, J. and Berki, R. (eds), *State and Society in Contemporary Europe* (Oxford: Martin Robertson).
Elton, G.R. (1977), *Reform and Reformation. England, 1509–1558* (London: Edward Arnold).
ESE (1979), Equipo de Sociología Electoral, Universidad Autónoma de Barcelona, 'El referendum del estatuto de autonomía en Cataluña', *Revista de Estudios Políticos* 12.
——— (1980), Equipo de Sociología Electoral, Universidad Autónoma de Barcelona, 'Las elecciones catalanes del 20 de marzo de

1980', *Revista de Estudios Políticos*, 14.
Esman, M.J. (1977a), 'Introduction', in Esman, M.J. (ed.), *Ethnic Conflict in the Western World* (Ithaca: Cornell University Press).
────── (1977b), 'Perspectives on ethnic conflict in industrialised countries', in Esman, M.J. (ed.), *Ethnic Conflict in the Western World* (Ithaca: Cornell University Press).
Esteban, J. de (1982), *Las Constituciones de España* (Madrid: Taurus).
Farneti, P. (1985), *The Italian Party System (1945–1980)* (London: Frances Pinter).
Federico de Carvajal, J. (1987), *El reto de las autonomías* (Barcelona: Plaza y Janes).
Felice, R. de (1983), *Storia dell'Italia Contemporanea, VI, 1956–76* (Naples: Edizioni Scientifiche Italiane).
Ferguson, W. (1968), *Scotland 1689 to the Present* (Edinburgh: Oliver and Boyd).
Flogaitis, S. (1979), *La Notion de Décentralisation en France, en Allemagne et en Italie* (Paris: Pichon et Duran-Auzias).
Folz, W.J. (1981), 'Modernization and nation building: The social mobilisation model reconsidered', in Merrit, R.L. and Russett, B.R. (eds), *From National Development to Global Community* (London: Allen and Unwin).
Frears, J.R. (1977), *Political Parties and Elections in the French Fifth Republic* (London: C. Hurst).
Frenkel, M. (1986), 'The distribution of legal powers in pluricentral systems', in Morgan, R. (ed.), *Regionalism in European Politics* (London: Policy Studies Institute).
Fusi, J.P. (1984), 'Teoría de Pais Vasco', *El Pais*, 13 February.
Fusi, J.P. (1985), 'Los nacionalismos en España, 1900–36', in *Nacionalismo y Regionalismo en España* (Cordoba: Diputación Provincial).
GEC (1976), *Gran Enciclopedia Catalana* (Barcelona).
Galasso, G. (1978), *Passato e presente del meridionalismo* (Naples: Guida).
Galli, G. and Prandi, A. (1970), *Patterns of Political Participation in Italy* (New Haven: Yale University Press).
Ganci, M. (1978), *La nazione siciliana* (Naples: Storia di Napoli e della Sicilia).
García Barbancho, A. (1979), *Disparidades Regionales y Ordenación del Territorio* (Barcelona: Ariel).
García Fernando, M. (1982), *Regionalismo y autonomia en España, 1976–1979* (Madrid: Centro de Investigaciones Sociológicas).
García Fernandez, J. (1980), 'Crónica de la descentralización: El

panorama descentralizador al acabar 1980 (1)', *Revista de Estudios Políticos*, 17.
Garvin, T. (1981), *The Evolution of Irish Nationalist Politics* (Dublin: Gill and Macmillan).
Gaspare, G. di (1985), 'Indirizzo politico e direzione amministrativa nell'intervento straordinario nel Mezzogiorno (dall'affirmazione alle crisi del 'Sistema Cassa'), *Le Regioni*, 5.
Giannola, A. (1982), 'The industrialisation, dualism and economic dependence of the Mezzogiorno in the 1970s', *Review of Economic Conditions in Italy*, 1.
Giard, J. and Scheibling, J. (1981), *L'enjeu régionale* (Paris: Messidor).
Giner, S. (1984), 'Ethnic nationalism, centre and periphery in Spain', in Abel, C. and Torrents, N. (eds), *Spain. Conditional Democracy* (London: Croom Helm).
Ginsberg, P. (1979), 'Gramsci and the era of bourgeois revolution in Italy', in Davis, J.A. (ed.), *Gramsci and Italy's Passive Revolution* (London: Croom Helm).
Gispert, G. and Prats, J. (1978), *España: un estado plurinacional* (Barcelona: Blume).
Gontcharoff, G. and Milano, S. (1983), *La décentralisation, nouveaux pouvoirs, nouveaux espoirs* (Paris: Syros).
González, M.J. (1981), 'El desarollo regional frustrado durante treinte años de dirigismo, 1928–58', in Acosta España, R. (ed.), *La España de las Autonomías*, Tomo 1 (Madrid: Espasa-Calpe).
Good, M. Hoover (1976), *Regional Reform in Italy: The Politics of Subnational Reorganisation*, Ph.D. thesis, Brown University.
Gourevitch, P.A. (1980), *Paris and the Provinces. The Politics of Local Government Reform in France* (London: Allen and Unwin).
Gramsci, A. (1978a), 'Some aspects of the southern question', in Hoare, Q. (ed.), *Antonio Gramsci. Selections from Political Writings (1921–1926)*, (London: Lawrence and Wishart).
―――― (1978b), 'Operai e contadini', from *L'Ordine Nuovo*, 3 January 1920, reprinted in V. Lo Curto (ed.), *La questione meridionale*, 2nd edition (Florence: G. D'Anna).
Granja, J.L. (1981), 'Autonomías regionales y fuerzas políticas en las Cortes constituyentes de 1931', *Sistema*, 40.
Graziani, A. (1979), *L'Economia Italiana dal 1945 a Oggi*, 2nd edition (Bologna: Il Mulino).
Graziano, L. (1984), *Clientilismo e Sistema Político. Il caso italiano* (Milan: Franco Angelo).
Green, V.H.H. (1965), *Renaissance and Reformation. Survey of European History between 1450 and 1660*, 2nd edition (London:

Edward Arnold).
Grémion, P. (1976), *Le Pouvoir Périphique. Bureaucrates et notables dans le système politique français* (Paris: Seuil).
—— (1981), 'Régionalisation, régionalisme, municipalisation sous la Ve république', *Le Débat*, 16.
Grémion, P. and Worms, J–P. (1975), 'The French regional planning experiments', in Hayward, J. and Watson, M. (eds), *Planning, Politics and Public Policy. The British, French and Italian Experience* (Cambridge University Press).
Grew, R. (1963), *A Sterner Plan for Italian Unity. The Italian National Society in the Risorgimento* (Princeton: Princeton University Press).
Guiral, P. (1977), chapter in Gras, G. and Livet, G. (eds), *Régions et Régionalisme en France* (Paris: Presses Universitaires de France).
Guillorel, H. (1981), 'Le Mouvement Breton', *Pouvoirs*, 19.
Gunter, R., Sani, G. and Shabad, G. (1986), *Spain After Franco. The Making of a Competitive Party System* (Berkeley: University of California Press).
Gyford, J. (1985), *The Politics of Local Socialism* (London: Allen and Unwin).
HLL (1916), *Highland Land League, Annual Report, 1916*.
Hachey, T. (1977), *Britain and Irish Separatism* (Chicago: Rand McNally).
Hanham, H.J. (1969), *Scottish Nationalism* (London: Faber).
Harvie, C. (1977), *Scotland and Nationalism. Scottish Society and Politics, 1707–1977* (London: Allen and Unwin).
Hayward, J. (1969), 'From functional regionalism to functional representation in France: The Battle of Brittany', *Political Studies*, XVII.
—— (1975), 'Change and choice: the agenda of planning', in Hayward, J. and Watson, M. (eds), *Planning, Politics and Public Policy. The British, French and Italian Experience* (Cambridge University Press).
—— (1979), 'Interest groups and the demand for state action' in Hayward, J. and Berki, R. (eds), *State and Society in Contemporary Europe* (Oxford: Martin Robertson).
—— (1981), 'France: histoire d'un échec', *Pouvoirs*, 19.
—— (1983), *Governing France: The One and Indivisible Republic*, 2nd edition (London: Weidenfeld and Nicolson).
—— (1986), *The State and the Market Economy. Industrial Patriotism and Economic Interventionism in France* (Brighton: Harvester Press).
Heald, D. (1983), *Public Expenditure* (Oxford: Martin Robertson).

Hebbert, M. (1987), 'Regionalism: a reform concept and its application to Spain', *Environment and Planning C. Government and Policy*, 5.

Hechter, M. (1975), *Internal Colonialism. The Celtic Fringe in British National Development, 1536–1966* (London: Routledge and Kegan Paul).

Hechter, M. (1985), 'Internal colonialism revisited', in Tiriakian, E.A. and Rogowski, R. (eds), *New Nationalisms of the Developed West* (Boston: Allen and Unwin).

Hepburn, A.C. (1980), *The Conflict of Nationality in Modern Ireland* (New York: St Martin's Press).

Hernández Lafuente, A. (1980), *Autonomía y integración en la segunda república* (Madrid: Encuentro).

Hernández, F. and Mercadé, F. (1983), 'Sociología del nacionalismo catalán', *Revista Internacional de Sociología*, XLI.45.

────── (1986), *Estructuras sociales y cuestión nacional en España* (Barcelona: Ariel).

Hunter, J. (1975), 'The Gaelic connection: Highlands, Ireland and Nationalism, 1873–1922', *Scottish Historical Review*, 59.

ICS (1975), *Compendio Statistico Italiano* (Rome: Istituto Centrale di Statistica).

Indovina, F. (1973), 'Le forze sociali e l'uso dell'ente regionale', in Rotelli, E. (ed.), *Dal regionalismo alla regione* (Bologna: Il Mulino).

Ingrao, P. (1973), 'Regioni per unire' in Rotelli, E. (ed.), *Dal regionalismo alla regione* (Bologna: Il Mulino).

Jiménez Blanco, J. (1977), *La conciencia regional en España* (Madrid: Centro de Investigaciones Sociológicas).

Johnson, R.W. (1981), *The Long March of the French Left* (London: Macmillan).

Jones, J.B. and Keating, M. (1982), 'The British Labour Party: Centralisation and devolution', in Madgwick, P. and Rose, R. (eds), *The Territorial Dimension in United Kingdom Politics* (London: Macmillan).

────── (1985), *Labour and the British State* (Oxford: Clarendon).

────── (1987), 'Beyond the Doomsday scenario. Governing Scotland and Wales in the 1980s', *Strathclyde Papers in Government and Politics* (Glasgow: University of Strathclyde).

Jones, J.B. and Wilford, R. (1986), *Parliament and Territoriality. The Committee on Welsh Affairs, 1979–83* (Cardiff: University of Wales Press).

Keating, M. (1975), *The Role of the Scottish MP*, Ph.D. thesis, CNAA.

────── (1976), 'Administrative devolution in practice. The Secretary of State for Scotland and the Scottish Office', *Public Administration*, 54.2.

────── (1985a), 'Whatever happened to regional government?', *Local Government Studies*, 11.6.

────── (1985b), 'Bureaucracy devolved', *Times Educational Supplement (Scotland)*, 5 April.

────── (1986a), 'Europeanism and regionalism', in Keating, M. and Jones, J.B. (eds), *Regions in the European Community* (Oxford University Press).

────── (1986b), 'Revendication et lamentation. The failure of regional nationalism in Languedoc', *Journal of Area Studies*, 16.

────── (1978), 'Parliamentary behaviour as a test of Scottish integration into the United Kingdom', *Legislative Studies Quarterly*, III.3.

────── (1988a), 'Does regional government work? The experience of Italy, France and Spain', *Governance*, 1.2.

────── (1988b), *The City that Refused to Die* (Aberdeen: Aberdeen University Press).

Keating, M. and Bleiman, D. (1979), *Labour and Scottish Nationalism* (London: Macmillan).

Keating, M. and Boyle, R. (1986), *Remaking Urban Scotland. Strategies for Local Economic Development* (Edinburgh University Press).

Keating, M. and Jones, B. (1986), *Regions in the European Community* (Oxford: Clarendon).

Keating, M. and Hainsworth, P. (1986), *Decentralisation and Change in Contemporary France* (Aldershot: Gower).

Keating, M. and Lindley, P. (1981), 'Devolution. The Scotland and Wales Bills', *Public Administration Bulletin*, 37.

Keating, M. and Midwinter, A. (1983), *The Government of Scotland* (Edinburgh: Mainstream).

Keating, M. and Rhodes, M. (1982), 'The status of regional government: An analysis of the West Midlands', in Hogwood, B. and Keating, M. (eds), *Regional Government in England* (Oxford University Press).

Kedourie, E. (1966), *Nationalism*, 3rd edition (London: Hutchinson).

Kee, R. (1976), *The Green Flag* (London: Quartet).

Kellas, J. (1986), *The Scottish Political System*, 3rd edition (Cambridge: Cambridge University Press).

King, R.L. (1987), 'Regional government: the Italian experience', *Environment and Planning C. Government and Policy*, 5.

LPSC (1919), Labour Party, Scottish Council, *Annual Report, 1916*, (Glasgow).
—— (1926), Labour Party, Scottish Council, *Annual Report, 1926*, (Glasgow).
Lafont, R. (1967), *La Révolution Régionaliste* (Paris: Gallimard).
—— (1972), 'Région, Occitanie, quelques perspectives', in *La régionalisation, espoirs ou illusions?* (Wanquetin: Mouvement d'Action Rurale).
Lebesque, M. (1970), *Comment Peut-on Être Breton?* (Paris: Seuil).
Lerner, H. (1980), Être de gauche dans le Midi' in G. Cholvy (ed.), *Histoire du Languedoc, de 1900 à nos jours* (Toulouse: Privat).
Levi, M. and Hechter, M. (1985), 'A Rational Approach to the Rise and Decline of Ethnoregionalist Parties', in Tiriakian, E.A. and Rogowski, R. (eds), *New Nationalisms of the Developed West* (Boston: Allen and Unwin).
Lemarchand, R. (1981), 'Comparative political clientilism: Structure, process and optic', in Eisenstadt, S.N. and Lemarchand, R. (eds), *Political Clientilism, Patronage and Development* (London: Sage).
Lindley, P. (1982), 'The framework of regional planning 1964–1980' in Hogwood, B. and Keating, M. (eds), *Regional Government in England* (Oxford University Press).
Linz, J. (1973), 'Early state building and late peripheral nationalism against the state: The case of Spain', in Eisenstadt, S.N. and Rokkan, S. (eds), *Building States and Nations* (Beverly Hills: Sage).
Lijphart, A. (1977), 'Political theories and the explanation of ethnic conflict in the western world: Falsified predictions and plausible postdictions', in Esman, M.J. (ed.), *Ethnic Conflict in the Western World* (Ithaca: Cornell University Press).
Lipset, S.M. (1985), 'The revolt against modernity', in *Consensus and Conflict. Essays in Political Sociology* (New Brunswick: Transaction).
Lipset, S.M. and Rokkan, S. (1967), 'Cleavage structures, party systems and voter alignments', in Lipset, S.M. and Rokkan, S. (eds), *Party Systems and Voter Alignments* (New York: Free Press).
Llera, F.J. (1986), 'Procesos estructurales de la sociedad vasca', in Hernández, F. and Mercadé, F., *Estructuras sociales y cuestión nacional en España* (Barcelona: Ariel).
López-Aranguren, E. (1983), *La conociencia regional en el proceso autonómico español* (Madrid: Centro de Investigaciones Sociológicas).

Lopez Rodo, L. (1980), *Las autonomías. Encruijada de España* (Madrid: Aguilar).
Lorca Navarete, J. (1987), *Crónicas políticas de la España actuál. El proceso autonómico andaluz* (Madrid: Piramide).
Lores, J. (1985), *La transicio a Catalunya (1977–1984)*, (Barcelona: Empuries).
Loughlin, J. (1985), 'A new deal for France's regions and linguistic minorities', *West European Politics*, 8.3.
Lucha Occitana (1975), *Milhau-Larzac*, brodadura n.1.
Lyons, F.S.L. (1971), *Ireland Since the Famine* (London: Weidenfeld and Nicolson).
Macdonagh, O. (1977), *Ireland: The Union and Its Aftermath* (London: Allen and Unwin).
MacLaughlin, J. (1986), 'The political geography of "nation-building" and nationalism in social sciences: structural vs. dialectical accounts', *Political Geography Quarterly*, 5.4.
Machin, H. (1977), *The Prefect in French Public Administration* (London: Croom Helm).
Madgwick, P. and Rawkins, P. (1982), 'The Welsh language in the policy process', in Madgwick, P. and Rose, R. (eds), *The Territorial Dimension in United Kingdom Politics* (London: Macmillan).
Maíz, R. (1986), 'El nacionalismo gallego: apuntes para la historia de una hegemonia imposible', in Hernández, F. and Mercadé, F., *Estructuras sociales y cuestión nacional en España* (Barcelona: Ariel).
Mangiatordi, B. (1985), 'Le regioni nel dibattito e nella ricerca', *Democrazia e Diritto*, XXV.1.
Martin Oviedo, J.M. (1980), 'El regimen constitucional de las comunidades autónomas', *Revista de Estudios Políticos*, 18.
Marx, K. and Engels, F. (1966), *The Communist Manifesto* (Moscow: Progress).
Mayo, P. Elton (1974), *The Roots of Identity. Three National Movements in Contemporary Politics* (London: Allen Lane).
Médard, J–F. (1981), 'Political clientilism in France: The center–periphery nexus reexamined', in Eisenstadt, S.N. and Lemarchand, R. (eds), *Political Clientilism, Patronage and Development* (London: Sage).
Mény, Y. (1974), *Centralisation et décentralisation dans le débat politique français (1945–69)* (Paris: Pichon et Duran-Auzias).
—— (1981), 'Crises, régions et modernisation de l'état', *Pouvoirs*, 19.
—— (1982a), 'Introduction', in Mény, Y. (ed.), *Dix Ans de*

Régionalisation en Europe. Bilan et Perspectives (Paris: Cujas).
―――― (1982b), 'Les relations État-Régions en France: l'échange inégal', in Mény, Y. (ed.), *Dix Ans de Régionalisation en Europe. Bilan et Perspectives* (Paris: Cujas).
Mercadé, F. (1982), *Cataluña: intelectuales, políticos y cuestión nacional* (Barcelona: Peninsula).
Merloni, F. (1982), 'Le Processus de création des régions en Italie', in Mény, Y. (ed.), *Dix Ans de Régionalisation en Europe. Bilan et Perspectives* (Paris: Cujas).
Merloni, F. (1985), 'Perché è in crisi il regionalismo', *Democrazia e Diritto*, XXV.1.
Miguelez Lobo, F. (1984), 'Sindicalismo y reconstrucción de Catalunya', *Papers*, 21.
Miller, W. (1981), *The End of British Politics? Scots and English Political Behaviour in the Seventies* (Oxford: Clarendon).
Miller, W., Sarlvick, B., Crewe, I. and Alt, J. (1977), 'The connection between SNP voting and the demand for Scottish self-government', *European Journal of Political Research*, 5.
Modica, E. (1972), *I Communisti per le Autonomie* (Rome: Edizioni per le autonomie e i poteri locali).
Moreno, E. and Marti, E. (1979), *Catalunya para Españoles* (Barcelona: Dopesa).
Morgan, K. (1980), *Wales in British Politics, 1868–1922*, 3rd edn (Cardiff: University of Wales Press).
Morgan, K. (1982), *Rebirth of a Nation. Wales, 1880–1980* (Oxford: Oxford University Press).
Morgan, P. (1986), 'Keeping the Legends Alive' in Curtis, T. (ed.), *Wales: The Imagined Nation* (Bridgend: Poetry Wales Press).
Morisi, M. (1982) 'L'osservazione "Politologica": alcune preliminari esigenze di ricerca sull'esperienza regionale', *Le Regioni*, X.6.
Mousnier, R. (1984), *The Institutions of France under the Absolute Monarchy, 1598–1789* (Chicago: University of Chicago Press).
Nairn, I. (1981), *The Break-Up of Britain. Crisis and Neo-Nationalism*, 2nd edition (London: Verso).
Neilsson, G. (1985), 'States and "nation-groups". A global taxonomy', in Tiriakian, E.A. and Rogowski, R. (eds), *New Nationalisms of the Developed West* (Boston: Allen and Unwin).
O'Callaghan, M.J.C. (1983), *Separatism in Brittany* (Redruth: Dyllansow Truran).
Olábarri Gortazar, I. (1981), 'La cuestión regional en España, 1808–1939', in Acosta España, R. (ed.), *La España de las Autonomías*, Tomo 1 (Madrid: Espasa-Calpe).
Oltra, B., Mercadé, F. and Hernández, F. (1981), *La Ideología*

Nacional Catalana (Barcelona: Anagrama).
Osmond, J. (1977), *Creative Conflict. The Politics of Welsh Devolution* (Llandysul: Gomer).
Pais Occitan (1978), prima.
Page, E. (1978), 'Michael Hechter's internal colonial thesis: some theoretical and methodological problems', *European Journal of Political Research*, 6.3.
Palard, J. (1982), *L'Identité Régionale. L'EPR et l'intégration régionale en Aquitaine* (Bordeaux: CERVL).
Parti Socialiste (1981), *La France au Pluriel* (Paris: Entente).
Pastori, G. (1980), 'Le regioni senza regionalismo', *Il Mulino*, 268.
―――― (1982), 'Gli studi di diritto amministrativo in materia regionale', *Le Regioni*, X.6.
Phlipponneau, M. (1977), 'La Gauche et le régionalisme', in Gras, G. and Livet, G. (eds), *Régions et Régionalisme en France* (Paris: Presses Universitaires de France).
―――― (1981), *Décentralisation et Régionalisation. La Grande Affaire* (Paris: Calmann-Levy).
Pi-Sunyer, O. (1985), 'Catalan nationalism. Some theoretical and historical considerations', in Tiriakian, E.A. and Rogowski, R. (eds), *New Nationalisms of the Developed West* (Boston: Allen and Unwin).
Poggi, G. (1978), *The Development of the Modern State. A Sociological Introduction* (London: Hutchinson).
Polese, M. (1985), 'Economic integration, national policies and the rationality of regional separation', in Tiriakian, E.A. and Rogowski, R. (eds), *New Nationalisms of the Developed West* (Boston: Allen and Unwin).
Porras Nadales, A. (1980), 'El referendum de iniciativa autonómica del 28 de febrero en Andalucía', *Revista de Estudios Políticos*, 15.
―――― (1984), 'Geografía electoral de Andalucía, *Revista Española de Investigaciones Sociológicas*, 28.
――――(1985), *Geografía electoral de Andalucía* (Madrid: Centro de Investigaciones Sociológicas).
(Madrid: Centro de Investigaciones Sociológicas).
Portelli, H. (1980), *Le Socialisme Français tel qu'il est* (Paris: Presses Universitaires de France).
Prescott, J. (1983), *Alternative Regional Strategy* (London: Parliamentary Spokesman's Group).
Prodi, R. (1985), 'Luigi Sturzo e l'intervento dello stato in economia', *Il Mulino*, XXXIV.
Pujol, J. (1976), *Una política per Catalunya* (Barcelona: Nova Terra).

Putnam, R., Leonardi, R. and Nanetti, R. (1985), *La Pianta e le Radici. Il radicamemto dell'istituto regionale nel sistema politico italiano* (Bologna: Il Mulino).
Reece, J.E. (1977), *The Bretons against France. Ethnic Minority Nationalism in Twentieth Century Brittany* (Chapel Hill: University of North Carolina Press).
Richardson, H.W. (1975), *Regional Development Policy and Planning in Spain* (London: Saxon House).
Rocard, (1981), 'La Région, une idée neuve pour la gauche', *Pouvoirs*, 19.
Rodriguez de la Borbolla, J. (1986), *Desde Andalucía* (Seville: Andaluzas Unidas).
Rogowski, R. (1985), 'Causes and varieties of nationalism. A rationalist account', in Tiriakian, E.A. and Rogowski, R. (eds), *New Nationalisms of the Developed West* (Boston: Allen and Unwin).
Roiz Celix, M. (1984), 'Los límites de la modernización en la estructura social de Cataluña y Euskadi', *Revista Española de Investigaciones Sociológicas*, 25.
Rokkan, S. (1981), 'Territories, nations, parties: Towards a geoeconomic–geopolitical model for the explanation of variations within western Europe', in Merrit, R.L. and Russett, B.R. (eds), *From National Development to Global Community* (London: Allen and Unwin).
Rokkan, S. and Urwin, D. (eds) (1982), *The Politics of Territorial Identity. Studies in European Regionalism* (London: Sage).
—— (1983), *Economy, Territory, Identity. Politics of West European Peripheries* (London: Sage).
Romano, S. (1977) *Histoire de l'Italie du Risorgimento à nos jours* (Paris: Seuil).
Rose, R. (1982a), *Understanding the United Kingdom. The Territorial Dimension in Government* (London: Longman).
—— (1982b), 'Is the United Kingdom a state? Northern Ireland as a test case', in Madgwick, P. and Rose, R. (eds), *The Territorial Dimension in United Kingdom Politics* (London: Macmillan).
Rose, R. and Urwin, D. (1975), 'Regional differentiation and political unity in western nations', *Professional Papers in Contemporary Political Sociology*, 06–007 (London: Sage).
Ross, J. (1981), 'The Secretary of State for Scotland and the Scottish Office', *Studies in Public Policy*, 87 (Glasgow: University of Strathclyde).
Rotelli, E. (1973), 'Dal regionalismo alla regione', in Rotelli, E. (ed.), *Dal regionalismo alla regione* (Bologna: Il Mulino).

Rudolph, J.R. and Thompson, R.J. (1985), 'Ethnoterritorial movements and the policy process', *Comparative Politics*, 17.3.
Ruffilli, R. (1970), 'La tradizione regionalista: crisi e rinnovamento', *Vita e Pensero*, 3.
SPS (1984), *Rapporto sullo Stato dei Potere Locali* (Rome: Sistema Permanente di Servizi).
Sadran, P. (1982), 'La régionalisation française: esquisse d'un bilan', in Mény, Y. (ed.), *Dix Ans de Régionalisation en Europe. Bilan et Perspectives* (Paris: Cujas).
Saenz de Buruaga, G. (1984), 'La planificación nacional y regional en la España de las autonomías', *Estudios Regionales*, 13.
Selan, V. and Donnini, R. (1975), 'Regional planning in Italy', in Hayward, J. and Watson, M. (eds), *Planning, Politics and Public Policy. The British, French and Italian Experience* (Cambridge University Press).
Salerno, G. (1983), 'Governo, Parlamento, Regioni ed Enti Locali', in *Annuario 1983 delle autonomie locali* (Roma: Edizioni delle Autonomie).
Salvadori, M. (1976), *La questione meridionale* (Turin: Loescher).
Salvemini, G. (1978), 'La questione meridionale', in *Educazione política*, December 1898, reprinted in V. Lo Curto (ed.), *La questione meridionale*, 2nd edition (Florence: G. D'Anna).
Santos, J.M. de los (1985), 'La conciencia andalucista', in *Nacionalismo y Regionalismo en España* (Cordoba: Diputación Provincial).
Sevilla Guzmán, E. (1986), 'Estructura social y identidad andaluza', in Hernández, F. and Mercadé, F. (eds), *Estructuros Sociales y Cuestión Nacional en España* (Barcelona: Ariel).
Shils, E. (1975), *Center and Periphery. Essays in Macrosociology* (Chicago: University of Chicago Press).
Smelser, N. (1966), 'Mechanisms of Change and Adjustment to Change', in Finkle, J.L. and Gable, R.W. (eds), *Political Development and Social Change* (New York: Wiley).
Smith, A.D. (1982), 'Nationalism, ethnic separatism and the intelligentsia', in Williams, C.H. (ed.), *National Separatism* (Cardiff: University of Wales Press).
Smith, A.D. (1971), *Theories of Nationalism* (London: Duckworth).
—— (1981), *The Ethnic Revival* (Cambridge: Cambridge University Press).
Smith, D. Mack (ed.) (1968a), The Making of Italy, 1796–1870 (London: Macmillan).
—— (1968b), *A History of Sicily. Modern Sicily after 1713* (London: Chatto and Windus).
—— (ed.) (1969), *Garibaldi* (Englewood Cliffs: Prentice Hall).

Solé Tura, J. (1985), *Nacionalidades y Nacionalismos en España. Autonomías, Federalismo, Autodeterminación* (Madrid: Alianza).
SPELEO (1985), *Le Languedoc–Roussillon fait son plan* (Aix-en-Provence: Edisud).
Stephens, M. (1976), *Linguistic Minorities in Western Europe* (Llandysul: Gomer).
Strubell, M. (1984), 'Evolución sociolinguistica a Catalunya', *Papers*, 21.
Sturzo, L. (1978), review of Dorso's *La rivoluzione meridionale*, reprinted in V. Lo Curto (ed.), *La questione meridionale*, 2nd edition (Florence: G. D'Anna).
Suarez Fernandez, L. (1981), 'Los raices históricas de la pluralidad', in Acosta España, R. (ed.), *La España de las Autonomías*, Tomo 1 (Madrid: Espasa-Calpe).
Tarrow, S. (1967), *Peasant Communism in Southern Italy* (New Haven: Yale University Press).
―――― (1977), *Between Center and Periphery. Grassroots Politicians in Italy and France* (New Haven and London: Yale University Press).
―――― (1978), 'Regional policy, ideology and peripheral defense. The case of Fos-sur-Mer', in Tarrow, S., Katzenstein, P.J. and Graziano, L. (eds), *Territorial Politics in Industrial Nations* (New York: Praeger).
Tezanos, J.F. (1984), 'Cambio social y modernización en la España actual', Revista Española de Investigaciones Sociológicas, 28.
Tilly, C. (1964), *The Vendée* (London: Edward Arnold).
Tiriakian, E.A. and Nevitte, N. (1985), 'Nationalism and modernity', in Tiriakian, E.A. and Rogowski, R. (eds), *New Nationalisms of the Developed West* (Boston: Allen and Unwin).
Torchia, L. (1984), 'La collaborazione fra stato e regioni nella politica di intervento straordinario del Mezzogiorno', *Le Regioni*, 5.
Torrealday, J.M. (1980), 'Territorio, Lengua y Migraciones en Euskadi', in Centre Internacional per a les minories etniques i nacionals, *Nactionalia V. Quartes Jornadadas de Ciemen, Abadia de Cuisca, 16–23 d'agost 1979* (Publicacions de l'Abadia de Montserrat).
Touraine, A., Dubet, F. and Hegedus, Z. (1981), *Le pays contre l'État. Luttes occitanes* (Paris: Seuil).
Trempé, R. (1980), 'Les industries d'un pays rural', in G. Cholvy (ed.), *Histoire du Languedoc, de 1900 à nos jours* (Toulouse: Privat).
Trias Fargas, R. (1972), *Introducción a la economía de Cataluña*

(Madrid: Alianza).
Tribunal Constitucional (1985), *Repertorio Aranzadi del Tribunal Constitucional* (Pamplona: Aranzadi).
Ulmo, Y. (1975), 'France' in Hayward, J. and Watson, M. (eds), *Planning, Politics and Public Policy. The British, French and Italian Experience* (Cambridge University Press).
Vallverdú, F. (1980), 'La Lengua Catalana' in Centre Internacional per a les minories etniques i nacionals, *Nactionalia V. Quartes Jornadadas de Ciemen, Abadia de Cuisca, 16–23 d'agost 1979* (Publicacions de l'Abadia de Montserrat).
Varela, S. (1976), *El problema regional en la segunda república española* (Madrid: Union).
Vasquez de Prada, V. (1981), 'La epoca moderna: Los siglos XVI a XIX', in Acosta España, R. (ed.), *La España de las Autonomías*, Tomo 1 (Madrid: Espasa–Calpe).
Vilariño, P. and Sequeiros, J.L. (1986), 'Determinantes sociales de la identidad nacional de Galicia', in Hernández, F. and Mercadé, F., *Estructuras Sociales y Cuestión nacional en España* (Barcelona: Ariel).
Villari, M. (1981), 'La Cassa per il Mezzogiorno e il problema dell'autonomia regionale', in Mori, G. (ed.), *Autonomismo meridionale: ideologia, politica e istituzioni* (Bologna: Il Mulino).
Villari, R. (1981), 'Autonomismo e Mezzogiorno', in Mori, G. (ed.), *Autonomismo meridionale: ideologia, politica e istituzioni* (Bologna: Il Mulino).
Vincens Vives, J. (1986), *Los catalanes en el siglo XIX* (Madrid: Alianza).
Weber, E. (1977), *Peasants into Frenchmen. The modernisation of rural France* (London: Chatto and Windus).
Welhofer, E.S. (1986), 'Class, territory and party: political change in Britain, 1945–1974', *European Journal of Political Research*, 14.
Wright, M. and Young, S. (1975), 'Regional planning in Britain', in Hayward, J. and Watson, M. (eds), *Planning, Politics and Public Policy. The British, French and Italian Experience* (Cambridge University Press).
Zagarrio, V. (1981), 'La tradizione meridionalista e il dibattito sulle autonomie nel secondo dopoguerra', in Mori, G. (ed.), *Autonomismo meridionale: ideologia, politica e istituzioni* (Bologna: Il Mulino).
Zariski, R. (1972), *Italy. The Politics of Uneven Development* (Hinsdale: Dryden).

Index

absolute monarchy, 25, 26, 35–6
Act of Union
　Scotland, 28
　Wales, 27
Agnew, J., 15
agriculture 3, 15, 59, 62, 63, 115, 154, 217
Alava, 145
Algeria, 13
Alianza Popular, 221, 227
Alianza Socialista de Andalucia, 218
Alsace, 34
Alsace-Lorraine, 1, 51, 108
Alto-Adige, 1, 139
An Commun Gaidhealach, 74
Anarchism, 70, 171, 181
anarcho-syndicalism, 93, 100
Andalusia, 10, 23, 60, 61, 102, 106, 145, 165, 217, 223, 226–8, 237, 239
Anglo-Irish agreement, 198
anticlericalism, 68, 69, 76, 100, 110, 111, 112
Aprile, A. Finocchiaro, 138
Aragon, 34, 36, 38, 39, 106
Arana, 101
Armée révolutionnaire breton, 203

Assemblea de Catalunya, 215
Asturias, 106, 212
Austria, 42
Auvergne, 35

Badajoz, 156
Balearic Islands, 36, 39
Barcelona, 70, 99, 101, 222
Basque Country, 10, 23, 36, 38, 39, 51, 52, 59–60, 69, 101–2, 103, 104, 106, 107, 108, 145, 156, 168, 209, 210, 211, 212, 216–17, 220–6, 229, 236, 241, 242, 243
Basque language, 37, 69, 70, 216
Basque Nationalist Party (PNV), 101, 216, 217, 221, 222, 224, 226, 236
Belfast, 84
Blas Infante, 102, 108
blocco agrario, 63, 136
Bonar Law, A., 84
Bonnets rouges, 203
Brand, J., 177
Braudel, F., 33
Bretagne et démocratie, 203
Breton Front, 110
Breuilly, J., 6

Index

Britain, 7, 25, 268, 269, 170
Brittany, 23, 34, 59, 67, 68, 69, 109–10, 151, 162, 171, 200–1, 210, 237, 238, 239
Bulpitt, J., 56, 57
bureaucracy, 20, 22, 26, 49, 119, 132, 133, 160, 163, 174, 243
Burgundy, 33, 34, 35
Burns, R., 74

caciques, 19, 53, 60, 61, 98, 99, 105, 219
Calabria, 234
Calvo Sotelo, 229
Cambó, F., 99
Campaign for a Scottish Assembly, 191, 238
Canada, 8
Canaries, 212
capitalism, 3, 6, 12, 13, 14, 15, 29, 58, 60, 62, 66, 86, 101, 114, 116, 123, 208, 209, 240
Carlism, 52, 69, 98, 102
Carmarthen, 279, 180, 181
Cassa per il Mezzogiorno, 17, 154, 155, 231
Castile, 36, 37
Castilian, 42, 69, 145
Catalan, 37, 41, 69, 145
Catalonia, 10, 12, 23, 34, 36, 37, 38, 52, 59–60, 61–2, 69–70, 77, 98–101, 102, 103, 106–8, 136, 145–6, 156, 165, 168, 171, 211, 212, 213–15, 220–2, 223–5, 237, 241, 243
Catanzaro, 234
Catharism, 34, 111
Catholic Church, 54, 68, 69, 76, 80, 105

Catholicism, 99, 101, 110, 111, 116, 117, 135, 136, 195
Catholics, 81, 85, 112, 131, 145, 192, 194, 199, 213, 217
Cavour, C., 41, 42, 43, 44, 53, 54
centralisation, 21, 47, 49, 52, 53, 55, 104, 135, 208, 211, 212
centre-periphery theories, 2–8, 11, 12, 19, 20, 21, 38
CERES, 210
CFDT, 207
Charlemagne, 33
Chamberlain, J., 87, 93
Charles I, 30
Charles V, 37
Christian Democrats, 135, 136, 139, 140, 141–3, 147, 148, 153, 154, 163, 164, 170, 232–3, 234
Church of Scotland, 28, 73, 87, 88
Churchill, Lord Randolph, 84
circonscriptions d'action régionale, 160, 161
CiU, 222, 224, 237
civil rights, 192–3, 199
civil society, 17, 28
Civil War
  English, 30
  Spanish, 101, 105, 106, 107, 216, 219, 224
Clark, G.B., 88
class, 3, 6, 13, 14, 19, 51, 58, 60, 121, 123, 172, 183, 217, 238
Clavero, M., 227
clientilism, 19, 21, 29, 53, 55, 56, 57, 117, 118, 122, 142, 144, 154, 170, 231, 232
Coalición Galega, 220

CODER, 160, 201
coercion, 81
Colajanni, N., 114
Colbert, 35
colonialism, 30, 37
  internal, 12, 13, 14, 59, 61, 102, 172, 209, 218
Comité d'Etudes et de Liaison des Intérêts Bretons (CELIB), 151, 160, 201–2
Comité occitan d'études et d'action (COEA), 204
commissaires de la république, 243
communes, 49, 50, 152, 161
communications, 3, 6, 11, 50
Communist Party
  Catalan, 215
  French, 132, 133, 202, 205, 207, 209, 239
  Italian, 136, 137, 138, 139, 140, 141, 143, 144, 163k, 169, 170, 232, 239
  Spanish, 215, 218, 220–1, 226, 227
Companys, L., 108
conciertos económicos, 52, 101, 225, 242
Confindustria, 153, 163
Connolly, J., 85
Connor, W., 9
Conservative Party, 82, 83, 84, 127, 130, 147, 149, 150, 159, 180, 183, 185, 186, 187–92, 194, 196, 197
consociationalism, 196
Constitution of Cadiz, 51
Convergència Democratica de Catalunya, 215
Coordinadora de Sortes Politiques, 215
corporatism, 157, 160, 163
Corsica, 109, 209, 235, 241

Covenant movement, 175
Cromwell, Oliver, 31
Cromwell, Thomas, 26
CRPE, 163
culture, 3, 6, 7, 8, 15, 16, 20, 23, 24, 30, 51, 59, 66, 69, 70, 72, 79, 92, 96, 98, 103, 165, 170, 173, 174, 179, 206, 208, 211
Cymru Fydd, 95

Darien venture, 28
DATAR, 151, 162
Dauphiné, 35
Debré, M., 133
decentralisation, 209
  administrative, 21, 174
  political, 52, 110, 134, 135, 141, 163, 202, 240
Declaration of Arbroath, 27
Defferre, G., 201, 204, 207
de Gasperi, 136, 142
de Gaulle, 161, 201, 204
democracy, 2, 7, 17, 49, 50, 240, 244
départements, 49, 50–1, 131–2, 152, 161, 162, 209, 210
deprivation, 11–12, 176
determinism, 4, 6, 8
Deutsch, K., 11
development
  economic, 3, 11, 12, 14
  political, 4, 18
  uneven, 12, 14
devolution
  administrative, 57, 87, 92, 126, 127–8
  political, 96, 97, 125, 177, 178, 182, 183–7, 188, 190, 191–2, 242
Dicey, A.V., 83, 96, 97, 198
diffusionism, 2–6, 11, 12, 13, 16, 19, 38, 66, 121
Diputación, 51

disestablishment, 72, 74, 87, 93, 94
divorce, 233
Dorso, 116, 136
Dublin, 8, 30
Dupuy, 19, 133
Dyson, 134

economic unification, 2, 3, 7, 48, 329
Edinburgh, 28, 128
education, 2, 6, 29, 46, 50, 51, 54, 56, 57, 67, 68, 69, 72, 73, 75, 87, 88, 92, 95, 96, 103, 127, 145, 174, 182, 212
eisteddfod, 72
Ellis, T., 94
empire
  British, 27, 29, 48, 56, 80, 86
  Spanish, 36, 37, 48, 52
emsav, 109, 110
England, 16, 25, 27, 29, 64, 150, 158, 175, 176, 185, 190, 191, 194
Esman, M.J., 16, 17
Esquerra Republicana de Catalunya (ERC), 100, 104, 105, 106, 215, 222
Estado Integral, 107
Estourbeillon, Marquis de, 109
ETA, 216–17, 222, 226, 235, 236
états, 35
ethnicity, 3, 10, 11, 12, 13, 15, 16
ethnonationalism, 9
European Economic Community (EEC), 91, 166, 168, 184, 200, 204, 237
European Regional Development Fund, 167

Evans, G., 179, 189
Extremadura, 60, 212

Falange, 218
famine, 32, 64–5, 80
Fanfani, A., 142, 154
farmers, 3
Fasci, 113, 118
Fascism, 111, 118, 119, 120, 136, 137, 156
federalism, 28, 44, 52, 53, 54, 96, 100, 103, 106, 107, 138, 209, 229, 241, 242
Félibrige, 68, 69, 111, 207
Fenianism, 83
feudalism, 3, 25, 36, 40, 46, 117
Fichte, 47
Fifth Republic, 49, 112, 134
First Republic (Spain), 52
folk song, 171, 177, 202, 213
Folz, W.J., 8
forces vives, 151, 160, 162, 201
Fortunato, G., 113, 114
Fourth Republic, 131, 132, 160
Fraga Iribarne, M., 220
Franchetti and Sonino, 113
France, 10, 13, 19, 23, 25, 27, 33–6, 38, 48, 49–51, 67–8, 108–13, 131–4, 146–8, 151–3, 160–3, 166, 169, 170, 200–11, 241–4
franchise, 29, 31, 48, 56, 65, 93, 95, 96, 114–15, 117, 118, 120
Franco, F., 106, 108, 145, 156, 211, 216, 219, 220, 224
free trade 20, 32, 37, 58, 61, 62, 63, 64, 98, 120, 136
French Revolution, 31, 35, 36, 40, 41, 47, 49
Friuli-Venezia-Giulia, 140

Front de Libération de
  Bretagne (FLB), 202
fueros, 17, 36, 39, 51, 52, 107,
  145, 224, 225

Gaelic, 29, 30, 73, 74, 89
Gaelic Athletic Association, 75
Gaelic League, 75
Galicia, 10, 23, 38, 61, 69, 70,
  98, 106, 107, 145, 211,
  212, 219–20, 223, 226
Gallego, 37, 69, 71, 145, 219
Gambetta, 49
Garantista tradition, 113
Garibaldi, 41, 42–3, 53, 116
Gaullist Party, 132, 134, 151,
  160, 169, 170
Generalitat, 39, 106, 107, 108,
  145, 222
Germany, 8, 33, 46, 58, 108
Gladstone, W.E., 82, 88
Glasgow, 29, 169, 175
Gonzalez, F., 218, 229, 239
Govan, 175, 183
Gramsci, A., 12, 115, 120
Grattan, T., 31
Grémion, P., 19, 133, 162
growth poles, 149, 151, 155

Hamilton, 175
Harvie, C., 73
Hayward, J., 33
Heath, E., 174, 185
Hechter, M., 12, 13, 16
Henry IV, 35
Henry VIII, 26, 30
Herri Batasuna, 217, 224, 225,
  235
Highland Land Law Reform
  Association, 65
Highland Land League, 66,
  89, 90
Highlands, 29, 30, 31, 64–6,
  73

Holland, 46
Holy Roman Empire, 33, 37
Home, Lord, 186
Home Rule, 91, 241
  for Ireland, 73, 81, 82, 83,
    84, 85
  for Scotland, 86–92, 129,
    159, 174–5, 176
  for Wales, 94, 95, 159

identity (territorial), 16, 17,
  19, 24, 31, 48, 51, 52, 67,
  76, 77, 78, 79, 93, 95, 97,
  99, 100, 104, 113, 146,
  171, 173, 176, 177, 181,
  183, 211, 219, 226, 235
ideology, 6, 9, 53, 56, 71, 79,
  99, 125, 172
immigration, 60, 69, 101, 216
industrial revolution, 11, 23
industrialisation, 3, 12, 14, 40,
  58–64, 70, 84, 98, 101,
  102, 121, 145, 151, 153,
  154–5, 156, 162, 217
Institut d'Etudes Occitans, 203
integration, 2–3, 4, 5, 6, 11,
  12, 17, 18, 19, 22, 24, 38,
  41, 45, 92, 121, 123, 95
intendants, 35
intergovernmental relations,
  241, 243
internment, 193, 197
Ireland, 1, 8, 13, 16, 23, 30–3,
  47, 57, 63–6, 75–6, 80–6,
  88, 96, 97, 125, 130–1,
  171, 192–200, 236
Irish National League, 65
Irish Parliamentary Party, 65,
  81, 82, 84, 178
Irish Republican Army (IRA),
  193, 195, 197, 198, 199,
  217, 235, 236
Irish Republican Brotherhood
  (IRB), 83, 85

Irish Volunteers, 84, 85
irredentism, 10, 108, 135, 192, 230
Isola, 114
Italy, 10, 19, 23, 25, 40–5, 48, 53–5, 76–7, 78, 113–20, 135–44, 146, 153–4, 163–4, 166, 168, 169, 230–4, 239, 241–4

Jacobinism, 19, 44, 47, 48, 50, 52, 53, 54, 68, 100, 102, 106, 123, 131, 132, 133, 135, 136, 141, 207, 210, 218, 220, 237
Jacobitism, 28, 29, 31, 52, 73, 98
Jaén, 156
jefes, 51
Johnston, T., 89, 127
Juegos Florales, 69
Justices of the Peace, 26

kailyard school, 74
Kedourie, E., 46, 47
Kellas, J., 129

labour movements, 3, 87, 88, 91, 93, 95, 122–3, 124
Labour Party, 57, 74, 84, 89–90, 91–2, 125, 126, 127, 130, 131, 146, 149, 157, 169, 174, 176, 178, 180, 181, 182–6, 187–92, 194, 197, 198, 239, 240
Lafont, R., 12, 13, 161, 204, 205, 206
land issue, 30, 58, 59, 61, 63, 64–6, 81, 82, 83, 88, 89, 90, 102, 107, 114, 115, 116, 118, 121, 135, 136, 139, 140, 154, 156
Land League, 65

language, 3, 16, 20, 24, 66, 67, 171, 173, 174
  in France, 35, 50–1, 67–8, 200, 202, 203–4, 208, 209, 211
  in Ireland, 32, 75
  in Italy, 40–1, 54, 76–7
  in Scotland, 73–4
  in Spain, 37, 38, 69, 70, 98, 99, 101, 145, 211, 213, 220, 222
  in Wales, 27, 71–2, 179, 180, 181, 182, 189
Languedoc, 23, 51, 59, 112, 152, 162, 168, 210, 239
Larzac, 204–5, 206
Latin, 41
Lebesque, M., 203
Leon, 36
Lerroux, A., 100, 104
Liberal Party
  Britain, 57, 82, 84, 87, 88, 89, 92, 93, 94, 95
  Italy, 118, 119, 137, 140
liberalism, 4, 5
Lijphart, A., 11, 14
Lipset, S.M., 6, 7
Lliga Catalana, 98–9
Lliga Regionalista, 99, 100, 103, 104, 105
Lloyd George, D., 94, 95
LOAPA, 228–9, 241
local government, 51, 53, 54, 55, 56, 92, 122, 125, 127, 128, 150, 151, 157, 158, 159–60, 161, 162, 163, 168, 169, 174, 233, 243
LOFCA, 228
Loi Deixonne, 211
Lombardy, 42, 62, 136
London, 8, 26, 30
Louis XIV, 39
Lutte occitane, 204, 206

MacLaughlin, J., 6
McCusker, H., 194
machine politics, 21, 53, 98, 120, 154, 155, 169, 232
Macià, F., 101
Madrid, 37, 60, 61, 102, 103, 156, 212, 214, 223, 225
Mafia, 55, 118, 137, 138, 155
Mallorca, 106
Mancomunitat, 100, 103, 145
markets, 3, 114
Marxism, 5–6, 7, 13, 100, 239
Mazzini, G., 41, 46, 47, 53
Médard, J.-F., 20
Mendès-France, P., 207
meridionalità, 77
Mezzogiorno, 12, 23, 43, 55, 77, 102, 113–20, 136, 140–4, 149, 154, 155, 168, 230, 239
military force, 4, 38
MIS, 233
Mistral, F., 68, 111
Mitterrand, F., 205, 207, 208
modernisation, 3, 4, 6, 17, 18, 19, 66–7, 77–8, 96, 103, 121, 122, 124, 149, 151, 153, 162, 201, 218, 219, 227, 235, 244
Monnet, J., 147
Montpellier, 205
Montserrat, 69, 213
Mouvement pour l'Organisation de la Bretagne (MOB), 202–3
Movimento per l'Independenza Siciliana (MIS), 138, 139
Movimiento, 164, 165, 170
Muirhead, R., 92
Murcia, 212
Mussolini, B., 137

Nairn, T., 6, 14

Nantes, 162, 210
Naples, 41, 42, 62, 155, 233
Napoleon I, 49, 69
Napoleon III, 42
nation-building, 6, 9, 11, 37, 39, 50, 79
National Front, 211
National League of Producers, 61
nationalisation, 211, 239
nationalism, 1, 9, 10, 13, 24, 26, 32, 40, 42, 45, 46–8, 50, 60, 66, 70, 76, 79, 82, 84, 95, 98, 101, 206, 235, 237
nationality, 10
nation-building, 6
nation-state, 5, 32
Navarre, 36, 37, 38, 39, 52, 105, 145, 224, 225, 242, 243
Neilsson, G., 16
Nice, 34, 41, 42
Nitti, 114
Normandy, 35, 162
Normans, 30
notables, 19, 20, 50, 53, 59, 112, 132, 133, 134, 151, 160, 161, 162, 168, 204, 210
notabili, 19, 140, 141, 142, 154
Nueva Planta, 39

O'Connell, D., 81
Occitan, 51, 67, 203–4
Occitania, 33, 34, 35, 59, 68, 111–12, 203–7, 237
Occitania, 33, 34, 35, 59, 88, 111–12, 203–7, 237
oil, North Sea, 176, 178, 183, 187
Olivares, 38
Omnium Cultural, 213

organisational analysis, 19, 20, 133
Ortega y Gasset, 105
Ossian, 73

Pact of San Sebastian, 104, 105, 106
Paisley, I., 193
Palermo, 155
Papacy, Pope, 34, 38, 109
Paris, 58, 151, 152, 205
parlements, 35, 49
Parliament
  British, 26, 28, 83, 128–9
  French, 134
  Irish, 30, 31
  Italian, 55, 118
  Scots, 27, 39
Parliament for Wales Campaign, 181
Parnell, C.S., 81, 83
Parti nationaliste breton, 110
Parti Nationaliste Occitan, 206
participation, 171, 181, 244
Partido Socialista de Andalucia (PSA), 218, 227, 228
Partido Popular Gallego, 218
parties, 7, 19, 20, 22, 121, 122, 163, 173, 212, 232, 238, 243
Partit Socialista de Catalunya, 215, 221
Partito d'Azione, 136, 137
Partito Popolare, 76, 116, 135, 140
Partito Sardo d'Azione, 120, 139
patronage, 19, 21, 29, 53, 55, 82, 112, 117, 118, 126, 142, 143, 154, 169, 170, 232
peasantry, 59, 61, 63, 64, 68, 75, 80, 81, 82, 96, 101, 102, 110, 112, 115, 116, 118, 120, 135, 136, 139, 140, 205
Philip IV, 38
Philip V, 39
Phlipponneau, M., 161, 201, 208
Piedmont, 41, 42, 43, 44, 62, 120
Plaid Cymru, 179–82, 237
planning
  indicative, 148, 156
  national, 156, 211, 242–3
  regional, 24, 124, 155, 157–65
  urban, 155
Pleven, R., 201
pluralism, 20, 211, 239
Pompidou, G., 161, 162, 205
Portugal, 36, 38
Poyning's Law, 30
Prat de la Riba, 99, 103
prefects
  France, 49, 50, 132, 133, 160, 161
  Italy, 54, 55, 243
Prescott, J., 191, 242
Prevention of Terrorism Act, 198
Primo de Rivera, 99, 100, 104
Prince of Wales, 181
protectionism, 20, 32, 37, 44, 59, 60, 62, 63, 98, 99, 114, 115, 145, 148, 207, 214
Protestants in Ireland, 76, 81, 84, 85, 86, 193, 194–5, 196, 198, 199
Provence, 35, 162
Prussia, 42
PSOE, 100, 101, 103, 104, 105, 106, 215, 217, 218, 220, 222, 224, 225, 226, 227, 228, 239
PSUC, 221

Pujol, J., 165, 214, 215, 221
Pym, F., 186

race, 16
Reconquista, 36
Redmond, C., 84, 85
Reformation, 27, 30
regeneracionistas, 52
Reggio Calabria, 233–4
Regional Economic Planning Boards, 158
Regional Economic Planning Councils, 157–9
regional government, 24, 52, 161, 162, 163–4, 173, 174, 210, 231, 232, 233, 240–4
regional planning, 24, 124, 155, 157–65
regional policies, 20, 24, 58, 124, 127, 147–56, 167, 168, 208, 231
regionalism, 9, 10, 18, 22, 24, 53, 98, 100, 102, 109, 110, 113, 122, 131, 161, 206, 211, 212, 220, 230, 235, 237–40, 239
religion, 3, 7, 16, 30, 31, 34, 38, 51, 53, 64, 66, 67, 70, 71, 72, 75, 84, 93, 95, 96, 98, 109, 120, 179
Renaixenca, 69
representation, territorial, 19, 21, 25, 62, 79, 113, 119, 120, 124, 129, 151, 157, 166, 167–71, 204, 242
Republic of Ireland, 193, 194, 195, 198–9, 236
Richelieu, Cardinal, 35
Rifkind, M., 189
Rising of 1916, 85
Risorgimento, 40, 41, 77, 117
Rocard, M., 208
Rokkan, S., 6, 7, 67

romanticism, 30, 69, 70, 72, 76, 77, 86, 103
Rome, 42, 55, 117, 118, 231
Rose, R., 8, 10
Roussillon, 34, 162
Royal Commission on the Constitution, 159–60, 182–3

Salvemini, G., 114, 115, 120
Saraceno, P., 153
Sardinia, 41, 118, 119–20, 136, 139, 140
saupoudrage, 162
Savoy, 34, 42
Scotland, 10, 13, 19, 23, 27–30, 57, 63–6, 73–4, 86–92, 96, 97, 127, 157, 159, 168, 170, 171, 172, 174–8, 182–92, 244
Scotland Act, 184–7, 241, 242, 243
Scots language, 73
Scott, Sir W., 73, 74
Scottish Council (Development and Industry), 150
Scottish Development Agency, 188
Scottish Home Rule Association, 88, 90, 91, 92
Scottish National Party (SNP), 92, 174–8, 186, 187, 192, 236
Scottish Office, 92, 127–30, 149, 150, 157, 159, 184, 188–9, 190
Scottish Trades Union Congress, 89, 90
secession, 2, 3, 47, 241
Second Empire, 50
Second Republic (Spain), 102, 103, 104–7, 221, 223, 224, 225
Second World War, 11

Secretary (of State) for
  Scotland, 87, 91, 127–9,
  183, 184, 194, 243
Secretary of State for Wales,
  183, 184, 190, 243
secularism, 4, 70, 109, 196,
  244
self-determination, 9, 46, 47
separatism, 9, 10, 20, 54, 60,
  90, 96, 100, 101, 102,
  103, 107, 110, 117, 120,
  135, 137–8, 139, 172,
  177, 178, 185, 192, 209,
  224, 235, 237, 238, 240
Servan-Schreiber, J-J., 207
Sicily, 10, 41, 42, 43, 44, 45,
  54, 55, 62, 77, 113,
  118–19, 136, 137–9, 140,
  142, 154, 233, 243
SFIO, 112, 132, 161, 162,
  170, 204, 202, 208, 210
Sinn Fein, 83, 85, 195, 199,
  235
Smith, A., 15
social democracy, 123, 171,
  239
Social Democratic and Labour
  Party (SDLP), 193, 196,
  198, 236
socialism, 13, 63, 70, 93, 100,
  102, 112, 178, 213
Socialist Party (French), 134,
  162, 170, 203, 205, 207,
  210, 211, 239, 240, 242
Socialist Party (Italian), 115,
  116, 136, 139, 140, 141,
  148, 164
Solidaridad Catalana, 99
sottogoverno, 143, 155
sovereignty, 26, 41, 46, 49,
  56, 96, 104, 105, 107,
  178, 191, 200, 241
Spain, 7, 10, 12, 19, 23, 25,
  36–9, 48, 51–3, 59–62,
  68, 97, 144–6, 147, 156,
  164–6, 168, 170, 211–30,
  237, 238, 239, 241–4
Srollad ar Vro, 203
state, 7, 9, 12, 18, 19, 22, 49,
  52, 97
  and autonomism, 237,
    240–4
  creation of, 1, 6, 21, 23,
    25–45, 54, 117
  and economy, 147, 153, 166
  and nation, 47, 48, 57
  and separatism, 236–7
Statute of Estella, 105
Statute of Nuria, 104, 105
Stormont, 130–1, 193, 194,
  195
Stuart, Mary, 27
Stuart dynasty, 28
Sturzo, L., 116, 117, 135
Suarez, A., 215, 218, 220, 222
suffrage, 8
Sunningdale, 196
SVIMEZ, 153
Switzerland, 8

Tarradellas, J., 214, 222
Tarrow, S., 20, 132
territorial management, 17,
  18–19, 24, 79, 86, 97,
  113, 121–46, 173, 176,
  187, 188, 190, 192, 199,
  200, 220, 229, 231
Third Republic, 50, 108, 109,
  208
Third World, 4, 6, 155, 195,
  215, 217
Thoenig, J-C., 19, 133
Thorez, M., 133
Togliatti, P., 141
Torras i Bages, J., 69, 99
Toulouse, 112, 162, 205

trade unions, 20, 63, 84, 89, 91, 151, 152, 156, 160, 191, 205
trasformismo, 54, 55, 63, 114, 118, 119, 136, 140, 141, 144, 163, 164, 169, 170
Turati, 114, 115
Tuscany, 42

UCD, 215, 218, 221, 222, 225, 227, 228
Ulster, 64, 84, 131
Ulster Defence Association (UDA), 193, 195
Ulster Political Research Group, 195
Ulster Unionist Party, 193, 194
Ulster Volunteers, 84
Unamuno, 70, 101
Union démocratique breton (UDB), 202
Union of Crowns, 27
Union of Parliaments, 27
Union régionaliste breton, 109, 110
unionism, 82, 83, 84, 90, 97, 127
United Irishmen, 31, 80
United Kingdom, 10, 13, 16, 23, 25–33, 36, 48, 56–8, 63–6, 71–6, 80–97, 125–31, 146, 149–50, 168–9, 174–200, 241
United States of America, 8, 13, 15, 56, 58, 171

Uomo Qualunque, 140
urbanisation, 2, 3, 121, 212, 216
Urwin, D., 7, 8, 67

Valencia, 36, 39, 106, 237
Valle d'Aosta, 139
Venice, 42
Vichy regime, 131
Victor Emmanuel, 11, 43, 44
viticulture, 111, 153, 168, 204, 206
Volem Viure al Pais, 205, 206, 209

Waldec-Rousseau, 49
Wales, 23, 27, 47, 63–6, 71–3, 77, 92, 97, 130, 159, 170, 171, 179–82, 189–92, 237
Wales Act, 184–7, 242
Wales Trades Union Congress, 181
Weber, E., 50
Welsh Language Society, 179
Welsh Office, 17, 130, 149, 181, 184
Welsh Parliamentary Party, 94
West Midlands, 158
Wilson, H., 183
working class, 60, 63, 64, 66, 70, 74, 90, 96, 100, 115, 116, 123, 195, 208

Yeats, W.B., 75
Younger, G., 188, 189